The Promotion of National Minorities by their "Mother Countries" in Central and Eastern Europe in the 20th and 21st Century

Edited by Tove Hansen Malloy, Stefan Oeter and Gerald Volkmer

Publications on the Culture and History
of the Germans in Eastern Europe

Volume 75

Edited by the Federal Institute
for Culture and History of Eastern Europe

DE GRUYTER
OLDENBOURG

The Promotion of National Minorities by their "Mother Countries" in Central and Eastern Europe in the 20th and 21st Century

Edited by

Tove Hansen Malloy, Stefan Oeter and Gerald Volkmer

DE GRUYTER
OLDENBOURG

Publications on the Culture and History of the Germans in Eastern Europe
Volume 75

Bibliographic information published by the Deutsche Nationalbibliothek
The Deutsche Nationalbibliothek lists this publication in the Deutsche Nationalbibliografie; detailed bibliographic data are available online at <http://dnb.ddb.de>.
Library of Congress Cataloging-in-Publication Data
A CIP catalog record for this book has been applied for the Library of Congress.

Published by De Gruyter/Oldenbourg, Berlin/Boston 2025

Cover layout: Lennart Hoes
Typesetting: Oliver Rösch
Printed and bound by Florian Isensee GmbH, Oldenburg

ISBN: 978-3-11-059716-5
ISBN E-Book: 978-3-11-075717-0

Contents

Appendices

Tove Hansen Malloy, Stefan Oeter, Gerald Volkmer

Introduction

About 90 languages are spoken in Europe, of which only 37 are so-called national languages. This shows the multiplicity and diversity of the groups that live as so-called linguistic or national minorities in the European states. Europe has always been characterised by enormous linguistic diversity; the term 'national minority' itself is a modern one, which evidently could only come into being after the concept of the nation was established more than two centuries ago. Even though the proportion of national minorities in the European population has steadily declined since the interwar period, the topic of 'national minorities' is still – or yet again – on the political agenda. An arc could easily be drawn from the Balkan wars of the early 1990s to Russia's current war of aggression against Ukraine. Indeed, the annexation of Crimea by Russia in 2014 prompted the Federal Institute for Culture and History of the Germans in Eastern Europe (Bundesinstitut für Kultur und Geschichte der Deutschen im östlichen Europa) and the European Network Remembrance and Solidarity to plan a conference to compare the different funding policy approaches of the so-called 'mother countries' in favour of 'their' national minorities living abroad. Especially for the member states of the European Network, i.e. Germany, Poland, Romania, Slovakia and Hungary, this question is interesting, as all these states support 'their own' minorities in neighbouring countries. The circle of kin-states that support their kin-minorities extends far beyond the EU in Eastern and South-Eastern Europe and also includes, as already mentioned, well-known actors such as Russia and Serbia. The policies of these states have repeatedly led to international tensions and wars, as cruelly demonstrated by the Russian attack on Ukraine since 2014 and especially 2022, underlining the fundamental need to address this issue. Despite numerous national and international norms on the protection of minorities, there is a lack of generally accepted guidelines for the support policies of European states towards their national minorities living abroad.

At least as difficult as determining such guidelines is defining the term 'minority'. The disciplines concerned – especially law, political science, history and the social sciences – take very different approaches. Even the legal sciences, which require a particularly exact definition, have varying provisions in specific legal systems. Accordingly, there is no generally recognised definition under international law. There is agreement that 'national' or 'linguistic' minorities are groups of people who are nationals of the state in question and thus do not fall under the laws on foreigners. People who have migrated to a particular state due to recent migration processes are also not included in this category. Finally, a 'minority' must be a group of people facing a majority in terms of numbers, and whose members share certain common characteristics that distinguish them from the majority. The most widely accepted definition in the international context comes from United Nations (UN) expert Francesco Capotorti. It states that a minority is "a group numerically inferior to the rest of the population of a state, in a non-dominant position, whose members – being nationals of the state – possess ethnic, religious or linguistic characteristics differing from the rest of the population and show, if only implicitly, a sense of solidarity directed towards preserving their culture, traditions, religion or language".[1]

Throughout the twentieth century, national minorities in Central and Eastern Europe were effectively not only the objects but, to some extent, also the subjects of nationalistic politics, wars and ideological influences. Under Soviet domination after the Second World War, these minorities ended up in dependent relationships; their cultural development was impeded and they were frequently exposed to ideological propaganda and oppression. In this way, their social structures were to a greater or lesser extent destroyed and cultural identities were damaged or even forcefully assimilated. The consequences of these experiences can still be felt today. The post-1989 political opening up in Eastern Europe led to a renaissance among these largely buried regional identities, in particular to a rediscovery and accentuation of the 'region'. National minorities, too, were now able to articulate themselves more strongly, cultivate their cultural identity, and exercise or demand rights of self-administration and political representation.

At the same time, the advancing of European integration and the growing shift among most of these countries towards the Council of Europe, the European Union and other supranational structures led to an increased production of norms at the European level. The protection of minorities and languages through international law became a central issue after 1989/90, which both the Organisation for Security and Co-operation in Europe (OSCE) and the Council of Europe took up. The OSCE's *Copenhagen Final Act (1990)*, which gave minimum standards for the protection of minorities, and the establishment of the Office of the High Commissioner on National Minorities at the OSCE are worth mentioning. A concrete result of the efforts in the Council of Europe were two international law instruments that entered into force in 1998. The Framework Convention on the Protection of National Minorities and the European Charter for Regional or Minority Languages. In 2008, the OSCE adopted the Bolzano/Bolzano Recommendations on National Minorities in Inter-State Relations, which emphasised the principle of non-interference: that programmes which serve to strengthen or preserve 'own' minorities in another state

1 Francesco Caportoti: The International Protection of Persons Belonging to Ethnic, Religious and Linguistic Minorities since 1919. In: United Nations Economic and Social Council 1977, P. 96.

must not violate the sovereignty of this 'host state'. The responsibility for dealing with minorities lies with the respective 'host state', with which agreements must be reached bilaterally. Care should always be taken to maintain good neighbourly relations, to which minority policy could contribute. Thus, at least the possibility of orienting the legal provisions to international standards was created. Parallel to these measures, new legal regulations were created at the state level, which in principle enable minorities to maintain or reassert their cultural identity. At the same time, a number of mainly bilateral agreements and neighbourhood treaties relating to the protection of national and linguistic minorities were concluded. Nevertheless, the current goals, contents and practices of nation-state policies in favour of and towards 'their' respective national minorities still differ considerably. So far, this topic has not been systematically and comparatively researched, especially in relation to Eastern Europe.

The European Network Remembrance and Solidarity (EN), the Federal Institute for Culture and History of the Germans in Eastern Europe in Oldenburg and the Institute for Foreign Cultural Relations in Stuttgart (Institut für Auslandsbeziehungen, IfA) quickly recognised the potential of this issue, which they wanted to take up in a multidisciplinary and international framework. The European Centre for Minority Issues in Flensburg (ECMI), the Chair of Public Law, International Law and Foreign Public Law at the University of Hamburg and the Chair of German Linguistics / German as a Foreign Language at the University of Bamberg, whose academic focus is in this field, came on as partners. From Eastern Europe, the Institute for Social Policy at the University of Warsaw, the Department of History at the University of Košice/Kaschau, and the Institute for Minority Studies at the Hungarian Academy of Sciences in Budapest joined the circle of project partners. Finally, this group was strengthened by two central players: the Office of the High Commissioner on National Minorities of the OSCE and the Federal Union of European Nationalities.

In preparation for the conference, a workshop was held in October 2014 at the University of Bamberg, hosted by Prof. Dr. Helmut Glück, and a second workshop in September 2015 at the University of Hamburg, organised by Prof. Dr. Stefan Oeter. Finally, the conference "The Promotion of National Minorities by their 'Mother Countries' in Central and Eastern Europe in the 20th and 21st Century", which this anthology records, took place from 9 to 11 November 2016 in the Representation of the Free State of Saxony to the Federation in Berlin. The conference was attended by almost 40 speakers, panellists and panel leaders from over a dozen European countries, who examined the topic in a multidisciplinary way from historical, legal, political, sociological, geographical, ethnological and linguistic perspectives. The exact proceedings of the conference can be found in the conference overview in the appendix of this volume. The geographical frame of reference was Central, Eastern and South-Eastern Europe. Unlike many regions in Western Europe, these areas have always been characterised by a great diversity of different ethnic groups, nations, languages and cultures.

Despite the comprehensive approach, the conference had to limit itself to a few striking examples, especially from among the member states of the European Network, in view of the large number of cases under consideration. It was therefore not possible to cover all 'mother countries' and 'their' minorities in Eastern Europe. Chronological focal points also had to be formed. Therefore, the timeframe of the study was limited to the period between the political changes of 1989 and the present – without, however, ignoring the historical background. The aim of the conference was not to fundamentally examine the relationship between state and minority, but to put the emphasis on the kin-states and 'their' kin-minorities. The focus was therefore not on domestic but foreign policy, although the triangular relationship between the external national homeland, the supported national minority and the state in which the minority lives was always considered. Since the scope of the term 'minority' was too wide, the conference concentrated on national minorities in the sense of the Framework Convention on the Protection of National Minorities of the Council of Europe, which places them under the special protection of the state. Only one case discussed at the conference does not fit into the scheme of the relationship between kin-state and kin-minority. It concerns the largest national or ethnic minority in Europe, which is at home in almost all European states but, as is well known, has no 'mother country' of its own: the Roma. Their case in particular should serve as a contrasting foil for the other examples discussed at the conference and sharpen the view of the ongoing changes across the entire subject.

To take account of this dynamic, the different perspectives on the topic were bundled into three panel discussions: "Multilateralism and Bilateral Approaches in the Promotion of Minorities", "German Minorities and their Media" and "Potential Discrepancies between the Goals and Actual Consequences in the Promotion of Minorities". The first panel debate compared the bilateral approaches (mainly governed by intergovernmental treaties) with the multilateral ones of the Council of Europe, the OSCE and, to a certain extent, the United Nations and the European Union. The second panel discussion singles out the media as a central instrument of minority promotion and illustrating it with the example of the German minorities in Eastern Europe. The focus on German minorities allowed for comparable examples with meaningful similarities and differences. In addition, it made use of the special expertise of our partner IfA, an intermediary organisation of the German Foreign Ministry that supports extensive programmes in the field of Germany's foreign cultural policy. In this framework, the interplay between the funding ministry, the implementing intermediary organisation, and the promoted minority was discussed. The third panel discussion took stock of the promotion of minorities by their 'mother countries' and, above all, attempted to reveal potential discrepancies between the goals pursued by the states and the concrete effects of minority promotion, especially on the legal, political and social situation of minorities in Eastern Europe. Finally, the question of possible 'European standards' in the promotion of minorities was also raised. The panel discussions provided a forum for representatives of European states and international organisations, civil society actors, and representatives of the scientific community and minority organisations from Central and Eastern Europe to address this multilayered, topical and often controversial issue in a multi-perspective and differentiated manner. The results of the discussions can be read in the conference report, which is printed in the appendix of this volume.

The papers which deal primarily with the objectives of state policy and its means of promoting minorities are summarised below under the heading "Concepts and Attitudes". In his introductory contribution, Stefan Oeter presents objectives, guidelines and standards in minority policy. Taking the whole of Europe from the perspective of political science are the contributions by Peter A. Kraus ("Sovereignty Options versus Autonomy Provisions: Minority Politics in Europe") and Karl Cordell ("Minorities, Immigrants and the Politics of Populism"), in which they deal in particular with frequently occurring attitudes towards minorities. Three central tools and applications of minority politics are presented in the second part of this volume. Tove Hansen Malloy examines unilateral legislation in favour of kin-minorities as a frequently used tool of European minority rights law. Kyriaki Topidi analyses the role of dual citizenship in the context of minority protection and sheds light on relevant cultural sensitivities. Finally, Helmut Glück discusses the connection between language and identity on the basis of historical and current developments of national minorities in Europe. The third part of this volume brings together the presentations of the third and fourth panel under the heading "Players". This refers primarily to the kin-states, their intermediary organisations and the kin-minorities interacting with them abroad. Zoltán Kántor presents the best-known example of this kind of relationship in East-Central and South-Eastern Europe by examining Hungary's kin-state policies between 2010 and 2018. In his contribution "Polish national minorities in post-Jagiellonian area", Cezary Żołędowski discusses Poland's relationship with Polish minorities living in Lithuania, Belarus and Ukraine. Gerald Volkmer analyses the situation of the German minorities in East-Central and South-Eastern Europe as well as in the states of the former Soviet Union and their promotion by the Federal Republic of Germany. Martin Klatt examines Germany's relationship to the German minority in Danish North Schleswig and Denmark's relationship to the Danish minority in German South Schleswig in the context of the 'European model' practised in the Danish-German border region. The latter two contributions were not presented at the conference, but supplement the examples introduced in this context with further relevant cases, especially since the conference papers presented by Jennifer Jackson-Preece ("The Historical Background of Current Minority Policy"), Károly-Kocsis ("Ethnic landscape of Europe"), Attila Papp ("Education") and Andris Spruds ("Russia and the Baltic States") could unfortunately not be written up. The volume concludes with the already mentioned contribution by Dieter W. Halwachs "Roma – a stateless European minority", which draws attention in particular to the numerous national or ethnic minorities in Eastern Europe that cannot fall back on the support of a 'mother country'.

The situation of the Roma in Romania was also addressed at a workshop for young academics that took place before the conference. Seven young academics from Germany, England, Hungary and Romania presented their current research projects, mainly dissertations in the fields of political science, law, history and European ethnology. The organisers wanted to emphasise the importance of promoting young academics for the further development of the research field. The results of this workshop can be read in the report prepared by Melanie Frank, which complements the conference report at the end of this volume, also written by Melanie Frank with thanks.

The publication of the papers and reports is intended to document the results of this conference and make them accessible to researchers and an interested public. This was made possible due to the generous funding of the conference by the Federal Government Commissioner for Culture and Media (BKM), who deserves great thanks for this. In addition, we would like to thank all our cooperation partners, in particular the Institute for Foreign Cultural Relations (IfA), which, through the Head of the Dialogues Department, Urban Beckmann, as well as Karoline Gil and Christian Stärk, played a decisive role making this conference happen. We would also like to include in these thanks the European Network Remembrance and Solidarity, namely the then-Chairman of the Steering Committee, Prof. Dr. Jan Rydel, and the Chairman of the Advisory Board, Markus Meckel, who contributed helpful initiatives and constructive advice to the planning of the event. We would like to thank Prof. Dr. Helmut Glück for organising the first preparatory workshop at the University of Bamberg in 2014 and the Representation of the Free State of Saxony to the Federation for providing the conference facilities. We are grateful to all the speakers, panellists and moderators, whose contributions made the conference and this volume possible in the first place. Finally, we would like to thank sincerely Sarah Patey for translating the German texts into English, McKinley Valentine for the proofreading and our colleagues at the Federal Institute for Culture and History of the Germans in Eastern Europe (BKGE) for their help in organising the conference and the inclusion of this volume in the series of publications of the BKGE, namely Anja Feldmann, Dr. Burkhard Olschowsky and especially the Director of the Institute, Prof. Dr. Matthias Weber.

Concepts and Attitudes

Stefan Oeter

Objectives, Guidelines and Standards in Minority Policy

1. Introduction

States and societies in Europe have been dealing with issues of minority policy for more than a hundred years. Pre-modern empires from their beginnings were conglomerates of disparate territories, highly diverse across language, culture, feudal organisation and constitution. The modern idea of the nation-state gained dominance in the 19th century, transforming the idea of statehood and propagating the ideal of unity of people, language and nation.[1] None of the (imagined) nation-states conformed in demographic composition to these ideals, since practically all were historical entities with diverse populations far from the ideal of cultural and linguistic homogeneity. The rapidly transforming structures of modern statehood, however, delivered the tools to change this situation. Compulsory military service, state-run school education, a cultural policy deeply coded in the idea of the uniform nation, and the growing penetration of society by dynamically developing bureaucracies were all used to forcibly homogenize the linguistic and cultural traits of the populations.[2] In other words: state power and its toolbox of forced transformation were able to create a social reality of nationhood from an idealised vision that, at its beginnings, had been pure imagination. In this state transformation, however, there was no place for the protection of resistant minorities.[3] Consideration of ethnic diversity only had a place in the (decaying) multinational empires of Central and Eastern Europe, such as the Habsburg monarchy. The situation changed partially with the new ordering of Central and Eastern Europe after World War One (1914–1918). The victorious Allied powers were aware that the creation of new nation-states in a territorial space where ethnic groups had been settling for centuries in very mixed patterns, with a resulting heterogeneity in linguistic, cultural and ethnic terms, would become a political and humanitarian catastrophe if strong safeguards were not put in place to prevent endless, bloody struggles for cultural and political dom-

1 See Joseph Marko, Edith Marko-Stöckl, Benedikt Harzl, Hedwig Unger: The historical-sociological foundations: state formation and nation building in Europe and the construction of the identitarian nation-cum-state paradigm. In: Joseph Marko (Ed.): Human and Minority Rights Protection by Multiple Diversity Governance. Abingdon 2019, P. 33–95, in particular P. 38et seq.

2 See Eric J. Hobsbawm: Nations and nationalism since 1780: Programme, myth and reality. 2nd edn, Cambridge 1992, P. 80–130.

3 See Marko et al.: Human and Minority Rights Protection (Footnote 1), P. 33 et seq.

inance.[4] In order to avoid that outcome, the Allied powers imposed far-reaching obligations of minority protection on the new states – obligations that, in practice, were only reluctantly implemented. These would later become the points of crystallisation for ardent internal and external conflicts with minorities and their kin-states.[5] Minority protection accordingly was perceived as a toxic concept after 1945, a perception that found its expression in the complete lack of any international standard for national minority policies.[6]

That extremely negative perception began changing in the 1980s. The gradual change towards a more positive attitude received a boost from the fall of the 'Iron Curtain' and the demise of the Soviet empire after 1990.[7] Minority conflicts, which had been suppressed with brutal force over decades in the one-party communist dictatorship, suddenly came to the surface and once again threatened to throw Europe into a series of bloody clashes. European states felt the need to act resolutely in countering such threats and agreed very quickly – in a forced attempt to achieve the necessary normative consensus – on a number of ambitious documents with new standards of minority protection. The first was the Copenhagen document of the Organisation for Security and Co-operation in Europe (OSCE), followed by the European Charter for Regional or Minority Languages and the Framework Convention on the Protection of National Minorities, both legally binding treaty regimes of the Council of Europe.[8]

With that development, Europe seemed to have found a new, all-embracing consensus on a number of important points – firstly, the need for institutionalized protection of traditional minorities from the strong pressure towards national homogeneity of language and culture, a pressure that inevitably results from legal and administrative systems oriented towards 'national unity'. However, looking in more detail tells us a disillusioning story about the precarious nature of the normative consensus achieved in the early 1990s. Below the surface of (seemingly agreed-upon) common objectives and guidelines there still persists a plethora of different percep-

4 See Stefan Oeter: Right to self-determination and the creation of new states. In: Société française pour le droit international (Ed.): Le traité de Versailles: Regards franco-allemands en droit international à l'occasion du centenaire. Paris 2020, P. 173–193.

5 See Peter Hilpold: Minderheitenschutz im Völkerbundsystem. In: Christoph Pan, Beate Sibylle Pfeil (Eds.): Handbuch der europäischen Volksgruppen. Vol. 3: Zur Entstehung des modernen Minderheitenschutzes in Europa. Wien 2006, P. 156–189; as well as Jennifer Jackson Preece: National minorities and the European nation-states system. Oxford 1998, P. 67 et seq.

6 See Marko et al.: Human and Minority Rights Protection (Footnote 1), P. 79 et seq.

7 See Sigrid Boysen: Einführung. In: Sigrid Boysen et al.: Europäische Charta der Regional – oder Minderheitensprachen: Handkommentar. Zürich, St. Gallen 2011, P. 23–39, in particular P. 28 et seq., and Marko et al.: Human and Minority Rights Protection (Footnote 1), P. 83 et seq.

8 For more on these two treaty regimes in detail, see Stefan Oeter: Conventions on the protection of national minorities. In: Stefanie Schmahl, Marten Breuer (Eds.): The Council of Europe: its law and policies. Oxford 2017, P. 542–571.

tions and political ideas about how to respond adequately to minorities in the legal and institutional system of modern statehood.[9] A closer look at the realities of national minority policy in the states of Europe reveals a broad range of policies, with a huge variety in concepts and approaches, but also in the toolbox of concrete instruments.[10] Completely different conceptualizations of statehood and of guiding ideas of what constitutes a nation find their expression in extremely varied views of the relationship between majority nations and minorities, leading to highly diverging legal and institutional arrangements for granting minorities a limited space for their own development and the preservation and promotion of their cultures and languages.

The national arrangements of minority protection today were not primarily formed by the overarching normative consensus at the European level, but from the varying traditions of the majority–minority relationship, from long-lasting path-dependencies in the concrete configuration of national minority policy, and from the linked political disagreements about what constitutes adequate protection of 'autochthonous' minorities.[11] The details of national developments and arrangements display a very broad range of solutions, which are difficult to bring under one common umbrella.

In a number of states, a radical transformation of state institutions has opened up space for self-determined shaping of local and regional political institutions in favour of certain ethnic groups and minorities. In the most advanced cases, this has involved ambitious constructions of autonomy for territorial entities that form the historical basis of 'nations' different from the respective state nation.[12] One might think here of the Autonomous Communities of Catalonia, the Basque Country and Galicia in Spain,[13] the autonomy arrangement for South Tyrol[14] and the Aosta Valley in Italy, or the special status of Scotland, Wales and Northern Ireland under British devolution policy.[15]

---

9 See Marko et al.: Human and Minority Rights Protection (Footnote 1), P. 87 et seq.

10 See Alexander Osipov: Diversity Management. In: Tove Malloy (Ed.): Minority issues in Europe. Vol. 1: Rights, concepts, policy. Berlin 2013, P. 273–300.

11 See Joseph Marko: Law and Ideology: the ideological conundrums of the liberal-democratic state. In: Joseph Marko (Ed.): Human and Minority Rights Protection by Multiple Diversity Governance. Abingdon 2019, P. 96–137.

12 See in detail Christian Schliemann Radbruch: Das völkerrechtliche Institut der Autonomie innerstaatlicher Gruppen. Tübingen 2017, in particular P. 27 et seq., P. 360 et seq.

13 See Eugenia López-Jacoiste Díaz: Autonomy and Self-determination in Spain. In: Peter Hilpold (Ed.): Autonomie und Selbstbestimmung. Baden-Baden 2016, P. 218–241.

14 See e.g. Esther Happacher Brezinka: Südtirols Autonomie in Europa. Wien 2012, P. 52 et seq., P. 87 et seq.

15 See Stephen Tierney: Giving with one hand: Scottish devolution within a unitary state. In: Sujit Choudhry (Ed.): Constitutional Design for Divided Societies: Integration or Accommodation? Oxford 2008, P. 433–460.

In many states we see a (more or less hesitant) change of the institutional and legal landscape, with some specific instruments of diversity management and minority protection being incorporated. Public policy in these cases reacts only very reluctantly to the normative quests for a comprehensive framework of minority protection, granting limited concessions piece by piece in a reactive mode instead of proactively developing a forward-looking comprehensive minority policy. Such piecemeal approaches are driven in part by pressure from below, in the form of outspoken demands of more and more self-confident minority groups, but also by pressure from outside – constituting reluctantly granted concessions to pushed for change voiced by international institutions. Sometimes both mechanisms work together to create a push for reform, putting the state under pressure to prove its willingness to achieve productive solutions.

Alongside these more positive cases, there are states that reject any move towards protecting minorities, states that are characterized by an outright rejection of any policy aimed at protecting and promoting minorities.[16] The idea of statehood in these cases is so deeply grounded in the understanding of a 'unitarian' nation, in which homogeneity must be created by any and all means, that any demand for protection of diversity, in the sense of minority protection, is read as a treacherous assault on the idea of the unity of state and nation.[17] Any concession to the normative demands for protection and promotion of minorities, their languages and cultures, is habitually rejected in these cases, even if the concession is grounded in European guidelines and standards – one might think of the hostile policies of Greece and Turkey towards their minorities.[18] Fundamental rejection of any type of minority protection at the level of central authorities and elites, however, may (as in France) go hand in hand with a remarkable openness to new solutions and models at the municipal and regional level. The opposite may also be found, where rhetorical openness towards the acceptance of European standards is coupled with persistent resistance of bureaucracy and administration to sustainable changes in the structures and practices of the state apparatus (Germany is like this to a degree).

The result of such a broad variety of ways of addressing minority issues in politics and administration is – as mentioned above – an enormous diversity in the approaches and concepts of minority policy. This diversity is clearly visible in any comparative study of minority policy across the states of Europe. The background and causes of such divergent approaches are multidimensional. They include differences in the elementary structures of political culture and traditions of statehood, but also the

16 See Marko: Law and Ideology (Footnote 11), P. 99–111.

17 See Marko: Law and Ideology (Footnote 11), P. 120–128.

18 For as a paradigmatic study on the minority policy of Turkey, see David Jacob: Minderheitenrecht in der Türkei: Recht auf eigene Existenz, Religion und Sprache nichtnationaler Gemeinschaften in der türkischen Verfassung und im Lausanner Vertrag. Tübingen 2017, P. 94–120.

huge divergence in the situation of various minorities. In part, these differences in approach and arrangement are the consequences of different historical and political coding of the models of statehood. Different practical situations pose different underlying challenge for minority policy. In some states, an ethnic group has traditionally formed the dominant segment of the population in a larger territory, and autonomy frameworks potentially create space for productive solutions developed by the group itself. In others, only a few members of a traditional minority group remain, scattered over a vast territory, which makes it difficult to create arrangements that adequately protect and promote the culture and language of the minority group.

I would like to demonstrate this point with some examples. The Sorbs in Lower Lusatia (in the German Land Brandenburg) and the Sami in Finland and Sweden are paradigmatic examples of one pole of the continuum, while Catalans and Basques in Spain, but also the South Tyrolians in the Autonomous Province of Bozen/Bolzano, are at the other extreme pole. The Sorbs in Upper Lusatia (in the German Land Saxony) still form – at least in the core regions – a partially closed social environment in which the (Upper) Sorbian language is used on a daily basis as a means of communication in village life and transmitted in families from generation to generation, but the corresponding social environments in Lower Lusatia have more or less faded away, so the language is no longer transmitted in families and is used only in very limited contexts and domains, mostly at a symbolical level.[19] If the survival of a minority language is to be safeguarded under such unfavourable conditions, proactive action from the state is needed to support the very essence of language transmission and (limited) use in social practice. That requires complex systems for teaching the language in school to children from the minority group, and also requires that families of the majority population are interested in having their children learning the language – language education must be of sufficient quality to enable language acquisition and run through the entire school career, so that language competence is developed and consolidated. The language must also be used extensively in print media, radio and television as well as on the internet and social media, and (state-funded) cultural activities must be able to take place in the minority language.[20] Comparable problems may be seen in Finland and Sweden concerning the Sami people, who are divided into a number of very small language groups with

19 On the different levels of linguistic competence in Upper and Lower Sorbian, see Thomas Menzek, Anja Pohontsch: Sorbisch. In: Rahel Beyer, Albrecht Plewnia (Eds.): Handbuch der Sprachminderheiten in Deutschland. Tübingen 2020, P. 227–270, in particular P. 251 et seq.

20 See Joseph Marko, Sergiu Constantin, Günther Rautz, Andrea Carlà, Verena Wisthaler: Against assimilation: the right to multiple identities. In: Joseph Marko (Ed.): Human and Minority Rights Protection by Multiple Diversity Governance. Abingdon 2019, P. 227–306; and Stefan Oeter: Mehrsprachigkeit als Last oder als Bereicherung?. In: Matthias Theodor Vogt, Jan Sokol, Dieter Bingen, Jürgen Neyer, Albert Löhr (Eds.): Minderheiten als Mehrwert. Frankfurt/Main 2010 (Schriften des Collegium Pontes 6), P. 139–158, in particular P. 143 et seq.

very low numbers of speakers in each group, spread out over a vast territory, making it very difficult to develop targeted models of schooling in the first language and to design focused provision of Sami-language media and cultural activities.[21] The situation is entirely different when we look at Catalans, Basques and South Tyroleans. As a result of the far-reaching institutional arrangements of territorial autonomy, these communities have gained their own regulatory space in their regions of settlement, enabling them to design an educational system tailored to their needs and to extend considerably the domains where their languages are used on a daily basis, including even official use in administration and (in the case of South Tyrol) in the judiciary. They are also able to develop targeted media in their languages and to support a rich and diversified cultural life in the regional language.[22] From the perspective of the relevant ethnic communities, the results of the autonomy arrangements have had very positive effects on language maintenance and on the further development of their languages – effects that resemble to a large degree what would be achieved if they had their own nation-states.

Accordingly, the question arises of whether it is even possible – under the prevailing conditions of extremely divergent approaches and solutions – to imagine common objectives, guidelines and standards of minority policy? In my eyes at least, the answer is yes, despite all the findings of an extremely heterogeneous landscape of national patterns of minority policy.

The basis of my positive answer may be found in the relevant documents and conventions of the OSCE and the Council of Europe, which comprise in essence:
- the Copenhagen Document of the OSCE of 1990[23]
- the Council of Europe's Framework Convention on the Protection of National Minorities of 1995 (FCNM)[24]
- the European Charter for Regional or Minority Languages of the Council of Europe of 1992.[25]

21 See for example Kristian Myntti, Pirkko Nuolijärvi: The case of Finland. In: Sia Spiliopoulou Åkermark, Leena Huss, Stefan Oeter, Alastair Walker (Eds.): International obligations and national debates: Minorities around the Baltic Sea. Mariehamn 2006, P. 171–225, in particular P. 175–76., 189 et seq.

22 See Peter Hilpold: Selbstbestimmung und Autonomie zwischen Sezession und innerer Selbstbestimmung. In: Peter Hilpold (Ed.): Autonomie und Selbstbestimmung. Baden-Baden 2016, P. 13–49.

23 OSCE, Document of the Copenhagen Meeting of the Conference on the Human Dimension of the CSCE, 29. June 1990, available at: https://www.osce.org/de/odihr/elections/14304 (last retrieval 18 Jan 2021).

24 Council of Europe, Framework Convention on the Protection of National Minorities, 1 February 1995, ETS No. 157, available at: https://rm.coe.int/168007cdac (last retrieval 1 Aug 2025).

25 Council of Europe, European Charter for Regional or Minority Languages, 5 November 1992, available at: https://www.coe.int/en/web/european-charter-regional-or-minority-languages/text-of-the-charter (last retrieval 18 Jan 2021).

All three documents share an overarching objective, namely the *preservation and promotion of cultural diversity* as a basic trait of pluralist modern societies. The classical, essentially authoritarian nation-state model of the 19th century was obsessed with 'unity' and forcible homogenisation of societies (including forcible assimilation of non-conforming ethnic groups and minorities), which is not really compatible with the modern model of liberal constitutionalism with its emphasis on individual freedom and its counter-majoritarian system of checks and balances intended to protect societal diversity and individual human rights.[26] In fact, the opposite: forced 'nation-building' that tries to eliminate the pre-existing ethnic, cultural and linguistic heterogeneity, in the interest of artificially creating a homogeneous 'people', bears totalitarian traits. Under conditions of modernity, it inevitably leads to massive political conflicts, with governments tempted to take recourse in policies of repression, which risk escalating violent conflicts. It was this aspect in particular which motivated the OSCE to deal with the issue of minority policy.[27] The Council of Europe was mainly motivated by the desire to safeguard the individual and collective rights of members of ethnic minorities, in order to protect them from the excesses of repressive policies of assimilation. This objective was pursued by the Framework Convention, which moved states to engage in an exercise of standard-setting. Another motivation for action was the consensus on cultural policy (reflected in the preamble of the Language Charter) that regional and minority languages (and the cultures they represent) constitute an endangered cultural heritage of an ever-more closely integrated Europe, the preservation of which is an important common task for the community of European states.[28] These three objectives and tasks, though at the outset rather different, converge in the overarching objective of preservation and promotion of cultural diversity that forms a common ground for the mentioned three documents.

Of course it is difficult to contest, if one looks more closely into the details of national policies towards minorities and their languages, that the practice on the ground is much more nuanced. Beyond the ritual of rhetorical declamations at political summits, the principled consensus tends to fade away in the nitty-gritty operations of daily administration – but is this not a regular phenomenon when the lofty air of political declamations meets the realities of routine practices of the bureaucracy? Operative realities demonstrate the perils of high-minded political principles and lay open the conflicting objectives that often are hidden in program-

26 See Marko: Law and Ideology (Footnote 11), P. 120–128.

27 See Krzysztof Drzewicki: Minority protection within the OSCE. In: Daniel Thürer, Zdzislaw Kędzia (Eds.): Managing diversity: protection of minorities in international law. Zürich, Basel 2009, P. 99–131, in particular P. 108 et seq.

28 See Boysen: Einführung (Footnote 7), P. 23–24., and Oeter: Conventions (footnote 8), P. 550 et seq.

matic language. Some member states of the Council of Europe evidently do not really share the common goal of preservation of cultural diversity, despite lip service at OSCE summits and in bodies of the Council of Europe. Other states seem to earnestly share the basic values underlying OSCE and Council of Europe, at least at the level of high politics, but the consensus starts to fade as soon as they get down to the level of drafting specific policies, and even more so at the level of administrative workings. One should also bear in mind that nearly all the member states of the two European organisations are in essence plural polities in which diverging forces coexist – a cosmopolitan strand of liberal politics that embraces and affirms cultural plurality, and countering forces that – as a reaction to the excesses of globalisation and multiculturalism – voice polemical critique at policies that seem to erode the protective shell of the inherited nation-state. Such contestation of globalization and multiculturalism all too often ends up in the atavisms of a dull right-wing populism – a populism that tends to bedevil any attempt at protecting cultural diversity.[29]

From the objective of preservation and promotion of cultural diversity there result guidelines for targeted minority policy that may be easily – assuming the commonly shared goal – be narrowed down to a set of concrete standards for operative policies and administrative practices. One should, however, not fall into the trap of imagining that such processes of 'concretisation' of policy guidelines into operative standards are a simple, merely deductive operation of formal logic where standards are easily produced from broader guidelines. Normative concretization always needs additional political judgements – and the permanent balancing of conflicting objectives in the details of concrete policy formulation.

Even if enriched with further political judgements and priority-setting, the described process of operationalizing very general objectives into normative guidelines and then concrete standards narrows down the margins for political decision-making. One should not underestimate the pitfalls that go along with gradually emerging densities of concreteness. In view of the very different problems and challenges of minority policy, there is a serious need for differentiating solutions. This need can be met by different means. One may – as in the construction of the OSCE standards or the normative requirements of the Framework Convention – take refuge in 'general clauses', kept in very abstract terms, which leave the task of concretization to the subsequent agents of interpretation, with remaining margins of quite considerable scope. One may also experiment, as was attempted in drafting the Language Charter, with an arrangement that tries to break down the guidelines into standards with a high degree of concreteness, which leads to complex 'menu' approaches (see, for example, the one underlying Part 3 of the Language Charter). The member states must, when ratifying the Charter, make a significant number of decisions of norma-

29 See the seminal study on modern populism by Jan-Werner Müller: What is populism? London 2017.

tive choice, in order to tailor their 'menu' of undertakings to the concrete needs of the protected languages and their groups of speakers.[30]

The following reflections will shed some light on the process of concretization that leads from agreed objectives to guidelines to concrete standards. The remarks will include a closer look at the political and administrative challenges that minority policy has to address in different states of Europe, and also the very different situations and problems resulting from the variety of institutional and legal frameworks and the enormous divergences in sociolinguistic constellations – a variety that calls for differentiated solutions.

2. Objectives of minority policy

We will first look into the objectives of minority policy (and of minority protection) as they develop from the context of European debates and documents. Starting with the basic European documents on the system of minority protection we can reformulate a common understanding of the objectives. We will see that the protection and promotion of cultural diversity is a formative trait of pluralist societies and modern constitutionalism based on democracy, the rule of law and human rights.

This overarching objective is expressed in the three major different documents with varying implications and has been given concrete shape in a number of differing sub-objectives.

- **Copenhagen Document of the OSCE:** The focus here is on the *prevention of minority-related conflicts* and on conflict management.[31]
- **Framework Convention on the Protection of National Minorities:** The central objective of this framework is the *protection of human rights of members of national minorities.* As their language and culture differs from the majority language and culture, national minorities must be safeguarded against pressure from the majority society and its institutions. The aim is to secure a safe space for further developing their specificities, their culture and language.[32]
- **European Charter for Regional or Minority Languages:** The primary focus of this instrument is the *protection of linguistic diversity as a central cornerstone of*

30 On this mechanism, see Boysen: Einführung (Footnote 7), P. 34; and Oeter: Conventions (Footnote 8), P. 558et seq.

31 See Drzewicki: OSCE (Footnote 27), P. 114 f.

32 See Rainer Hofmann: Das Rahmenübereinkommen zum Schutz nationaler Minderheiten: Einführung, Überblick, Würdigung. In: Rainer Hofmann, Doris Angst, Emma Lantschner, Günther Rautz, Detlev Rein (Eds.): Rahmenübereinkommen zum Schutz nationaler Minderheiten: Handkommentar. Baden-Baden, Wien, Zürich, St. Gallen 2015, P. 68–86; and Patrick Thornberry, Maria Amor Martín Estébanez: Minority rights in Europe: A review of the work and standards of the Council of Europe. Strasbourg 2004, P. 89–136.

the cultural heritage of Europe and the preservation of historically grown multilingualism.[33]

In the subsequent paragraphs I will elucidate the explicitly formulated objectives of minority policy contained in the three major documents, looking more closely at some specific relevant passages.

Copenhagen Document of the OSCE

The history of the Copenhagen Document of the OSCE highlights its clear focus on questions of conflict prevention and conflict management. The document was developed in the immediate aftermath of the end of the East–West conflict and the shift towards democracy and the rule of law in Central and Eastern European states. With the demise of the Soviet empire and the overthrow of its one-party dictatorship, old inter-ethnic rivalries and conflicts that had been held below the surface broke out again.[34] In some cases, this was already happening in the final phase of the Soviet empire in the 1980s, for example in Nagorno-Karabakh; in many more, the old ethnic rivalries came to the fore with the (re-)gaining of sovereign statehood, for example the Baltic states and the Republic of Moldova saw disputes with the sizeable Russian minorities. In other cases, in particular in Eastern Central Europe, the unresolved legacies of the various post-World War One peace treaties, such as the Treaty of Trianon with Hungary, troubled the transforming societies and states of the region – not to mention the violent conflicts in the former Yugoslavia, which soon escalated into dramatic bloodshed. Given this political situation at the beginning of the 1990s, it is not surprising that the European states saw the minority question as a Pandora's box of potential ethnic conflicts, a disquieting danger for the security and stability of the community of European states.

This worry – and the resulting motivation to deal proactively with issues of minority policy – found its expression in Section 30 of the Copenhagen Document, which reads as follows:

> The participating States recognize that the questions relating to national minorities can only be satisfactorily resolved in a democratic political framework based on the rule of law, with a functioning independent judiciary. This framework guarantees full

33 See Boysen: Einführung (Footnote 7), P. 23f.; in addition Jean-Marie Woehrling: Introduction. In: Alba Nogueira López, Eduardo J. Ruiz Vieytez, Iñigo Urrutia Libarona (Eds.): Shaping language rights: commentary on the European Charter for Regional or Minority Languages in light of the Committee of Experts' evaluation. Strasbourg 2012, P. 11–31, in particular P. 16 et seq., and Thornberry, Martín Estébanez: Minority rights in Europe (Footnote 32), P. 137–168.

34 See Alan Phillips: The Fall of the Iron Curtain and its significance for the establishment of minority rights regimes in Eastern Europe. In: European Yearbook of Minority Issues 13 (2014), P. 5–29.

respect for human rights and fundamental freedoms, equal rights and status for all citizens, the free expression of all their legitimate interests and aspirations, political pluralism, social tolerance and the implementation of legal rules that place effective restraints on the abuse of governmental power.

The idea that minority rights are "an essential factor for peace, justice, stability and democracy in the Participating States" was also expressed in the creation in 1992 of a specific OSCE organ dedicated to minority issues: the office of the High Commissioner for National Minorities (HCNM).[35] Over the following decades, the institution of the HCNM developed numerous conflict prevention and conflict management operations and contributed decisively to the development of a targeted minority policy in a great number of Balkan, Central and Eastern European states. Perhaps more importantly, the HCNM also helped develop a normative consensus on the basic structures of a modern minority policy, mainly by drafting a series of Guidelines and Recommendations dedicated to various aspects of minority policy.[36]

Framework Convention on the Protection of National Minorities

The Framework Convention constitutes the Council of Europe's main answer to the challenge of formulating guidelines for a modern minority policy adapted to the current problems. At the beginning of the 1990s, various bodies of the Council of Europe had put forward plans and projects for new treaty documents on minority protection, aiming to set binding standards for minority policy. Some of these projects were quite ambitious, such as the Additional Protocol to the European Convention on Human Rights. Most of them were perceived by the member states as going too far and being excessively ambitious. They were only able to reach agreement on the version with the lowest ambition, the draft of the Framework Convention on the Protection of National Minorities.[37] As the title suggests, the Framework Convention sets out a very broad normative frame, formulated in vague and abstract terms. Details and concrete operational rules must be shaded in by member states and tailored to the needs of the specific situation of each minority on the spot. Member states did, however, entrust a newly created treaty body with an important role: monitoring the implementation of the guidelines and rules of the convention. This new body was named the Advisory Committee. The Advisory Committee is

35 On the institution of the High Commissioner, see Lamberto Zannier: Integration of diverse societies as a tool for conflict prevention: the experience of the OSCE High Commissioner on National Minorities. In: OSCE Yearbook 25 (2019), P. 235–245; and Drzewicki: OSCE (Footnote 27), P. 121 et seq.

36 See Drzewicki: OSCE (Footnote 27), P. 123 et seq.

37 See Oeter: Conventions (Footnote 8), P. 543 et seq.

tasked with reporting on the strengths and weaknesses of implementation to the Committee of Ministers of the Council of Europe. The Advisory Committee plays an important role, not only in monitoring national implementation of the Framework Convention, but also in the interpretation and 'concretisation' of the rules set out in the treaty, in particular through its Thematic Commentaries.[38]

The Framework Convention is primarily oriented towards the protection of the human rights of members of national minorities. The extent of these protections has already been formalised in the existing European system of human rights protection, in particular the European Convention on Human Rights. It is further adapted to the needs and specific problems of minorities (and their members) in the Framework Convention.[39]

The central objective of the Framework Convention is formulated explicitly in its preamble, in the typical prose style of such documents:

Being resolved to define the principles to be respected and the obligations which flow from them, in order to ensure, in the member States and such other States as may become Parties to the present instrument, the effective protection of national minorities and of the rights and freedoms of persons belonging to those minorities, within the rule of law, respecting the territorial integrity and national sovereignty of States.[40]

The Framework Convention is addressing a basic problem that results from the established institutional and legal setting of the classic nation-state. From a human rights perspective, but also from the viewpoint of the (democratically needed) respect for the preferences and liberties of all citizens, there is a significant problem with the inherited institutional and legal framework of the traditional nation-state. The nation-state model of the 19th and early 20th century has a rather repressive attitude towards its minorities, at least from a human rights perspective. In pursuit of its central aim of 'nation-building' – that is, the creation of a society as homogenous as possible in conformity with the *Leitidee* ('dominant idea') of national culture. The nation-state tended to (and sometimes still does) pressure its culturally and linguistically diverse citizens into assimilation, implying that they should adapt completely to the values, norms, culture and language of the majority society. There is no room for diverging preferences in such a model of statehood – it is based on a given *Leitkultur* ('guiding culture' or 'leading culture') and normatively fixed 'national language', which inevitably creates a strong linguistic and cultural asymmetry,

38 On this issue, see Emma Lantschner: Evolution and value of the thematic commentaries of the Advisory Committee of the Framework Convention for the Protection of National Minorities. In: European Yearbook on Human Rights 2 (2010), P. 275–284.

39 See Oeter: Conventions (Footnote 8), P. 552 et seq.

40 See Gerhard Hafner: Präambel. In: Rainer Hofmann, Doris Angst, Emma Lantschner, Günther Rautz, Detlev Rein (Eds.): Rahmenübereinkommen zum Schutz nationaler Minderheiten: Handkommentar. Baden-Baden, Wien, Zürich, St. Gallen 2015, P. 154–156.

embodied in rules on official use of the 'national' language in the administration, the judiciary, schools, media and economic and social life. Divergent minority cultures are assessed as inferior and backwards by the national elites and seen as lacking in loyalty to the ideals of the 'nation'.

Notwithstanding the functional necessity of a simplified language administration in modern centralised states, monolingualism of institutions and social infrastructure imposed by the state will often cause significant human rights problems for members of minorities. Lacking access to state institutions and public services, minorities will face discrimination and exclusion in the structures of modern society. Such discrimination and exclusion is in direct conflict with the principles of equality found in modern constitutions (and international human rights regimes).[41] Socialization in a language different from the national language leads to problems in numerous fields of modern life, such as:

- criminal proceedings
- exercise of the freedoms of association and assembly
- in the context of freedom of expression and information, and in particular with regard to the media
- in the conflict between parental authority and state control of the school system, and the duty to send children to state schools;
- in the health sector (hospitals) and in the realm of elderly care.

The safeguards of general human rights protection under the ECHR address these problems only to a very limited extent and do not really cope with these minority-specific human rights problems, especially the always delicate questions of equality.[42] As a result there is a need to develop and guarantee specific rules for the protection of human rights of members of minorities, with a particular focus on real-world discrimination. The Framework Convention on the Protection of National Minorities should be seen as a targeted response to these specific problems.

European Charter for Regional or Minority Languages

The European Charter for Regional or Minority Languages (the "Language Charter") explicitly formulates some specific objectives. Its focus is the protection of the inherited linguistic diversity as a central building block of Europe's cultural her-

41 See Marko: Law and Ideology (Footnote 11), P. 128–132; and Stefan Oeter: Der Schutz nationaler Minderheiten im Völkerrecht: In: Rüdiger Wolfrum Ed.), Gleichheit und Nichtdiskriminierung im nationalen und internationalen Menschenrechtsschutz. Berlin 2002, P. 187–214.

42 See Thornberry, Martín Estébanez: Minority rights in Europe (Footnote 32), P. 39–87, and Christian Hillgruber, Matthias Jestaedt: Die Europäische Menschenrechtskonvention und der Schutz nationaler Minderheiten. Bonn 1993, in particular P. 33 et seq., 89 et seq.

itage.[43] The preamble of the Language Charter sets out its central aim: "Considering that the protection of the historical regional or minority languages of Europe, some of which are in danger of eventual extinction, contributes to the maintenance and development of Europe's cultural wealth and traditions."[44]

In pursuing this objective, the Language Charter is accordingly focused on measures designed to protect linguistic diversity. The safeguards and measures provided for in the Language Charter are oriented towards the protection and promotion of minority languages, enabling speakers' historically developed bilingualism to be part of their daily life, while opening up additional domains for communicating in minority languages.[45]

The Language Charter tries to facilitate daily use of minority languages (and other communication opportunities) by putting a differentiated set of measures at member states' disposal – a menu of possible safeguards and tools of promotion from which the states must select, at the moment of ratification. Each state therefore creates a set of protective and promotional measures that are tailored to the specific situation of each minority language. The Language Charter is divided, in its essential mode of construction, into two different categories of obligations. These are laid out in Parts 2 and 3 of the charter.

Part 2 lists a number of general guidelines, formulated in very broad terms, that serve as programmatic points of orientation for the minority policies of member states, independent of the specific situation and the priorities set by national minority policy.[46] The objectives of Part 2 are very general, and intended as guidelines for national minority policy with regard to all languages that fall under the authoritative definition of the term 'regional or minority language' contained in Article 1 lit. (a) of the Language Charter. They are deliberately decoupled from the priorities of national minority policy, and apply independently of the nationally defined preferences for certain minorities and languages.[47]

Part 3, on the contrary, sets out a menu of granular, technically formulated standards on language protection and promotion, from which states must – according

43 See Sigrid Boysen: Präambel. In: Sigrid Boysen et al.: Europäische Charta der Regional oder Minderheitensprachen: Handkommentar. Zürich, St. Gallen 2011, P. 40–55.

44 See also Boysen: Präambel (Footnote 43), P. 44 et seq.

45 See Sarah McMonagle: Autochthone Minderheiten und ihre Sprachen – eine europäische Perspektive. In: Ingrid Gogolin, Antje Hansen, Sarah McMonagle, Dominique Rauch (Eds.): Handbuch Mehrsprachigkeit und Bildung. Wiesbaden 2020, P. 31–37, in particular P. 33–34.

46 Concerning Part 2 of the Charter see Peter Hilpold: Artikel 7. In: Sigrid Boysen et al.: Europäische Charta der Regional oder Minderheitensprachen: Handkommentar. Zürich, St. Gallen 2011, P. 112–182, in particular P. 115 et seq., and also Robert Dunbar: Article 7. In: Alba Nogeira López, Eduardo J. Ruiz Vieytez, Iñigo Urrutia Libarona (Eds.): Shaping language rights: commentary on the European Charter for Regional or Minority Languages in light of the Committee of Experts' evaluation. Strasbourg 2012, P. 185–244, in particular P. 187 et seq.

47 See Hilpold: Artikel 7 (Footnote 46), P. 116–17.

to specified requirements – select a set of measures. These measures will, in line with the state's assessment of the situation of the various languages, do justice to the problems and challenges that arise in relation to the languages concerned. In the context of Part 3, states are allowed to choose which languages will profit from the specific protection, and also which concrete measures of protection and promotion will apply to each of the languages chosen.[48] In its essential modes of construction, the mechanism is designed according to the example of the European Social Charter. Such inspiration makes sense since Part 3 largely sets out positive measures of protection and promotion to be tailored to the specific needs of the languages concerned, in substance thus closely resembling the choice required from states under the Social Charter.[49]

Interim findings: convergence of objectives

If one analyses the above documents in their entirety, we need not discuss at length the question of common objectives of the policy guidelines at European level which are set out in them. The lead documents of European minority protection that were analysed in some detail in the first parts of this paper share a common understanding and a common objective – the protection and promotion of historically grown cultural and linguistic diversity. That objective may be expressed with slightly different nuances depending on the specific document, but it underlies all of them nonetheless. The point of departure for the relevant OSCE documents is the insight that only respect for this inherited diversity can secure the basic preconditions for European stability and preservation of peace. The Framework Convention is founded on the understanding that forced suppression of the given diversity will inevitably lead to significant violations of minorities' basic human rights, and that these violations will endanger society's peace and stability. The Language Charter centres protection of inherited linguistic diversity as a key building block of preserving the wealth of European culture. It sees targeted protection and promotion measures in favour of regional and minority language as crucial for preserving inherited linguistic diversity as a constitutive part of the intangible cultural heritage of Europe.[50]

These objectives, deriving from the general aim of preserving and promoting historically grown cultural and linguistic diversity, have found more concrete shape

48 See Sigrid Boysen: Artikel 2. In: Sigrid Boysen et al.: Europäische Charta der Regional oder Minderheitensprachen: Handkommentar. Zürich, St. Gallen 2011, P. 78–87.

49 See Oeter: Conventions (Footnote 8), P. 551.

50 On the relationship between Language Charter and UNESCO Convention on the Protection of the Intangible Cultural Heritage, see Stefan Oeter: Intangible cultural heritage in need of protection: the case of regional and minority languages. In: Evelyne Lagrange, Stefan Oeter, Robert Uerpmann-Wittzack (Eds.): Cultural heritage and international law. Cham 2018, P. 59–83.

in the specific objectives of various regimes. These more specific objectives have developed out of state practice and expressed as specific points of orientation in the wording of the relevant policy and treaty documents. The activities of the OSCE High Commissioner and the relevant monitoring bodies of the Council of Europe[51] have been developed through close interaction with the organs concerned with the member states, and through these activities, we have a considerable body of experience at our disposal that might tell us which instruments might function well under what conditions – and what the central problems and challenges of a sustainable minority policy might be.

3. Guidelines

The common objectives of minority policy, based upon a broad European consensus, find their expression in a number of guidelines for national minority policy. These guidelines transform the broad objectives into specific procedures of national policies. The guidelines set out in the fundamental policy documents of the OSCE and the treaty regimes of the Council of Europe are a reaction to the specific challenges of minority policy in the context of nation-state based legal and institutional frameworks. The primary matter of concern, the preservation and promotion of historically grown patterns of cultural and linguistic diversity, stands in a marked contrast and friction to established ideological codings of the nation-state model. Minority protection runs counter to the programme of creating a state of cultural and linguistic homogeneity, which has always been the ideal of nation-states. Safeguarding the human rights of members of minority groups raises particular challenges for states obsessed with 'unity', since the individual preferences and liberties of minority members all too often suffer under the unitarian tendencies of nation-states, as a kind of collateral damage of imposing a nation's lead culture *(Leitkultur)* on the legal and institutional system of the state.[52]

Formal equality vs. substantive equality

Article 7 of the Framework Convention enshrines *inter alia* the following right: "The Parties shall ensure respect for the right of every person belonging to a national

51 On the construction of the monitoring bodies under the Framework Convention and the Language Charter, see the contributions of Alan Phillips and Stefan Oeter in: Gaetano Pentassuglia (Ed.): Mechanisms for the implementation of minority rights. Strasbourg 2004, P. 109–129 and P. 131–157.

52 See Marko: Law and Ideology (Footnote 11), P. 112–120.

minority to freedom of peaceful assembly, freedom of association, freedom of expression, and freedom of thought, conscience and religion."[53]

One might ask why the Framework Convention reiterates these classic safeguards of general human rights in its minority-related canon. Freedom of assembly and association, freedom of speech and freedom of thought, conscience and religion are already protected under the ECHR and under the International Covenant on Civil and Political Rights of the United Nations. What value does their inclusion in the Framework Convention add? The answer is that obligations under general human rights protection are not enough. Certain minority-specific dangers of individual and collective rights prove difficult to address under the perspective of general human rights protection.[54] A number of states in Europe, in particular those 'belated nations' with a programme of catching up on 'nation-building', have some difficulties with accepting open articulation of and collective organisation around minority-specific concerns. The legislation of these states often contains limitation clauses that prohibit 'separatist tendencies' and activities threatening the unity of the nation or, going further, even put them under criminal sanctions. A broad interpretation of such prohibited activities, in the sense of protecting the 'unity of the nation', treats as a crime any kind of collective organisation and open articulation of the existing diversity of a cultural, linguistic or ethnic nature – a crime against the sacred values of the nation and against national unity. Corresponding restrictive clauses are found in legislation on civil-society associations and assemblies.[55] The same can be found in some states with regard to limits on individual freedom of speech, even more so regarding freedom of the press and of the media. Even the practice of a different religious faith to the majority nation is massively limited in some configurations, in the interest of preserving the cultural and religious homogeneity of the 'nation-state'. Along the same lines is legislation that makes the national (official) language mandatory for associations and assemblies or that restricts or even entirely prohibits the use of regional or minority languages in the public sphere, even in the context of minority-specific associations and assemblies. The state defends itself in these cases against the accusation of excessive restriction of civil and political rights with the argument of the (purported) 'neutrality' of the state and its equal treatment of all citizens. The state claims to safeguard only the basic preconditions of functioning, the smooth operation of its public sphere, and protects itself against 'divisive' activities of a subversive nature, all on the basis of equality and non-discrimination towards all its citizens.

---

53 On Article 7 FCNM, see Anna Fontaine: Artikel 7: Allgemeiner Teil – Europarat. In: Rainer Hofmann, Doris Angst, Emma Lantschner, Günther Rautz, Detlev Rein (Eds.): Rahmenübereinkommen zum Schutz nationaler Minderheiten: Handkommentar. Baden-Baden, Wien, Zürich, St. Gallen 2015, P. 262–270.

54 See also Marko et al.: Against assimilation (Footnote 20), P. 273 et seq.

55 See. Marko et al.: Against assimilation (Footnote 20), P. 274 et seq.

If, however, one looks more deeply into the basic epistemic structure of such argumentation under a lens of modern equality doctrine, the arguments tend more to disguise the problems than to lay them open and deal with them productively. The state with its legal and institutional framework is *not* neutral with regard to the cultural and linguistic characteristics of its population, by definition cannot be, because its legal and institutional system is deeply coded in preferential terms in favour of the nation that it embodies as a 'nation-state'. The European 'nation-state' is coded in such a way that structural discrimination of minorities is inevitable.[56] What is at stake here is the (in structural terms) discriminatory nature of purely formal equality. The question, then, is how to establish substantive equality, leading to the quest for equal opportunities and an equal scope for self-realization, independent of the cultural and linguistic characteristics of citizens.[57]

The Framework Convention reacts to this challenge of freedom of expression and information with a specific safeguard of the rights in view of minority-related threats by formulating in Article 9 (1) of the convention: "The Parties undertake to recognise that the right to freedom of expression of every person belonging to a national minority includes freedom to hold opinions and to receive and impart information and ideas in the minority language, without interference by public authorities and regardless of frontiers."

Guidelines on free use of minority languages in the private and public sphere

This raises the issue of free use of the minority language in the closed, intimate sphere of private life, and even more centrally, its use in public space. While there have been few attempts to limit the private use of minority languages (with the notorious exception of Turkey in recent history[58]), restrictions on minority language use in the public sphere are not as rare as one might think. Public use is sometimes subject to very harsh restrictions.[59] A fundamental guideline of all the documents used here to reconstruct the basics of European minority policy follows from that fact. Both the Language Charter, in its programmatic provision of Part 2 on

56 See Marko: Law and Ideology (Footnote 11), P. 112–120, esp. P. 118f.; compare also Will Kymlicka: Multiculturalism. In: Will Kymlicka (Ed.). Contemporary Political Philosophy: An Introduction. 2nd ed. Oxford 2002, P. 327–376, in particular P. 343 et seq.

57 See Joseph Marko: Against discrimination: the right to equality and the dilemma of difference. In: Joseph Marko (Ed.): Human and Minority Rights Protection by Multiple Diversity Governance. Abingdon 2019, P. 307–339, in particular P. 311 et seq.

58 See Marko et al.: Against assimilation (Footnote 20), P. 239–40; Christian Rumpf: Das türkische Verfassungssystem. Wiesbaden 1996, P. 104–05; Jacob: Minderheitenrecht in der Türkei (Footnote 18), P. 227–229.

59 See Marko et al.: Against assimilation (Footnote 20), P. 273 et seq.

the issue, namely Article 7 (1) lit. (d) Language Charter, and Articles 9–11 of the Framework Convention, and also Section 32.1 of the Copenhagen document of the OSCE explicitly state that the free use of the minority language in the private and public sphere constitute a guiding and foundational principle. Such fundamental orientation around the principle of 'language freedom' *(Sprachenfreiheit)* may be sub-divided into various aspects:

- A core element of individual use in the private sphere is already guaranteed under the ECHR (a test case of this element was Turkey's prohibition of the use of Kurdish).[60]
- 'Use in the public' concerns in particular freedom of expression and freedom to access any kind of information, where it is undisputed (at least in the outcome) that these freedoms include the choice of language as a means of communication.[61]
- Freedom of assembly and freedom of association protect the collective dimensions of the use of a language in community with a group of like-minded individuals – here we also find a normative consensus that both safeguards include the freedom to choose which language that will be used in the group.[62]
- Particular problems arise when it comes to minority language speakers' right to communicate with state authorities and judicial courts and tribunals. Article 10 para. 1 and para. 2 FCNM address this topic, as well as Articles 9 and 10 of the Language Charter, and to a certain degree Section 34 of the OSCE's Copenhagen Document.[63]

The issue of communication in regional or minority languages with authorities and the judiciary is legally delicate, because the special status of the national language as (often the exclusive) official language is a legitimate point of reference for differentiations in language legislation. Given the state interest in a functioning and efficient organisation of administrative authorities and judicial courts, there are valid grounds to determine one (or at the utmost two) languages as a standard medium of communication between citizens and the authorities, and even more as standard forms of communication within the administration (and for keeping official records).[64] It is not possible for the internal communications of authorities and judicial courts to be in a multitude of languages – the internal communication and records must be accessible for all the personnel of state institutions. As a result, there is a functional

60 See Thornberry, Martín Estébanez: Minority rights in Europe (Footnote 32), P. 57 et seq.

61 See only Marko et al.: Against assimilation (Footnote 20), P. 273 et seq.

62 See Fontaine: Artikel 7 (Footnote 53), P. 262 et seq.

63 On the problem of official use of minority languages in general, see Marko et al.: Against assimilation (Footnote 20), P. 243 et seq.

64 See Jean-Marie Woehrling: The European Charter for Regional or Minority Languages – a critical commentary. Strasbourg 2005, P. 159 et seq.

need to limit the number of official languages to one or two. A closer look to the particular situation of multilingual states shows that, in specific situations, the functional need to limit linguistic diversity might be overcome by additional regional arrangements in the language areas of important regional or minority languages. These arrangements typically supplement the general scheme of the official language with an additional official language at the regional level – usually the dominant regional language of the specific region.[65]

The functional need to restrict language use in internal administrative and judiciary communications does not, however, tell us anything about the linguistic regime applicable in contact between administration, courts and citizens. With extended services of translation and interpretation it is obviously possible to be more generous than in the internal sphere, allowing the use of a greater number of languages as possible means of communication with the authorities. Where administrative personnel have facility or fluency in the regional or minority languages, other forms of direct communication without translation might be possible.[66] Multilingual communication with the external sphere, however, must then be translated in the internal communications language of the institution.

In other words: under certain conditions it might make sense to allow citizens to communicate with the administration and judicial courts in minority languages. In this context, the functional needs of states (determined by their available resources) must be balanced with the legitimate communication needs of minorities – and in view of this balancing process the states enjoy a certain margin of appreciation (or margin of state discretion).[67] The situations are very different in detail – both in regards to the communication needs of minority members and the availability of state resources, in particular the existing or potential linguistic resources of administrative personnel. A good illustration of this point is given by Article 10 para. 2 FCNM:

> In areas inhabited by persons belonging to national minorities traditionally or in substantial numbers, if those persons so request and where such a request corresponds to a real need, the Parties shall endeavour to ensure, as far as possible, the conditions which would make it possible to use the minority language in relations between those persons and the administrative authorities.[68]

65 See Marko et al.: Against assimilation (Footnote 20), P. 244 et seq.

66 See Jutta Engbers: Artikel 10. In: Sigrid Boysen et al.: Europäische Charta der Regional oder Minderheitensprachen: Handkommentar. Zürich, St. Gallen 2011, P. 250–284, in particular P. 260f.

67 See Engbers: Artikel 10 (Footnote 66), P. 256 f.

68 See Rainer Hofmann: Artikel 10: Allgemeiner Teil – Europarat. In: Rainer Hofmann, Doris Angst, Emma Lantschner, Günther Rautz, Detlev Rein (Eds.): Rahmenübereinkommen zum Schutz nationaler Minderheiten: Handkommentar. Baden-Baden, Wien, Zürich, St. Gallen 2015, P. 317–326.

Very specific problems arise in the context of judicial proceedings, in particular regarding the use of first languages in criminal proceedings. The dilemma that states must resolve in this context is illustrated by Article 10 para. 3 FCNM which states:

> The Parties undertake to guarantee the right of every person belonging to a national minority to be informed promptly, in a language which he or she understands, of the reasons for his or her arrest, and of the nature and cause of any accusation against him or her, and to defend himself or herself in this language, if necessary with the free assistance of an interpreter.[69]

The functional logic of this provision is immediately convincing. Criminal proceedings are usually of imminent importance for the accused, so it must be made possible for the accused to understand the reasons for their arrest and the nature and the cause of the accusations raised against them, to follow the proceedings and be able to defend themself in a language in which they can express themself adequately. Where the speakers of the minority language have only limited (or perhaps even no) knowledge of the official language, this forces the state to provide translations of relevant documents and call in interpreters for the accused – if the court is not capable (or allowed) to conduct the proceedings in the first language of the accused. This guideline corresponds to the requirements for a 'fair trial' under general human rights protection, as laid down in Article 6 para. 3 lit. (a) and (e) ECHR.[70] Beyond this core obligation of procedural rights in criminal proceedings, states have a considerable leeway in determining the adequate arrangements, and must balance the functional grounds for and against the admission of regional or minority languages in front of courts and tribunals. In most cases, the balance falls against the admission of regional or minority languages. In a great majority of cases in Europe, this is because members of minorities are brought up and socialised bilingually and can articulate themselves without any problem in the official language of the state concerned.

There are some specific problems in the realm of basic social infrastructure, such as the hospital and aged care sectors. By and large these are comparable to the delicate situation of criminal proceedings.[71] Linguistic difficulties are often relevant to the basic legal rights of the people receiving health care (for example, to understand and consent to medical interventions). In high-stress medical situations like an accident or severe illness, care must be taken to ensure smooth communication

69 See Hofmann: Artikel 10 (Footnote 68), P. 324f.; and Woehrling: European Charter (Footnote 64), P. 164.

70 See for e.g. Wolfgang Peukert, Artikel 6. In: Jochen Abraham Frowein, Wolfgang Peukert: Europäische Menschenrechtskonvention: EMRK-Kommentar. 3. Aufl. Kehl 2009, P. 142–268, in particular P. 253–258, P. 266–67.

71 See Dagmar Richter: Artikel 13. In: Sigrid Boysen et al.: Europäische Charta der Regional oder Minderheitensprachen: Handkommentar. Zürich, St. Gallen 2011, P. 323–348, in particular P. 341 et seq.

between patients and medical personnel. In aged care, this challenge is aggravated by the fact that elderly people, in particular in cases of dementia, fall back into their first language, the language of childhood, despite having been functionally bilingual throughout their active life.

Guidelines on use of minority languages in the media

The earlier examination of issues of freedom of expression and information reminds us that language use in the media is of utmost importance for the social use of regional and minority languages – and especially for their presence in the public sphere. The presence of minority languages in print media and electronic media is not only of fundamental importance to the exercise of speakers' communication freedoms, it is also of enormous importance to the perception of the minority language as a relevant medium of social communication – crucial for maintenance and further development of the language. Use of a language in the media creates a need to further develop the language and adapt it to modern conditions.[72] Such a functional multiplicity of the needs for minority language use in media lead to a wide range of specific guidelines.

First and foremost, there is a legitimate demand from the side of the speakers, based upon the communication freedoms of human rights protection, to find media communication in minority languages. Only with such use in the media is it possible to exercise the right to active freedom of speech, and also freedom of information – the freedom to access information in the language that speakers prefer.

In addition, media diversity should be as broad as possible in regional and minority languages, in order to secure their presence in public life. In this context we find quite different challenges and also limits to what is possible, according to the specific characteristics of the relevant media and the varying situations of the languages.

For the case of classical 'linear' television, we can easily conclude that the limits of the possible are rather narrow, at least for the smaller language groups. The creation and maintenance of separate TV channels broadcasting in a minority language is quite difficult for a number of reasons and poses an enormous challenge in terms of the resources needed.[73] It is far easier to meet the demand for regular pro-

72 See Marko et al.: Against assimilation (Footnote 20), P. 281 et seq., and Robert Dunbar, Tom Moring: Article 11 – Media. In: Alba Nogueira López, Eduardo J. Ruiz Vieytez, Iñigo Urrutia Libarona (Eds.): Shaping language rights: Commentary on the European Charter for Regional or Minority Languages in light of the Committee of Experts' evaluation. Strasbourg 2012, P. 373–424, in particular P. 375 et seq.

73 See Marco Körfgen: Artikel 11 – Medien. In: Sigrid Boysen et al.: Europäische Charta der Regional oder Minderheitensprachen: Handkommentar. Zürich, St. Gallen 2011, P. 285–305, in particular P. 293–94; and Dunbar, Moring: Article 11 (Footnote 72), P. 381 et seq.

grammes in minority languages – but even to meet this lower commitment there remain a number of questions which are not easy to answer (When should such programmes be broadcast? How many programmes, at what intervals? What types of programmes, in which quality?) These open questions often reduce the utility of such programmes considerably.[74]

Minority language radio is much easier, as the resource requirements are much lower than for television. It is possible for trained volunteers to produce and air minority language programmes, with only a small amount of support from the public authorities. There is a much smaller risk of overextending public resources.[75]

In the case of print media (newspapers and journals) it is quite difficult to uphold and sustain the publication of a sufficient offering in minority languages. In particular, the low number of speakers that is typical of most of minority languages makes such offerings commercially unappealing, resulting in a need for rather high subsidies from the state. Online formats – news feeds that are similar to the printed press but do not have printing and distribution costs – might offer new options, but it is far from clear whether they can replace the missing offerings in traditional print media.[76]

In general, one can say that the internet and social media provide new platforms and formats for communication with a broad public. Whether these new offerings can satisfy the underlying rationale of securing the presence of the languages in the public space remains unclear and is a question not sufficiently researched.[77]

As a hard baseline for all the minority policy guidelines on the use in the media one could posit a (defensive) safeguard that prevents the state from excessively legislating to restrict the production and distribution of media formats in minority languages. This hard baseline safeguard is only of limited use, however, since most minorities in Europe are quite small, with low numbers of language speakers, making it difficult to sustain commercial offerings in purely economic terms.[78] A sufficient offering of productions and programmes thus needs a considerable amount of

74 See Dunbar, Moring: Article 11 (Footnote 72), P. 396 et seq.; and Körfgen: Artikel 11 (Footnote 73), P. 295–96.

75 See also Dunbar, Moring: Article 11 (Footnote 72), P. 394 et seq.

76 See Dunbar, Moring: Article 11 (Footnote 72), P. 403 et seq.; and Körfgen: Artikel 11 (Footnote 73), P. 298 et seq.

77 See Jennifer Jackson Preece: "Taking Oslo Online": Minority language policy and the internet. In: Iryna Ulasiuk, Laurenţiu Hadîrcă, William Romans (Eds.): Language Policy and Conflict Prevention. Leiden 2018, P. 231–250; and Tom Moring: New media and the implementation of instruments in support of minority rights related to media. In: European Yearbook on Minority Issues 6 (2007), P. 19–50; see also Elin Haf Gruffydd Jones, Jarmo Lainio, Tom Moring, Fatma Resit: New technologies, new social media, and the European Charter for Regional or Minority Languages. Report for the Committee of Experts. Strasbourg 2019, available at: https://rm.coe.int/new-media-report-web-en/168098dd88 (last retrieval: 18 Jan 2021).

78 See Marko et al.: Against assimilation (Footnote 20), P. 284 et seq.

state support. That support can mean treating such programmes as a public good and including them in the mission of public broadcasters, as part of the public infrastructure *(Grundversorgung)*, or it can mean (heavily) subsidising independently operated platforms.[79] The basic finding is that there will always be considerable demand for positive action from the side of the state – a demand that in legal terms (if not laid down as explicit obligation in international legal documents) can only be deduced indirectly from the state's *duty to protect* the communication freedoms of the members of minorities.[80]

Guidelines on school and education

Judging from my own experience, by far the most important sector for the medium- and long-term survival of smaller regional and minority languages is the realm of schooling, or (in more abstract terms) the education sector.[81] The reason is simple: most speakers of regional and minority languages in Europe live in a situation of progressed diglossia, which means a situation of strongly asymmetric bilingualism. When diglossia comes with a strong language hierarchy, the domains of minority languages shrink and shrink ever more, until they are limited to the intimate space of family use (perhaps in rural areas still also some village use). The practical value of the language is very much reduced, with a subsidiary emotional value as a language of close communication; transmission in families becomes precarious. Without external support for language acquisition, mostly via school offerings, the very survival of the language cannot be guaranteed any more.[82] Since adequate offerings in the education system are often the only way to confront the menace of language death, targeted support for language acquisition in schools constitutes a legitimate demand. The question of adequate educational offerings is an issue of fundamental importance for minority policy.

The legal guidelines developed for this sector can be described as a graduated system of requirements building upon each other. The starting point, deriving from the general system of human rights protection, is the right to education, as provided for in Article 2 of the First Additional Protocol of the ECHR. This general right, however, is non-specific and does not help much with the specific challenges of language maintenance for minority languages. It therefore does not provide us with clear guidelines on educational matters in relation to minority languages.[83]

79 See Körfgen: Artikel 11 (Footnote 73), P. 299.
80 See Marko et al.: Against assimilation (Footnote 20), P. 286.
81 See Oeter: Mehrsprachigkeit (Footnote 20), P. 149 et seq.
82 See Heiko F. Marten: Sprach(en)politik: eine Einführung. Tübingen 2016, P. 65 et seq., P. 92 et seq.
83 See also Thornberry, Martín Estébanez: Minority rights in Europe (Footnote 32), P. 60 et seq.

Already more specific is the programmatic guideline of Part 2 of the Language Charter, where Article 7 para. 1 lit. (f) requires "the provision of appropriate forms and means for the teaching and study of regional or minority languages at all appropriate stages".[84]

More explicit in its function as a guideline is Article 14 para. 1 FCNM, which states: "The Parties undertake to recognise that every person belonging to a national minority has the right to learn his or her minority language."[85] This is supplemented by the guideline of Article 12 Abs. 3 FCNM: "The Parties undertake to promote equal opportunities for access to education at all levels for persons belonging to national minorities."[86]

Even more precise are the guidelines in The Hague Recommendations Regarding the Education Rights of National Minorities of the OSCE High Commissioner for National Minorities of October 1996, in particular the guiding principles formulated in paragraphs 11, 12 and 13 on the organisation of the school system in relation to children from minority families.[87]

The guidelines in the Hague Recommendations of 1996 are very helpful, because they elaborate with utmost clarity the fundamental rationale which should form the underlying basis of the organisation and structure of a minority-related schooling system. On the structures of pre-school education, the Hague Recommendations call in paragraph 11 for the following:

> The first years of education are of pivotal importance in a child's development. Educational research suggests that the medium of teaching at pre-school and kindergarten levels should ideally be the child's language. Wherever possible, States should create conditions enabling parents to avail themselves of this option.[88]

In the realm of primary school education, paragraph 12 of the Hague Recommendations formulates the following guideline:

---

84 See Hilpold: Artikel 7 (Footnote 46), P. 136 et seq., and Dunbar: Article 7 (Footnote 46), P. 217 et seq.

85 See Claudine Brohy: Artikel 14: Allgemeiner Teil – Europarat. In: Rainer Hofmann, Doris Angst, Emma Lantschner, Günther Rautz, Detlev Rein (Eds.): Rahmenübereinkommen zum Schutz nationaler Minderheiten: Handkommentar. Baden-Baden, Wien, Zürich, St. Gallen 2015, P. 414–422.

86 On this, see Charlotte Altenhoener-Dion: Artikel 12: Allgemeiner Teil – Europarat. In: Rainer Hofmann, Doris Angst, Emma Lantschner, Günther Rautz, Detlev Rein (Eds.): Rahmenübereinkommen zum Schutz nationaler Minderheiten: Handkommentar. Baden-Baden, Wien, Zürich, St. Gallen 2015, P. 371–379.

87 OSCE High Commissioner on National Minorities: The Hague Recommendations regarding the education rights of national minorities, October 1996, available at: https://www.osce.org/hcnm/hague-recommendations (last retrieval: 18.01.2021).

88 See also the explanation in para. 11 in the 'Explanatory Notes' – Hague Recommendations (Footnote 87), P. 13 f.

> Research also indicates that in primary school, the curriculum should ideally be taught in the minority language. The minority language should be taught as a subject on a regular basis. The official state language should also be taught as a subject on a regular basis preferably by bilingual teachers who have a good understanding of the children's cultural and linguistic background. Towards the end of this period, a few practical or non-theoretical subjects should be taught through the medium of the State language. Wherever possible, States should create conditions enabling parents to avail themselves of this option.[89]

Regarding secondary schools, paragraph 13 of the Hague Recommendations takes up and continues the basic approach of school education in the first language of the child, with a gradually extended share of education in the official language throughout the different phases of education. Paragraph 13 states:

> In secondary school, a substantial part of the curriculum should be taught through the medium of the minority language. The minority language should be taught as a subject on a regular basis. The State language should also be taught as a subject on a regular basis, preferably by bilingual teachers who have a good understanding of the children's cultural and linguistic background. Throughout this period, the number of subjects taught in the State language, should gradually be increased. Research findings suggest that the more gradual the increase, the better for the child."[90]

If one looks into the details of the various problems and the specific education needs of minority languages, one sees that what constitutes 'adequate arrangements' will depend on the size of the minority, the number of speakers, the sociolinguistic situation of the language (how many domains are still available?), the extent of language transmission in families, the degree of language development (particularly in modern domains), and the structure of the school system. Different situations will require different arrangements, each adapted to the specific circumstances.[91] The following examples will illustrate the variations in both the challenges faced and in the solutions needed to cope with them.

Let us take as an example of a 'small language', i.e. a language with a small number of speakers, such as North Frisian. North Frisian is the traditional regional language of the Northern Sea coast area of the old Duchy of Schleswig in the German Land Schleswig-Holstein, covering the major parts of the county of Nordfriesland. This is a Western Germanic language, halfway between Low German and 'Old English'. It

89 See also the 'Explanatory Notes' – Hague Recommendations (Footnote 87), P. 14.

90 See the 'Explanatory Notes' – Hague Recommendations (Footnote 87), P. 14.

91 See Christine Langenfeld: Artikel 8 – Bildung. In: Sigrid Boysen et al.: Europäische Charta der Regional oder Minderheitensprachen: Handkommentar. Zürich, St. Gallen 2011, P. 183–221, in particular P. 192 et seq.; in addition Stefan Oeter: Aus europäischer Sicht: Die Regional und Minderheitensprachen und ihr Platz in den deutschen Schulsystemen. In: Bundesraat för Nedderdütsch (Ed.): Mit den Regional und Minderheitensprachen auf dem Weg nach Europa. Leer 2011 (Schriften des Instituts für niederdeutsche Sprache 43), P. 34–62.

is today spoken (and used as a daily language) only by a small group of some thousands of speakers, mostly on the islands around Föhr. The speakers all live in a situation of progressed diglossia, with the dominant language being Standard German.[92] School education in the minority language, in particular the teaching of reading and writing, would probably make no sense here in functional terms. As a result, the educational authorities of Schleswig-Holstein limit themselves to a scheme of teaching the minority language in a number of selected schools in the language area, as a second language taught as a separate subject. This solution could have been adequate, in principle, if the state were to ensure that there are sufficient (and easily accessible) classes meeting children's needs at a sufficient quality to secure language acquisition and further development of the language. Language learning as a separate subject should be integrated in the curriculum as an ordinary class *(Schulfach)*, and the subject should be taught consistently throughout the school career of the children. Unfortunately, these conditions were not met, which endangers the potential success of the model. The offering for a long time was haphazard, limited to schools where a trained North Frisian teacher was (more or less accidentally) available, and offered only for some school years. Practically no targeted teaching material existed, teacher training in Frisian was underfunded and produced only a very few qualified teachers, and so on. Under these conditions, a model of teaching the language, adequate in principle, was doomed to failure and could not meaningfully contribute to the objective of language maintenance, let alone further language development.[93]

The situation is quite different for the Danish minority in Schleswig-Holstein. From the start, the situation is already very different, since we are dealing here with a fully developed national language serving as official language in the neighbouring Kingdom of Denmark. The Danish language is actively used in nearly all formal domains in Schleswig-Holstein and serves as the routine means of communication in the public space of Danish associations and in the cultural life of the minority. The school system for the Danish minority is outsourced to a separate (and independent) Danish school association, massively supported by the Danish state (in addition to the support given by the Land Schleswig-Holstein as a part of the financial scheme for private schools replacing state schools). The language of instruction at the Danish schools – ranging from kindergarten and pre-schools to two grammar schools leading to the matriculation exam (the *Abitur*) – is Danish; only the classes in German are taught in German as the language of instruction. The result of the

92 See in detail Alastair Walker: Die Friesen und das Friesische in Nordfriesland. In: Rahel Beyer, Albrecht Plewnia (Eds.): Handbuch der Sprachminderheiten in Deutschland. Tübingen 2020, P. 65–138, in particular P. 111 et seq.

93 See Walker: Friesen (Footnote 91), P. 94 et seq.,and Stefan Oeter: Die Europäische Charta der Regional oder Minderheitensprachen: zum Beispiel Nordfriesisch. In: Thomas Steensen (Ed.): Nationale Minderheiten: Beiträge zum 9. Internationalen Ferdinand-Tönnies-Symposium. Bredstedt 2017, P. 137–163.

system is impressive: school children who, at the beginning of their school career often have only shaky knowledge (if any) of the Danish language, leave the school with an advanced degree of bilingual competence, with Danish often being the stronger language over German, despite the overwhelming dominance of German in daily life in the surrounding society.[94]

It is also interesting to examine the contrasting case of German language in South Tyrol. In general, one can say that the linguistic situation in the Autonomous Province of Bozen/Bolzano is characterised by marked societal bilingualism. In daily life, however, there is a strong tendency to retreating into monolingual social spaces. This tendency can be seen in the school system, where German and Italian schools form two separate branches of school education neatly separated from each other.[95] Children from (German-speaking) South Tyrolean families go to schools where the medium of instruction is – Standard German, notwithstanding the fact that the local idioms show a marked difference from Standard German, being dialects of the Bavarian variety of German. Only the additional subject of Italian language (as the official language of the state) is taught with Italian as the medium of instruction, and there are a lot of complaints about the deficient quality of this teaching. As a result of these problems, local South Tyroleans often have difficulty mastering the Italian official language – a rather absurd result in functional terms, but one that can be found in other minority regions with school systems segregated along national lines. From a functional perspective it would be much better to educate children in such situations in a bilingual school model following the guidelines of the Hague Recommendations, in particular for secondary schools where the share of teaching in the official language should expand in a gradual way in the higher grades of secondary education. Unfortunately, there are few examples of such bilingual models of teaching in Europe – one could only mention the model of the Spanish Autonomous Community of Galicia, where the regional language Gallego and the national language Castellano are taught side by side (and the teaching takes place in both languages as the medium of instruction). Another case worth mentioning might be the '2plus' model in the Saxonian region of Upper Lusatia (teaching in both German and Upper Sorbian).[96]

---

94 See Karen Margrethe Pedersen, Doris Stolberg: Dänisch als Minderheitensprache in Deutschland. In: Rahel Beyer, Albrecht Plewnia (Eds.): Handbuch der Sprachminderheiten in Deutschland. Tübingen 2020, P. 17–63; see also Stefan Oeter: Die Entwicklung der europäischen Sprachenvielfalt und die Rolle der Minderheiten. In: Christoph Bergner, Matthias Weber (Eds.): Aussiedler und Minderheitenpolitik in Deutschland. München 2009 (Schriften des Bundesinstituts für Kultur und Geschichte der Deutschen im östlichen Europa 38), P. 151–175, in particular P. 161–62.

95 See Marko et al.: Against assimilation (Footnote 20), P. 293–94, and Siegfried Baur, Dietmar Larcher: Fit für Europa: Erfahrungen mit Mehrsprachigkeit in Südtirol. Meran 2011.

96 See – as far as the case of the Autonomous Community Galicia is concerned – the 2nd Evaluation Report of the Committee of Experts fort he Language Charter– Council of Europe/European

The example of school education points again to the fact that the construction of specific standards for an adequate minority policy in given cases is highly dependent on the specific circumstances of the minority (and the sociolinguistic conditions of the minority language). There is an irrefutable need to find solutions adapted to the specific situation. This basic observation applies not only to the education system, but also to areas such as the inclusion of minority languages in the media and the official communication in minority languages with administration and judicial courts, in addition to the solutions needed in social services, support of cultural activities, and so on.

A fundamental consequence results from these insights: if one is not willing to rely on very broad and sweeping clauses that give a general orientation but do not indicate any specific measure, then a highly differentiated instrument that puts out a range of specific measures adapted to different situations is needed. Otherwise the decision of what to do, in light of the prevailing circumstances, is largely left to the member states, with international institutions having only very loose control over the details. The decisions needed to operationalise the general guidelines involve a number of rather delicate issues of political choice – a political choice states are not willing to entrust to international institutions with only a very broad indication of where to go. The lack of trust in international institutions (and the unwillingness to give up control) was probably the main reason why the proposal of an Additional Protocol to the ECHR met such outright rejection in the early 1990s – and the atmosphere in international fora has not become better in the meantime. States want to keep control of the delicate matters of political choice that are involved in operationalising the general guidelines into specific standards, which sets clear limits to the ambition of steering national minority policy.[97] The mode of construction borrowed from the European Social Charter, namely the provision of a 'menu' of potential measures set out in the undertakings of Part 3 of the Charter, has a number of advantages in that regard. The 'menu' from which states must select at the time of ratification – the set of building blocks they believe correspond to the needs of each language chosen for special protection under Part 3 – allows exactly the kind of differentiated measures that fit to the specific circumstances. Admittedly, this requires some degree of goodwill on the part of states in selecting the adequate undertakings. In most cases, however, empirical evidence shows us that states do

---

Charter for Regional or Minority Languages: Report of the Committee of Experts on the Application of the Charter in Spain,2nd Monitoring Cycle, 11 Dec. 2008, available at: https://rm.coe.int/CoERMPublicCommonSearchServices/ DisplayDCTMContent?documentId=09000016806dba68 (last retrieval: 18 Jan 2021); concerning the 'Two+' model in Upper Lusatia see Christoph Gantefort, Natalia Migal, Ingrid Gogolin, Hans-Joachim Roth: Ein Weg zur Zweisprachigkeit: Bilanz des Modellprojekts "2plus" sorbisch-deutsche Schulen in Sachsen nach sechs Jahren wissenschaftlicher Begleitung. Abschlussbericht an das Land Sachsen. Münster 2011.

97 See Oeter: Mehrsprachigkeit (Footnote 20), P. 150 et seq.

try to do their best in selecting from the 'menu'. The 'menu approach' also allows international institutions to formulate rather specific, technical undertakings in the list of options which, once chosen by a state, become relatively stringent obligations. For the monitoring body, it is much easier to assess whether such a concrete obligation has been fulfilled or not than it is for a monitoring body under a convention full of broad and sweeping guidelines (such as the Framework Convention). At the same time, states retain a certain degree of control over the specific composition of the menu of ratifications – it is their decision (at ratification) that determines the set of undertakings against which they are measured. This choice makes it possible for the treaty body to enter into a dialogue with the state concerned if they come to the conclusion that the undertakings chosen make no sense under the specific circumstances – the body may at least propose that the state change its instrument of ratification.

4. Standards

The guidelines for an adequate minority policy that have been formulated in numerous documents at the European level need to be broken down into specific standards. One of the major aims of at least partially concrete standards is that international institutions will be able to control the compliance and adequate implementation of such standards. The European instrument that is most advanced in accomplishing the desired steps of operationalisation to specific standards is the European Charter for Regional or Minority Languages, but it has to pay a price for this achievement. The price to be paid is the menu approach, which leaves a considerable degree of control to the states in selecting the specific standards they will implement. In the following passages, we will first revisit the standards for schooling and education that have particular relevance to the maintenance of minority languages. Following that, we will look into the standards on the use of minority languages in the media and the issue of official use of minority languages in the judiciary and administration.

Standards for education

Probably the most crucial way that a state's minority policy can contribute to the maintenance of languages is via adequate education infrastructure at all levels: kindergarten and pre-school, primary school, secondary school and tertiary education. This infrastructure has the potential to secure the transmission of a language from generation to generation, especially for small languages with a low number of speakers and a progressed shrinking of domains. For these languages, the point will come when the practical value of the language is so diminished that speakers no longer find it worthwhile to keep the language alive, and they will stop transmitting it within their families. If this happens on a wide scale, the mode of natural language acquisition in early childhood might become precarious, or even be lost.[98] But even for larger language communities, with several million speakers, where the language still serves as a dominant means of communication in the daily life of speakers, there might still be a need to support the language by means of education. Even more widely spoken languages must strive to enable speakers to use the language in as many domains as possible, including the broad variety of specialised technical languages of expert communities. To be used in a broad variety of domains, a language requires not only constant expansion *(Ausbau)*, i.e. development of grammar and of the lexicon of available words, but also requires speakers to develop the capacity to use their first language in the highly technical domains of modern life. This capacity is usually acquired in school education.

The objective of stabilisation and expansion into a variety of domains demands a series of coordinated measures of minority policy in school education.[99] The types of measures needed will depend very much – as elaborated above – on the demographic, social and sociolinguistic situation of a minority (and its minority language) and also on the institutional arrangements of the national educational system.

The Language Charter is instructive in that regard, with its elaborate menu of different levels of undertakings for education adapted to different circumstances. Article 8, the provision of Part 3 of the Charter that deals with matters of education, distinguishes in principle three different levels of promoting languages in school – levels which can be chosen according to the specific situation of each language:
- Education given in the minority language, using it as a medium of instruction
- Bilingual forms of teaching in both the minority and the official language
- Teaching of the minority language solely as a subject matter.[100]

These different forms of educational promotion of language acquisition and development make very different demands on the school system, and also on the system of teacher training. For the school system and the curriculum, it makes a big difference whether one or more languages are used as medium of instruction, affecting both the composition of the teaching staff, and also the degree of flexibility a school will have in employing the teachers for different classes. When a school system merely teaches the language, it requires only on the group of teachers who

98 See McMonagle: Autochthone Minderheiten (Footnote 45), P. 33–34.

99 See Oeter: Mehrsprachigkeit (Footnote 20), P. 149 et seq.

100 See on the graduated scale of options of Art. 8.1 ECRML Alba Nogueira López: Article 8.1 – Education (I). In: Alba Nogueira López, Eduardo J. Ruiz Vieytez, Iñigo Urrutia Libarona (Eds.): Shaping language rights: commentary on the European Charter for Regional or Minority Languages in light of the Committee of Experts' evaluation. Strasbourg 2012, P. 247–288, in particular P. 256 et seq.

are qualified to teach the minority language as a second language. Under the more ambitious options, there is a need for a broad range of specifically trained teachers, enabling them to teach the substantive content of a variety of subject matters in the minority language.[101] The need for a broad variety of qualifications places particular demands on the system of teacher training – it is not sufficient any more to train a limited amount of language teachers; rather, a broad range of teachers specialising in a variety of subjects must be trained to teach their specialities in the minority language. This is quite an ambitious endeavour for educational systems that traditionally have operated in a monolingual fashion.[102]

The weakest version of the options (teaching the minority language exclusively as a subject matter) is in organisational terms the easiest path. In practice, this option proves to leave language education in precarious position, because the offerings tend to remain under the minimum conditions required by the Charter. These minimum conditions are designed to ensure that such a model can achieve a sensible result at all.[103] The basic preconditions of the option, at least if the model is to make sense in terms of language maintenance, are the following:

- Language offered as a separate subject (problematic case of Low German)
- Regular component of the curriculum (at least as an elective subject [*Wahlpflichtfach*])
- Sufficient number of teaching hours (more than just one or two hours per week)
- Continuity of the offering throughout the grade levels
- Sufficient-quality teaching materials available for all grades
- Basic and further training of teachers adapted to the needs of the education system (in terms of quantity and quality of teachers trained).

The monitoring reports of the Committee of Experts for the Language Charter deliver quite telling examples of the numerous challenges of such a targeted promotion of minority languages in the education system.[104] A closer look to the exemplary case of the teaching of Low German in northern German schools may illustrate the point. In 1998, Germany recognised Low German – with the ratification of the Language Charter – as a separate regional language, distinct from 'German' (meaning Standard German). In most of the federal states *(Länder)* of northern Germany the state accepted the obligation to offer Low German as a separate subject in

101 See Langenfeld: Artikel 8 (Footnote 91), P. 217 et seq.

102 See also Oeter: Mehrsprachigkeit (Footnote 20), P. 153.

103 See Nogueira López: Article 8.1 (Footnote 100), P. 260–262; Oeter: Mehrsprachigkeit (Footnote 20), P. 152.

104 The monitoring reports of the ComEx are available at https://www.coe.int/en/web/european-charter-regional-or-minority-languages/reports-and-recommendations#{%2228993157%22:[20]} (last retrieval: 18 Jan 2021).

schools in the traditional language area.[105] However, in many federal states (Länder), the teaching of Low German is not offered as a separate subject, a visible part of the curriculum, but rather remains integrated into the classes of German, with a minimal, largely symbolic share of the hours of teaching. This solution is an odd legacy of the times when Low German was perceived as a dialect rather than as a separate language. Even in the situations where Low German *is* offered as a separate subject, it usually remains marginalised as a purely elective course outside the regular curriculum. This means it is given outside the regular timetable, thus imposing an additional burden on pupils. This (irregular) model of teaching usually remains precarious, is not backed up sufficiently with trained teaching staff and operates with an insufficient number of teaching hours per week. The offering in most regions is limited to a small number of schools, without any systematic coordination of the relevant offerings throughout the various grades and levels of education. The range of teaching materials is not of an adequate quality, and the basic and further training of teachers for the teaching of minority languages is obviously insufficient to sustain a consistent offering throughout the traditional language area.[106] However, if a language like Low German, which is under serious threat of extinction, is taught only in a haphazard way at some places in some grade levels, with an insufficient number of hours and a precarious integration into the overall curriculum, without a sufficient number of adequately trained teachers and without teaching materials of the necessary quality, the model is doomed to failure – it cannot achieve the intended result of language maintenance. Such a precarious offering is reduced to a mere exercise in symbolism, an attempt to disguise the lack of political will to take resolute action and to develop a sustainable minority policy that really contributes to the survival of the language.

In addition to these core undertakings in the field of education, experiences of monitoring the two Council of Europe conventions and also the practice of the OSCE High Commissioner for National Minorities demonstrate that there are other issues of importance in educational matters. These issues play a certain role in safeguarding the success of minority policy in matters of education. One might point here to the need to further intercultural understanding via targeted measures in school education. Pursuing such an objective requires some specific components in teaching, components specifically dedicated to teaching the culture and history of the relevant minorities, as is provided for in Article 8 para. 1 lit. (g) of the Language Charter.[107] Establishing such units of teaching is often difficult in the framework of traditional

105 See Stefan Oeter: Status der Regional und Minderheitensprachen aus verfassungs- und völkerrechtlicher Sicht. In: Niederdeutsches Jahrbuch 130 (2007), P. 127–150, in particular P. 132 et seq.

106 See Oeter: Platz in den deutschen Schulsystemen (Footnote 91), P. 50 et seq.

107 See e.g. Langenfeld: Artikel 8 (Footnote 91), P. 216–17.

nation-state school systems and has to confront strong ideological barriers. The typical history curriculum is all too often focused on very traditional forms of one-sided narratives of a glorious national history. This tradition is still very dominant in history teaching. As an additional challenge, a focus on mutual understanding tells us that teaching the history and culture of minorities should not be limited to specific minority schools, where it is taught only to children from minority families, but should be offered for all children going to school in the regions where the minority traditionally lives, thus covering also the children from the majority population – this, at least, is the standard set up under Article 12 (1) FCNM.[108]

A further lesson drawn from experiences of dedicated minority schooling points to the functional need to establish targeted mechanisms for internal monitoring of the minority language components in the school system. This is very helpful if one wants to detect qualitative deficiencies in the system of school organisation und the schemes of teaching, in order to react in an early phase and take measures improving the system.[109] Such an educational monitoring with a focus on the minority-related endeavours in school education serves two objectives at the same time. On the one hand, it helps to establish a mechanism of quality assurance that is urgently needed in a system that still bears traits of an experimental arrangement (without long-standing experience how the different components work together); on the other hand, it delivers linkage points for a public debate on the objectives, the necessary quality, but also the deficiencies of the existing system of educational promotion of minority languages – and thus helps to create some kind of a 'learning system'.

Standards for media

A similar need for differentiated solutions can be seen in the field of media offerings in regional and minority languages. The different menu options of the Language Charter provided for in Article 11 illustrate the problems involved and the potential solutions.

The strongest option under the Language Charter, the option set out in Article 11 (1) lit. (a) (i) ECRML, provides for the creation of at least one radio station and one television channel broadcasting in the regional or minority language. This is a quite challenging endeavour, at least for television, since a dedicated television channel requires considerable resources – financial as well as human resources. In most national contexts these resources will not be easily available, which makes such a highly ambitious project not a very sensible political target.[110] The broadcasting of

108 See Nogueira López: Article 8.1 (Footnote 100), P. 265–66.
109 See only Langenfeld: Artikel 8 (Footnote 91), P. 219–20.
110 See Dunbar, Moring: Article 11 (Footnote 72), P.381 et seq.

television programmes in regional and minority languages on a regular schedule is a much more realistic and practicable option.[111] This option has a number of practical questions with the potential to hamper its ability to promote and maintain the minority language: How regularly should programmes be broadcast – once a month, once a week, or even daily? What timeslot should these programmes be broadcast in, and which channels of transmission should be used? Difficult-to-watch timeslots and problematic channels of transmission may significantly hamper the practical use of such offerings for minority members. How about the quality of the programmes? Who is producing them, under the conditions of scarcity of trained personnel with knowledge of the minority languages?

These problems are easier to solve for radio, since the technical and logistical requirements are much lower.[112] With some support from the state it is even possible to put civil-society organisations in a position to produce and broadcast radio programmes in the minority language. An interesting example of this is the Northern Frisian radio programmes produced (with support from state authorities) by the Frisian Fering Foundation on the island of Föhr.[113] Radio Rumantsch in the Swiss canton of Grisons (Graubünden), a quite extreme example admittedly, demonstrates the potential pitfalls of overambitious endeavours in this field. Broadcasting entirely in Romansh (Rumantsch Grischun), with a 24-hour programme, Radio Rumantsch was created some ten years ago as a separate radio station for the Romansh community, as part of the network of Swiss public broadcasters. The station has attracted a significant number of academically trained members of the minority, with the downside of cannibalising the other institutions and organisations of the Romansh community.[114]

Print media, in particular newspapers and journals in regional or minority languages, have their own problems. The human resources problem is less of an issue since print media can operate with quite a small staff. However, the economic viability of print media in minority languages is often highly fragile. The high distribution costs of traditional print media, combined with the very small number of readers, presents significant economic obstacles for the sustainable operation of periodical

111 See Dunbar, Moring: Article 11 (Footnote 72), P. 396 et seq.

112 See. Dunbar, Moring: Article 11 (Footnote 72), P. 394 et seq.

113 See the 5th evaluation report of the Committee of Experts for the Language Charter on Germany – Council of Europe/European Charter for Regional or Minority Languages: Report of the Committee of Experts on the Application of the Charter in Germany,5th Monitoring Cycle, 28 May 2014, available at: https://rm.coe.int/CoERMPublicCommonSearchServices/DisplayDCTMContent?documentId=09000016806d8829 (last retrieval: 18 Jan 2021).

114 See the 3rd evaluation report of the Committee of Experts for the Language Charter on Switzerland – Council of Europe / European Charter for Regional or Minority Languages: Report of the Committee of Experts on the Application of the Charter in Switzerland, 3rd Monitoring Cycle, 12 March 2008, available at: https://rm.coe.int/CoERMPublicCommonSearchServices/DisplayDCTMContent?documentId=09000016806dba92 (last retrieval: 18 Jan 2021).

print media. As a consequence, there is often an urgent need for significant state subsidies if such periodicals are to survive.[115]

Online media creates a number of new opportunities in that regard, particularly because it reduces distribution costs and facilitates the distribution of content in minority languages.[116] A fundamental problem remains, however: who is capable of producing the necessary content? At least for small minorities, with a limited reservoir of adequately trained persons, this is a considerable challenge.

The Language Charter does contain some standards requiring a certain degree of state support for the production and distribution of audio-visual works in minority languages (and also for translation in the field of book production).[117]

Standards for official language use

We can find, at least in principle, comparable requirements for a range of differentiated standards for the adequate arrangements of official use of regional and minority languages in administration and the judiciary, mostly around the rules on language use for citizens communicating with state authorities.

Use of regional and minority languages in communication between citizens and authorities varies significantly in practice, depending on the sociolinguistic situation of the languages and their speakers, as well as the internal logic (and organisational tradition) of the state apparatus. The underlying problem in most states is the legacy of the traditional nation-state, usually founded on a policy of strict monolingualism.[118] This raises considerable obstacles for any attempt to develop constructive arrangements allowing some (limited) use of minority languages with state authorities. These obstacles vary, however, with the different levels of public authority. We quite often find situations in Europe where oral use of minority languages in communication with local authorities is possible.[119] In traditional settlement areas of minorities with a relatively high proportion of relevant language speakers, it is relatively likely that speakers of such minority languages may be found among the administrative staff of municipalities. From a purely functional perspective, it is easy here to enable use of the minority language in communication with the municipal

115 See Körfgen: Artikel 11 (Footnote 73), P. 299.

116 See the references supra in Footnote 77.

117 See Körfgen: Artikel 11 (Footnote 73), P. 297–98, 300–01.

118 See Marko et al.: Against assimilation (Footnote 20), P. 243 et seq.

119 Art. 10.2.b ECRML; see Jutta Engbers: Article 10 – Administrative authorities and public services. In: Alba Nogueira López, Eduardo J. Ruiz Vieytez, Iñigo Urrutia Libarona (Eds.): Shaping language rights: commentary on the European Charter for Regional or Minority Languages in light of the Committee of Experts' evaluation. Strasbourg 2012, P. 337–424, in particular P. 351–52.

administration, even in administration responses to letters and applications in minority languages. The core obstacle here is not logistical, but rather the persisting ideology of monolingualism that lingers in the legal framework of municipal administration.

The same functional logic might also lead to situations where the use of the minority language as an (additional) official language at the municipal level might make sense. In states with a multi-ethnic self-understanding, it is possible to open the path towards such local arrangements of official language use, even within the municipal administration. As an example I would like to mention the case of the Romansh municipalities in Grisons (Graubünden) that have the option to operate in the language of the local Romansh majority.[120]

Much more difficult is the inclusion of regional and majority languages in communication arrangements for the state administration. If allowed at all, the use of minority languages is usually limited to submitting applications and documents in the minority language.[121] Where administrative staff with the necessary linguistic capabilities are available, the applications and documents can be processed directly within the administration. Quite often, however, the administration will have to rely on translation services. Accordingly, the 'menu option' set out in Article 10 (1) lit. (a) (iii) of the Language Charter, which guarantees a response in minority language by the administration, is not often selected by states.

The Language Charter includes some ambitious menu options, which provide for a genuinely bilingual administration. However, these are quite challenging to implement (and exist only in a very limited number of cases).[122] For most national administrations, such a path seems far too costly and difficult. The existing empirical evidence shows that the creation of an administration that processes administrative actions in more than one language makes sense only in the context of territorial autonomies where the regional language becomes a second official language. In these cases, the option has proven to function well and be useful from a political perspective.

From a broader perspective, one might ask what would justify such additional efforts. From a functional perspective, these arrangements do not seem to be necessary – the members of minorities are usually bilingual anyway and in most cases have perfectly mastered the national language (in addition to their minority language). They do not need arrangements for official use of minority languages in order to communicate effectively with the administration. The value of such arrangements of official use lie less in the communication needs of daily life and more in symbolism – it signifies the state's recognition of the minority, expands the practical value

120 Art. 10.2.a ECRML; See Engbers: Article 10 (Footnote 119), P. 350–51.

121 Art. 10.1.a (iv) and (v) ECRML; see Engbers: Article 10 (Footnote 119), P. 345–46.

122 Art. 10.1.a (i) ECRML; see Engbers: Article 10 (Footnote 119), P. 344–45.

of the language, and conveys a message to the members of the minority that this is also their state. The minority language also gains new domains, forcing it to develop further the language, in the sense of *Sprachausbau*. This increases the value of the language, and not just symbolically.[123]

5. Conclusion: What do we still need?

In reviewing the findings of this study, we can conclude that the community of European states has progressed quite far in narrowing down shared objectives into specific guidelines and standards. Over the past three decades, the states of Europe have, through the OSCE and Council of Europe, developed an impressive set of objectives, guidelines and standards for issues of minority policy. With such an array, it can be seen that we do not need further guidelines and standards. All we need in this domain is out there already. The guidelines and standards set out in this paper in some detail cover the problems sufficiently. What is missing is something else, something different.

If we look in detail at minority policy in European states, we can see that missing 'something else' is an operative consensus covering the details of administrative practice, beyond the ritual repetition of declamations at political summits and working bodies of government experts in the framework of the OSCE and the Council of Europe. We can openly observe the lack of political acceptance of the guidelines and standards analysed here when we look at the (deficient) state of ratification of the two Council of Europe conventions dealing with minority protection.

Even more sobering is the implementation practice of states that *have* accepted and ratified the Framework Convention and the Language Charter. The implementation practice for the two conventions is easily analysed by examining the evaluation reports of the two relevant treaty bodies. Doing so, we can easily see that there are a lot of practical obstacles hindering adequate development of minority policy, even in the like-minded states that have ratified the Framework Convention and the Language Charter. The implementation of the guidelines and standards – guidelines and standards that appear plausible and seem to offer reasonable solutions to the difficult problems we have been dealing with here – is not proceeding smoothly. The model of the nation-state, based on an ideology of requisite homogeneity of language and culture, has left deep traces in the institutional and legal order of the states of Europe. This helps to explain the alarming findings from a deep look into the machine room of European minority policy. In the details of administrative practices, the political will to transform the monolingual and monocultural institu-

123 See Oeter: Mehrsprachigkeit (Footnote 20), P. 156.

tions of the nation-state proves to be underdeveloped. A will to enact radical transformation is necessary for any serious pursuit of the project of 'diversity governance'. The lack of political will is fatal, because it abandons national minority policy to be caught in the dead ends of traditional policies of nation-building, policies that definitively miss the necessary departure to new horizons. Given this, we can only remind states that they long ago agreed to guidelines and standards that we all agree are sensible –that simply need to be implemented. States do not like such reminders, but we should not hesitate to recall how far they lag behind on doing what is necessary – implementing the objectives, guidelines and standards that simply reflect the overwhelming consensus on what should be done.

Peter A. Kraus

Sovereignty options versus autonomy provisions: minority politics in Europe

This chapter begins by briefly discussing some key conceptual and theoretical problems connected with the definition of national minorities and minority nations. Typically, a minority is conceived of as a structurally disadvantaged group whose members share a distinctive ethnic or national identity that cannot be subsumed under the identity of the majority or 'titular nation' in a given state. However, 'minority' and 'majority' are *relational* concepts. They point at a fluid situation, in which defining the size, boundaries, and identity of groups is basically a question of political power. With this caveat in mind, it will be argued that, in comparative terms, *nationality* (or rather *nationness*, in the sense of constituting a 'nation', rather than an 'ethnic' group), *territoriality*, and *external protection* are strategic resources that strengthen the capacity of a minority to defend its cause from a majority.

Second, the chapter will give an overview of majority-minority relations in Eastern and Western Europe, focusing on the characteristic features of each region. These are closely linked to historical ways of state- and nation-building. In the West, minority conflicts are in most cases seen as the internal affair of a particular state. In the East, in contrast, they are frequently based on a triangular configuration involving a national minority, a (re)nationalising state, and a kin state that may act as an external national homeland for the minority.

Third and finally, the new framework of minority politics in Europe today (compared with Europe twenty-five years ago) will be put under scrutiny. A critical element is the trend towards 'renationalisation' of decision-making in the context of the European Union. This trend has been accompanied by the rise of secessionist demands in 'consolidated' Western European states. Meanwhile, the political cycle initiated in 1989 has apparently come to an end in Eastern Europe, and the region must confront Russia's increasing territorial revisionism. Thus, the range of challenges connected with minority conflicts in Europe is broadening. It remains to be seen whether the ongoing dynamic will entail a reassessment of the notion of sovereignty in minority policies and in the development of a transnational rights regime.

Theoretical and conceptual issues

Minorities are fuzzy entities. Coming up with a clear-cut definition of them is therefore arduous. In the most general terms, when we focus on society and politics, the minority concept refers to a situation where a particular segment of the population in a given state or a state-like context is at a structural disadvantage, if only due to numerical inferiority. The disadvantaged group must have distinctive identity features – based on language, religion or other collective attributes – whose origin is linked to *cultural diversity* rather than to the mechanisms that cause *socio-economic inequality*, although in many cases maintaining the distinction in empirical analysis is a difficult task.[1] Accordingly, we speak of a minority if the members of the group in question share a specific ethnic or national identity that differs from the identity of the majority or the state's 'titular' nation[2] in ways that typically trigger demands for institutional non-discrimination, recognition, or protection.

Both the political and the legal discourse on minorities tend to draw a clear line differentiating 'ethnic' from 'national' minorities. Ethnic minorities are generally considered a by-product of the dynamics of migration, and thereby as an aggregate effect of multiple voluntary individual decisions to move from Country A to Country B. Due to the comparatively recent mass migration to Europe, they are also sometimes referred to as 'new' minorities. 'Old' minorities, in contrast, are groups of historically autochthonous origin, which were often incorporated to a nation-state against their will. They form territorially concentrated groups, and their members often see themselves as minority nations or national minorities, the latter being linked to a kin state in a contiguous geographical area. While distinguishing between ethnic and national minorities has for a long time been a common approach in both sociological and normative literature,[3] it has not been uncontested, as the attribution of such labels and of the corresponding group status is ultimately the result of political choices with contingent connections to the 'objective' criteria used in academic debates. It is therefore paramount to bear in mind that minority and majority are *relational* concepts. They refer to dynamic and changing contexts; how a group's size and boundaries are defined largely reflect power relations. With this caveat in mind, we can still outline three general factors of great relevance to developing a systematic approach to the study of minority issues.

The first factor, *nationness*, is implied in the distinction between ethnic and national minorities we just discussed. Groups formed by people of Maghrebi origin in France or by 'German Turks' can hardly claim a homeland 'of their own' in the

1 Think of groups such as the Roma, indigenous communities, or immigrant minorities – cases in which the two dimensions have become inextricably intertwined. For a more general discussion of this point, see Peter A. Kraus: The politics of complex diversity: A European perspective. In: Ethnicities 12 (2012) No. 1, P. 8–9.

2 This is the national collectivity that gives the state its official name, such as the Greeks in Greece, the Spanish in Spain, or the Slovaks in Slovakia, to give but a few examples.

3 A standard reference is Will Kymlicka: Multicultural Citizenship: A Liberal Theory of Minority Rights. Oxford 1995.

countries to which their grandparents or great-grandparents migrated. To the extent they mobilise as ethnic minorities at all, their agenda aims at non-discrimination and achieving equal socio-economic status, rather than the protection of a historically anchored cultural identity. In contrast, under today's democratic standards, the often problematic and conflict-ridden absorption of long-established territorial minorities by a hegemonic nation-state offers a strong normative template for demands for institutional autonomy. Institutional autonomy is considered a prerequisite for the reproduction of a particular cultural identity in modern societies. At any rate, this is the logic that underlies the legal and political criteria that the European Union (EU) and the Council of Europe (CoE) have been putting forward for dealing with minority issues over the last four decades. Both the European Charter for Regional and Minority Languages and the Framework Convention for the Protection of National Minorities, introduced by the CoE in 1992 and 1995 respectively, reflect this logic. While the CoE and the EU occupy clearly separate realms in European politics, EU organs have nonetheless been clearly supportive of the Charter and the Framework Convention. In the context of post-communism, the regulations outlined in these documents became an important part of the conditions that Eastern European states were expected to meet if they wanted to attain EU membership.[4]

The second factor is *territoriality*. The articulation of minority demands and the implementation of minority rights are easier if groups have a stable territorial basis. Territory is a political resource that minorities can use to threaten a state with exit strategies if their demands for autonomy are ignored. It is worth keeping in mind that non-territorial groups cannot secede. Although Black nationalists in the USA were equally justified in their grievances against the state as Québec sovereigntists were against the Canadian state, their mobilisations during the 1970s show that the lack of a clear-cut territorial base is an impediment for stabilising group cohesion. In Europe, we can compare the situation of two socio-economically disadvantaged groups – the Albanians in North Macedonia and the Roma – to see the impact of having territorial strongholds (or lacking them). Ultimately, under conditions of autonomy or multinational federalism, a minority may in theory even enjoy a political status that comes close to the position the majority or titular nation has at the level of the state as a whole.

A third factor is whether there is an *external national homeland* for the minority. This factor is especially salient in cases where a minority in state A and the titular nation in neighbour state B regard themselves as parts of the same national community, as the consequence is a potential overlap of 'internal' and 'external' conflict dimensions. As with the other factors discussed here, it is important to stress the

4 Peter A. Kraus: A Union of Diversity: Language, Identity and Polity-Building in Europe. Cambridge 2008, P. 109–110.

contextual aspects that inscribe higher or lower degrees of salience into such a conflict. For example, while Sweden does not play any interventionist role in the situation of the Swedish-speaking minority in Finland, Serbia has been proactively addressing the concerns of the Serbs in Kosovo. The respective dynamics may change with time, as many other examples show: what actors consider internal and external is a function of power relations altered by the forces of history.

With all necessary caution, we may assume that nationness, territoriality, and external protection are resources that strengthen the capacity of a minority group to defend its cause in situations of conflict. These factors can therefore be used as template for a first empirical analysis. At one end of the scale, we can locate groups such as the Roma, or small minorities with a precarious territorial base such as the Aromanians; at the other end, we find minority groups with a comparatively strong territorial base, such as the German speakers in South Tyrol.

Minority politics in contemporary Europe

Nation-state formation in Western and Eastern Europe reflects different historical trajectories. Hence, it is hardly surprising that the two regions are also characterised by different majority-minority relations. Western Europe gave birth to polities structured as state-nations: the states that emerged in Sweden, Britain, and France in the late Middle Ages turned out to become the main architects of a protracted period of nation-building, the key point being its historical timing.[5] State structures erected by hegemonic political centres were used by rulers to fuel a top-down dynamic of nation-building and to introduce common linguistic and cultural standards among a vastly rural population, which would become the national citizenry centuries later, in the age of democratic transformations.[6] Under conditions of path-dependency, the state-nation set the standard parameters of political modernity in the Western half of Europe. However, that these standards became dominant does not imply that they were uncontested. Their implementation created minorities who interpreted the language of equal citizenship on their own grounds, claiming cultural rights that could offer them some compensation for the wrongs inflicted on them as victims of the state- and nation-building plans machinated by the central powers. The strength of the respective mobilisations varies radically from case to case, to some extent reflecting the weight of the three factors discussed above. An additional factor to be included in our analysis is the new setting offered by the EU, which for some time nourished hopes that the states would lose former prerogatives in a Europe in

5 Stein Rokkan: State Formation, Nation-Building, and Mass Politics in Europe. Oxford 1999.

6 The quasi-paradigmatic example of republican France is portrayed in rich detail in Eugen Weber: Peasants into Frenchmen. Stanford, CA 1976.

which supranationalism would open up new spaces for subnational actors. For some of these, the emergence of a Europe of the Regions was ultimately even associated with the option of 'independence in Europe', as the Scottish National Party (SNP) phrased it several decades ago.

For different reasons, Western European state-nations may have undergone a dynamic of destabilisation, but this dynamic has not counterbalanced all effects of the assimilationist *longue durée*, during which the Westphalian system of states strongly exposed all minority identities to the culture of the majority. Thus, Scottish independentists today speak English rather than Gaelic, and the language policy of the Spanish state has turned Catalonia, where Catalan was the main vehicle of everyday communication well into the 20th century, into a bilingual territory. Getting back to our three factors, it is worthwhile emphasising that a minority such as the Catalans, who managed to resist the homogenising push of Spanish authorities over a long time-span, had to rely exclusively on their own strength. As with other Western European minorities that we may classify as comparatively 'strong', and in contrast with important minority groups in the East, the Catalans lack a kin state that gives support to their cause before the European Union or the international community. Even if the Westphalian state system was supposed to pacify a continent torn apart by decade-long religious wars, its peace-bringing effects were limited. In Western Europe, violent disputes over borders and over geopolitical hegemony only came to an end after World War II. For the architects of European integration, the path taken up in the 1950s was the way to go, if the more virulent tensions built into the Westphalian system had to be overcome once and for all. At the same time, from the perspective of those minorities who had managed to survive under Westphalian conditions, Europe represented an opportunity to loosen up the institutional straitjacket of the nation-states.

While the political map of present-day Europe shows a remarkable territorial continuity of state-nations that inherited and reframed former dynastic domains of rule in the West, it is characterised by the vanishing of former imperial legacies in the East, in ways that have dramatically and repeatedly altered state borders over the last hundred years. The entrenched power of the Tsars, the Ottomans, and the Habsburgs slowed down the nationalisation of politics among the subjects over whom they ruled. This changed dramatically in the period leading up to World War I and during its aftermath. The national principle spread like wildfire. After the dissolution of the old empires, the democratic appropriation of nationalism, in a somewhat paradoxical way, set apart the new titular nations created after 1918 from mobilised minorities – the Germans being the most notorious example – for whom 'their' homeland was not the newly established state they now belonged to, but rather a neighbouring state. What came into being under these circumstances was a triangular configuration of majority-minority conflicts. To some extent, it became salient again after 1989 and has kept shaping politics in Central and Eastern

Europe (CEE) into the present.[7] The conflictual triangle is constituted, first, by a state that has (re)initiated a process of nationalisation. Its second angle are this state's minorities, whom the nationalising state sees as communities 'external' to the nation, especially because their sense of loyalty may be directed towards a neighbouring country rather than the nationalising state whose citizens they officially are. And third, the neighbouring country that is a kin-state to the minority. As Hungary's approach towards Magyar minorities in Slovakia and Romania shows, such a neighbouring country may indeed act as a patron polity that conflates ethnonational and political attachments. In the case of the CEE countries that joined the EU since 2004, it has been thus far possible to contain minority conflicts to a level that is significantly less virulent than that of the interwar period. Further to the east, attempts at de-escalating triangular nationalist conflict have been much less successful. This is particularly the case in Ukraine, where the perception of Russian-speaking minorities as 'external' forces has been reinforced by the Russian state's attempts to instrumentalise these groups for its neo-imperial purposes.[8]

In the decades since the establishment of the EU and its expansion to include Eastern members, minority configurations on the continent have become dynamic and complex. There have been major changes in both the East and West. Europe around 1992 is a good starting point for grasping these changes. Three decades ago, the basic objective of Western Europe's minority movements was achieving or deepening autonomy provisions. In important cases, such as Corsica or Scotland, such provisions had not materialised in any substantial form yet. For comparatively strong minorities, such as the Catalans and the South Tyroleans, the order of the day was to consolidate and expand their territorial autonomy arrangements. In general terms, the hopes of minority activists lay in the construction of a 'Europe of the Regions', which was expected to become a third level of governance on equal grounds with the intergovernmental Europe of the States and the supranational Europe represented by the Commission. We should not forget, however, that there were also two extremely tension-ridden areas of minority activism, namely the Basque Country and Northern Ireland. The political status quo in these two territories was radically challenged by militant movements giving support to the political violence of underground organisations such as the Irish Republican Army (IRA) and Euskadi Ta Askatasuna (ETA, translation: "Basque Homeland and Liberty"). The violent exception of the Basque Country and Northern Ireland seem now to belong to the past, even if peace remains highly precarious in the Northern Irish case after the shock of Brexit.

7 Rogers Brubaker: Nationalism reframed: Nationhood and the national question in the New Europe. Cambridge 1996.

8 Kostiantyn Fedorenko and Andreas Umland: A Triadic Nexus Conflict? Ukraine's Nationalizing Policies, Russia's Homeland Nationalism, and the Dynamics of Escalation in 2014–2019. In: Aadne Aasland, Sabine Kropp (Eds.): The Accommodation of Regional and Ethno-cultural Diversity in Ukraine. Cham 2021, P. 53–82.

In the East, in the years after the fall of the Berlin wall in 1989, the situation was considerably more turbulent than in the West, due to the chain of ethnonational conflicts triggered by the dissolution of Yugoslavia and the collapse of the Soviet Union. The breakdown of the two states, allegedly constructed as multinational federations, led to a spiral of protest mobilisations in former federal units or sub-units, whose citizens blended democratic demands with national ones,[9] paving the way for the constitution of a great number of new states invoking the principle of national sovereignty in Europe's Eastern half. As a result of this crisis and re-equilibration, on a map that in 1992 comprised 26 states, we count 36 in 2021.[10] In several cases, independence could only be reached at the cost of severe conflict – a conflict that entailed traumatic consequences with the ethnic cleansing in the Balkan wars.

Thirty years later, in 2021, the situation in the CEE area looks less grim. It seems obvious that the EU accession of most countries in the region has been a crucial factor in containing ethnonational strife. In the 1990s, EU and CoE made considerable efforts to work out the parameters of a European human rights regime in which the protection of minorities within and between nation-states had a pivotal role. The EU's Eastern Enlargement has certainly not eradicated minority conflicts in CEE. In most states of the area, minority issues remain open, as is evidenced by the ongoing discrimination of Roma people, the discussions on the linguistic rights of Russian speakers in Latvia and Estonia, and the unfinished business regarding the status of the Hungarian minority in Romania all show. Nonetheless, the 'Europeanisation' of minority politics in the new member states has contributed to setting up a framework for negotiated conflict resolution. The situation looks way more troublesome further to the East, due to the new geopolitical revisionism that has emerged in Russia, which contributed decisively to the territorial destabilisation suffered by Ukraine since 2014, which culminated in the country's invasion by Putin's troops in 2022.

In the three decades since the Maastricht Treaty and the establishment of the EU, minority politics in the West have developed in a somewhat different direction, in ways few observers would have anticipated in 1992. The end of violent conflict in Northern Ireland and the Basque Country, as already mentioned, indicates important turning points. What was once mainly militant protest is now channelled through institutional politics. The institutionalisation of conflict by conventional means has, on the other hand, been less successful in Scotland and Catalonia, where

9 On the complex relationship of democracy and nationalism see, among many others: Craig Calhoun: Nations Matter: Culture, History, and the Cosmopolitan Dream. New York 2007; Egbert Jahn: Nationalismus und Demokratie – Einheit oder Widerspruch? Frankfurt a. M. 1992 (Untersuchungen der FKKS 4/1992); and Sir Ivor Jennings: The Approach to Self-Government. Cambridge 1956.

10 The count does not include the former Soviet republics that became independent in the Caucasus and Central Asia.

secession has been the main issue on the political agenda for more than a decade now. Successive elections have confirmed the hegemony of the Scottish National Party and of Catalan independentism. While gravitating to the centre-left on social and economic affairs, both Scottish and Catalan sovereignty movements reflect a growing frustration with the minimal leeway the Europe of the Regions offers minority nations for working against the concentration of powers between Brussels and state governments in an EU facing a long period of crises. The clash of demands for independence with nation-state prerogatives has been particularly dramatic in Catalonia, where hopes have been dashed that Europe would mediate between the sovereigntist forces and Spanish authorities after the October 2017 referendum on secession, considered illegal by Spain.[11]

All in all, the main developments in minority politics since the end of the Cold War and the establishment of the European Union reveal a peculiar interplay of continuity and discontinuity. The East has remained a region characterised by the persistence of traditional ethnonational cleavages, frequently played out by majorities rather than by minority activists. Minority issues tend to overlap with the triangular configuration that turns minority protection into a matter of monitoring between states, which act, however reluctantly, under supervision by the EU. Minorities that do not fit into this triangular pattern confront severe obstacles when looking for political gateways that will allow them a forceful articulation of their demands.

A West that initially put pressure on CEE countries to adopt its standards has meanwhile come closer to the approach to political integration prevalent in the East, with regard to important aspects of majority-minority relations. To varying degrees, its state-nations have adopted a discourse that emphasises the role of cultural belonging in relation to a shared civic identity, at any rate when it comes to their interactions with immigrant ethnic groups. It is unclear if the change in the normative framing of integration is more than a short-term move by political elites eager to appease a public increasingly tempted by right-wing populists who denounce migration and asylum policies. Neither does the change necessarily affect the standing of autochthonous minorities. Nevertheless, it is noteworthy that some of these minorities seem to have shifted in quite the opposite direction.[12] Thus, in the Scottish and Catalan referendum campaigns, local activists put much effort into substantiating the 'civic' foundations of their cause, which they considered to be diverse and equally open to newcomers as to supposed insiders. With the rise

11 Peter A. Kraus, Joan Vergés Gifra (Eds.): The Catalan Process: Sovereignty, Democracy and Secession in the 21st Century. Barcelona 2017. https://presidencia.gencat.cat/web/.content/ambits_actuacio/desenvolupament_autogovern/iea/publicacions/01_IEAg/IEAg_arxius-i-vincles/IEAg_05.pdf.

12 Núria Franco-Guillén: Immigració i independència. Els casos de Quebec, Escòcia i Catalunya. Barcelona 2017.

of new sovereigntist forces in its Western half, a new layer of complexity has been added to the already complex tableau of majority-minority relations in Europe. In this tableau, minority rights continue to be critical for the survival of particular groups. However, in the long term, these rights must not be reduced to superficial relief for the status inequality experienced by groups whose grievances are basically a consequence of a prolonged minoritisation. Sovereigntism ultimately is the expression of a struggle that aims to replace 'mere' minority protection with full equal empowerment.

From minority rights to sovereignty claims

With the European Charter of Regional or Minority Languages and the subsequent Convention for the Protection of National Minorities, the CoE set the foundations for a European minority rights regime that has ultimately received the active support of the bulk of EU member states.[13] The developments in the 1990s reflected a tendency among liberal democracies in Europe and elsewhere: while democracy remains unquestionably based upon the principle of majority rule, such majority rule does not legitimate the unilateral domination of structural minorities. Indigenous groups, national minorities, and minority nations were typically not incorporated into the domain of the majority state under conditions of mutual consent. The logic of the rule of the – supposedly 'one' and 'homogeneous' – people cannot be used to justify political measures that have substantially negative consequences for the reproduction of identity markers that these groups consider distinctive, such as religion or language. In other words: there is no legitimate democratic basis for criminalising the public use of Kurdish in Turkey, nor is there a legitimate basis for impeding the use of Romani as a language of instruction in primary schools in CEE countries. The symbolic violence of blunt majoritarian approach that negates the existence of a minority readily turns into conflict, a conflict that can generate new violence in political contexts where the very notion of a pre-given and inalterable national unity has been a subject of vehement contestation from the beginning.

Political scientists and legal scholars are increasingly prepared to concede that compulsory assimilation is not a legitimate means for guaranteeing democratic stability.[14] Pioneering voices in a debate aimed at the reconciliation of contemporary constitutionalism and diversity have argued that assimilation is a mechanism of domination hardly better than exclusion. This is because assimilation denies citizens

13 Although there are notorious exceptions. France, for instance, still has to ratify the Charter.

14 John McGarry, Brendan O'Leary, Richard Simeon: Integration or Accommodation? The Enduring Debate in Conflict Regulation. In: Sujit Choudhry (Ed.): Constitutional Design for Divided Societies: Integration or Accommodation? Oxford 2008, P. 41–90.

the very freedom to determine who they are and want to become.[15] Once we accept this logic, it becomes clear that minority rights lack normative thrust if they are just goodwill concessions from a majority to a minority expected to remain a 'minor' player in articulating the constitutional foundations of a common polity. If we take the normative rationale of minority rights seriously, their ultimate goal should not be to perpetuate the status of minorities, but to put the members of different cultural groups, be they majorities or minorities, on equal ground for making substantive political choices, irrespective of the group's size and the resources that can be mobilised on their behalf.

Seen from this perspective, Europe's current minority rights regime, as important at it doubtlessly is for taming majority domination, can hardly be considered a neat departure from the Westphalian order erected in early modernity with the ultimate purpose of concentrating power in the hands of a set of discrete political centres that became sovereign nation-states.[16] Four centuries after the Peace of Westphalia, minority provisions as codified in the Charter, the Convention, and various autonomy regulations introduced by several European countries, do soften the assimilationist pressures minorities have been – and mostly continue to be – exposed to. While such softening may make for a better modus vivendi between majority and minorities than harsh assimilationism, it does not redefine group relations in a democratically innovative way. The decentralising reforms put in place during the last decades in Eastern and Western Europe should not be underrated, even less so in a time when a reactivated populism of the majorities is jeopardising earlier advances. We must also keep in mind, though, that the concessions some European governments were prepared to make decades ago were not meant to challenge the Westphalian principles underlying the system of sovereign nation-states. Providing minorities with rights, whether on the basis of cultural group autonomy (as is to some extent the case of the Hungarians in Slovakia and Romania) or on the basis of territorial autonomy (as with the Basques and Catalans in Spain), does not put these minorities on an equal standing with the majority group that considers itself the 'titular' nation. Irrespective of whether a group enjoys territorial autonomy or some other form of protection, the condition of this group as a minority unavoidably involves it not being sovereign.[17]

But why is it important to become sovereign in a 21st century world, anyway? For many scholars of contemporary politics and law, the very concept of sovereignty

15 James Tully: Exclusion and Assimilation: Two Forms of Domination in Relation to Freedom. In: Melissa S. Williams, Stephen Macedo (Eds.): Political Exclusion and Domination. New York 2005, P. 191–229.

16 Stephen D. Krasner: Sovereignty: Organized Hypocrisy. Princeton, NJ, 1999.

17 For a more elaborate version of this argument, see Peter A. Kraus: Caught in the Minority Trap: Normative Limits of Territorial Autonomy. In: Karlo Basta, John McGarry, Richard Simeon (Eds.): Assessing Territorial Pluralism: Empirical and Normative Perspectives. Vancouver 2015, P. 82–86.

has become obsolete, at any rate if one wants to properly understand the forces at work in political environments subject to the massive impact of globalisation and Europeanisation.[18] If we look at issues such as the environmental crisis and climate change, national sovereignty does not seem to be of the utmost relevance for successfully coming to grips with what is at stake for humanity as a whole. But there are many other issues, linked to language use, education, access to public media, and the control of territorial resources, to name but a few, that continue to offer ample space for discussing the critical question of who should be entitled to decide on which matter on behalf of whom. The perennial problem of determining the 'proper' shape of the demos[19] is inextricably tied to questions of majority-minority relations and their impact on designing legitimate political constituencies. Against this background, the main reason for claiming sovereignty today, as in previous periods of political modernity, is the will to not only be able to decide on the matters that affect one's immediate individual interests, but also to have a say on matters that link these interests to the irreducibly collective dimension of group membership.[20] From this angle, the key point is that classifying such a group as a minority, even if the minority is 'protected' or 'autonomous', is ultimately equal to saying that the group lacks sovereignty.

Even in a world in which sovereignty may have lost much of the political edge it had at the peak of state nationalism, minority protection still addresses the symptoms rather than the roots of majority domination and the ills inscribed into the Westphalian state system. If you are Catalan, Welsh, or a Bulgarian Turk, you are likely to prefer any level of territorial or cultural autonomy to direct oppression. Autonomy, however, is primarily designed to alleviate the effects of a minority's incorporation into the nation-state; it does not give you the levels of cultural and political recognition enjoyed by those who are 'plainly' Spanish, British, or Bulgarian. The language of minority rights thereby continues to be the language of unequal recognition, although the recognition of a minority as a relevant collective subject may mitigate the political consequences of majority domination. It is therefore understandable that indigenous activists in Canada, for instance, reject their very inclusion in a citizenship regime that would grant them comparatively generous minority rights. Accepting such inclusion would imply accepting the Canadian state's constitutional authority for conceding such rights, which is problematic, to put it mildly, from the perspective of the people who inhabited the country long before it

18 A discussion of the use of different views on sovereignty and post-sovereignty in the analysis of EU politics is given by Richard Bellamy: Sovereignty, Post-Sovereignty and Pre-Sovereignty: Three Models of the State, Democracy and Rights within the EU. In: Neil Walker (Ed.): Sovereignty in Transition. Oxford 2003, P. 167–190.

19 Robert A. Dahl: Democracy and its Critics. New Haven, CT,1989, P. 193–209.

20 Michael Walzer: Spheres of Justice: A Defense of Pluralism and Equality. New York 1983.

was colonised by white settlers.[21] It would be a mistake to compare the grievances of Europe's national minorities and minority nations to the injustices committed against groups that became the victims of the West's colonial expansion.[22] There is one element, however, that the restitution of the rights of indigenous peoples and autonomy regulations for minority nations both have in common: the respective arrangements are put in place on the basis of a recognition that is not mutual – as in the case of two states that take up diplomatic relations – but rather stands on uneven ground. This ground is the ground of a politics that relies on the institutional template of the nation-state.

Let us turn to a concrete example to elucidate what such inequality implies. In the Western European context, a typical mechanism for recognising minority demands is the introduction of regional autonomy arrangements. It is true that such arrangements give minoritised cultural groups official recognition: the Catalan language enjoys co-official status in the Autonomous Community of Catalonia, as does Welsh in Wales, and German in South Tyrol. The minority policies of the Spanish, Italian, and British state must therefore be considered more generous than the policies of the Turkish state towards the Kurds, if we remain in the area of those states that are CoE members. That the Welsh or the Catalans are better off than the Kurds, however, does not mean they share the privileges of sovereign statehood. A Welsh speaker in Aberystwyth must cope with the challenges of cultural diversity and multilingualism, for instance, as she has no choice but to become fluent in English in addition to Welsh. Her fellow citizen in London, in contrast, will easily make do with English only, and is freed from the effort of acquiring a bilingual repertoire. The example may sound hair-splitting and somewhat beside the point. In fact, I would immediately agree with those who argue that being bilingual is not an annoyance, but an asset. Still, this fairly banal example shows how the 'burden' of learning is distributed unevenly between a member of a linguistic majority and a member of a linguistic minority. Here, I am obviously paraphrasing Karl Deutsch's famous definition of power as 'the ability to afford not to learn'.[23] In consequence, even if the Welsh woman may ultimately benefit from this unequal burden, at least via her increased cognitive options, if we follow Deutsch, the relationship is still one of power asymmetry.

It is true that in the cases of the Welsh or the Catalans, the power asymmetry does not coincide with socio-economic deprivation. The crucial difference between these

21 Glenn Coulthard: Red Skin, White Masks: Rejecting the Colonial Politics of Recognition. Minneapolis 2014.

22 The term 'internal colonialism' has been used to describe the dynamics of minoritisation in Europe too: Michael Hechter: Internal Colonialism: The Celtic Fringe in British National Development. Berkeley 1975.

23 Karl W. Deutsch: The Nerves of Government: Models of Political Communication and Control. New York 1963, P. 111.

minorities and indigenous groups is that the latter have been suffering enduring and encompassing exclusion since colonisation, an exclusion which has no equivalent for most European minorities. But not having been subject to socio-economic discrimination does not imply equality of access to political and cultural resources. From Max Weber we have learnt that class equality should not be conflated with status equality.[24] In a poignant analysis paying respect to the Weberian legacy, the late Finland-Swedish political sociologist Erik Allardt showed that the mobilisation of minority groups such as the Welsh, Catalans, and Basques was not driven by primarily socio-economic motives, but by the desire for cultural and political status equal to that of the majority – in other words, the desire for *recognition*.[25] Introduced by Allardt as a sociological rather than a philosophical category,[26] equal recognition is about forcing the dominant group to accept the self-categorisation of a minority in a way that enables the minority to attain a position of equal dignity to the majority. Achieving such equal dignity at all relevant levels of public institutions cannot be realised under the asymmetric conditions of autonomy provisions and minority protection. It requires a sovereign empowerment of groups in ways that ultimately render categories such as majority and minority obsolete.

This is certainly not a small task. In the universe of political modernity, the exercise of sovereignty is intimately connected with the amalgamation of territory, identity, and power represented by the nation-state, a nation-state whose very existence has created the preconditions for the status inequalities experienced by those groups who do not fit in the nation's majority identity frame. Some of these groups may have obtained a more or less generous protection, which allows them to sustain a frame of their own. However, this frame lacks the robustness reserved for those institutions that represent not just players at the regional level, but players at the level of sovereign states. To remark that the very concepts of minority, of protection, and of autonomy ultimately indicate the subordinate political status of those who are a non-majority and thereby 'protected' and 'autonomous' - yet not sovereign! - can hardly be considered an exaggeration in such a context.

For those who had hoped that the EU would give rise to a system of polycentric, multilayered, and 'post-sovereign'[27] governance, in which the role of states would

24 Max Weber: Wirtschaft und Gesellschaft. Gemeinschaften. MWS I/22-1. Tübingen 2009, P. 78–88.

25 Erik Allardt: Implications of the Ethnic Revival in Modern, Industrialized Society. A Comparative Study of the Linguistic Minorities in Western Europe. Helsinki 1979 (Commentationes Scientiarum Socialium 12).

26 A normative view of how dealing constructively with diversity requires practices of mutual recognition can be found in the work of the Canadian philosopher Charles Taylor: Charles Taylor: Multiculturalism and "The Politics of Recognition". Princeton, NJ, 1992.

27 Neil MacCormick: Questioning Sovereignty: Law, State, and Nation in the European Commonwealth. Oxford 1999.

be sharply counterbalanced by the role of regions and social groups, the situation thirty years after the Maastricht Treaty is sobering. The Committee of the Regions (CoR) has not even remotely reached an institutional standing that could give it a corrective role in relation to intergovernmental Europe, which is but a euphemism for the Europe of the states. Since it came into being, the CoR has had mere consulting functions. Its political relevance has only decreased with the renationalisation of EU politics observable after the Eastern enlargement. It seems therefore questionable whether the EU can be seen as a novel kind of multilevel federation, where a reconciliation of unity and diversity beyond Westphalian patterns is possible.[28] The EU's response to the rise of independentism in Scotland (before the UK ceased to be a member state) and in Catalonia can certainly not be taken as an evidence that European institutions are willing to give support to minority nations who attempt to reframe the power structures of established nation-states. While independence in Europe has become a symbolic political option at best, independence without Europe does not look promising either. It is unrealistic to think of a transformation of minority politics that does not use Europe as its main stage. On the other hand, the political opportunities to use this stage for minority purposes have not exactly flourished since the initial euphoria of the Maastricht period.

The last twenty years can hardly be taken as an evidence that a post-sovereign order is emerging in Europe.[29] Integration started as a process that was intended to pave the way for the "European rescue of the nation-state",[30] whose structures lay in ruins after two world wars. Regardless of the discourse of Euro-federalism, the goal of taming the nation-state through integration was not synonymous with superseding it with a novel kind of polity representing a clean break with the legacies of Westphalia. This is not to say that European politics, even if conceived as intergovernmental – i.e. interstate – politics, has not undergone sweeping changes in the course of integration. The transformative impetus reached its peak in the Maastricht period. Since then, however, the Eastern enlargement, the financial crisis, and the deep controversies around the distribution of refugees after 2015 have been accompanied by the successive renationalisation of decision-making in the EU, and the corresponding weakening of it at the supranational and subnational levels. Governments have complained that they are being sandwiched between 'Brussels' on one side and the regions on the other. However, if there has been any sandwiching at all, it has been a sandwiching of the citizens and non-state bodies by the nation-states. It has to be stressed that the 'hijacking' of integration by intergovernmentalism is not a

28 Michael Keating: Europe as a multilevel federation. In: Journal of European Public Policy 24 (2017) No. 4, P. 615–632.

29 This paragraph draws from Peter A. Kraus: Between Minority Protection and Linguistic Sovereignty. In: Revista de Llengua i Dret. Journal of Language and Law 69 (2018), P. 15. http://dx.doi.org/10.2436/rld.i69.2018.3122.

30 Alan S. Milward: The European Rescue of the Nation-State. Second edition. London 2000.

symptom of the health and robustness of the nation-states, which are actually losing control over their internal affairs and confronting massive legitimation problems.[31] Nonetheless, for complex reasons that vary from region to region, these problems have triggered a revival of state-endorsed nationalism all over Europe, which in turn has contributed to the creation of a fertile soil for identity politics orchestrated in the name of majorities. The generosity a significant number of European governments showed towards minority concerns in the 1990s, in the times of the Charter of Regional or Minority Languages and the Convention for the Protection of National Minorities, seems to be a thing of the past. The leaders who have withdrawn from a diversity-sensitive vision of integration include allegedly liberal politicians such as Emmanuel Macron. While the President of France claims that he stands firmly against the identity politics of right-wing populism and is defending Europe against the evils of nationalism, he is reluctant to set the foundations for a Europe of diverse citizens, the contours of which might counterbalance entrenched national identities from above as well as from below, as his refusal to accept Corsica as a diverse part of the Republic evidenced.

In a globalising transnational order, in which the governments of nation-states remain the main political agents, minority rights and autonomy provisions are limited in their ability to safeguard the institutional presence and unhindered reproduction of minority identities. If all citizens – irrespective of their cultural origin and collective attachments – are to be granted equal dignity, this transnational order requires more than expanded minority protection and additional concessions regarding regional autonomy. It requires nothing less than a radical reconsideration of the meaning of sovereignty today, a reconsideration along lines that transcend the inherited hierarchical dichotomies upon which the very logic of 'minorities' and 'majorities' has been built. While diversity exhibits ever more complex patterns, the legal and institutional provisions designed to govern its multiple manifestations are caged by the framework of nation-states representing monochrome collective identities. The best approach to protecting diverse citizens is to empower them. To make such empowerment a reality, the mechanisms created to monitor the respect and implementation of minority rights through trans-European bodies are an important and necessary point of departure. But such mechanisms alone will not do, as the ongoing and intensifying minority conflicts in different parts of Europe show. What is required is a fresh approach to promoting sovereignty options for minoritised groups. It must be based on a collective pluralism[32] that goes beyond the traditional majority-minority frame. Adopting such an approach would make the very notion

31 Manuel Castells, Olivier Bouin, Joao Caraça, Gustavo Cardoso, John Thompson, and Michel Wieviorka (Eds.): Europe's Crises. Cambridge 2017.

32 Peter A. Kraus: Popular Republicanism versus Populism: Articulating the People. In: Social Sciences 10 (2021) No. 366, P. 6. https://www.mdpi.com/2076-0760/10/10/366.

of 'minority' ultimately pointless. Sovereignty is a concept that was invented in Europe. Europe therefore seems an especially apt setting for empowering groups and democratising sovereignty. Sovereignty can then be a means to promote equal levels of dignity across individuals and peoples. However, if we want to make progress in this direction, Europe and we as Europeans still have a long way to go.

Karl Cordell

Minorities, Immigrants and the Politics of Populism

Traditionally, those interested in minority rights provision in Europe have focussed on the rights of indigenous minorities. However, in recent years most Western European countries have witnessed significant immigration, that has led to the creation of large migrant communities that in their number and in most cases their political impact greatly exceeds that of established indigenous (minority) counterparts. Bearing that in mind, this chapter aims to assess a number of issues related to ethnic minorities, both migrant and indigenous. However, greater emphasis will be placed on migrant communities, precisely because of their size and consequent political salience.

The chapter begins with an overview of recent migration patterns into Western Europe. Second, an assessment is made of the political salience of indigenous minorities in contemporary Europe. Lastly, I attempt to assess the factors that have prompted the rightward populist shift that has been underway in recent years throughout Europe. Three causal factors lying behind this shift will be identified; immigration, discontent with globalisation and concern about the nature and pace of European integration. That these elements are symbiotically linked to one another is evidenced through the contemporary debate on immigration. Consequently, consideration of immigration constitutes a thread that links the various topics considered in this chapter with one another.

Patterns of immigration

Clearly, we are all the descendants of immigrants as is obvious to even the most casual observer of current affairs, societies are rarely viewed as an undifferentiated homogenous mass. For a variety of reasons, societies are classified and categorised in numerous ways, whether it be by gender, by class, by religious affiliation or indeed between the 'indigenous' population and 'immigrant' groups. At what point an immigrant group, such as the Huguenots who migrated to Prussia in the seventeenth century, or the Irish who migrated to Scotland in the nineteenth century, becomes indigenous is an open question. The former group is present in Germany today only in terms of surnames, museums and historical memory. Yet the latter is still visible and not fully comfortable with assuming a wholly Scottish identity, as – despite recent marked enthusiasm for (cultural) Catholics in the West of Scotland for the cause of Scottish independence – a visit to the home of the Celtic football club will testify.

If it is difficult to identify the point at which a group or indeed an individual becomes indigenous, the popular imagination has little difficulty in determining who is an immigrant. Skin colour may be one factor. Language and religion are others. The essential point is this: that in order to identify and locate *indigeneity*, a set of characteristics is ascribed to the *immigrant* – the 'Other'. As noted earlier, mythologising cannot disguise the fact that all societies are marked and indeed created by migration. However in recent years in Europe, immigration has become an increasingly contentious subject and has stimulated the growth of right-wing populist political parties and movements. Who then are these immigrants and what are the issues that so excite the minds of the populists?

If we turn first with migrants to (Western) Europe, we could if we so desired, divide and sub-divide them endlessly into any number of sub-groups. In order to maintain some sense of perspective, it is perhaps more useful to divide them into a small number of broad categories. The first, so often conveniently forgotten, is those millions of Europeans who were the victims of often legally sanctioned forced migration during and after the Second World War, who came to settle in those countries that were willing and able, or indeed morally obliged as a kin-state, to offer sanctuary. Here we are referring principally to ethnic Germans, but also to smaller numbers of, for example, Ukrainians, Lithuanians and Slovaks. The second is migrants who have exercised their right to settle on the territory of formal colonial powers. Since the late 1940s, France, the United Kingdom, Belgium and the Netherlands have witnessed waves of migration from the African, Caribbean and Asian countries that they formerly occupied.[1] Third, we may identify migrants from the less-developed world who migrated to Western Europe between the 1950s and 1970s in search of work: the so-called 'guest workers' and their descendants, for example, Turkish and Kurdish migrants to Germany and Moroccan migrants to the Netherlands. Fourth, since the late 1980s there has been large-scale migration on the part of refugees who do not necessarily have any colonial or ancestral connection to the countries to which they have fled, but who in their home country would face either a life of unremitting misery or death. We must also note two particularly contentious waves of migration that have occurred in more recent years. The first is the mass movement of Eastern Europeans to richer Western European countries since 2004, when free movement of labour came into force within the European Union (EU). The second is the arrival of approximately one million migrants into Europe in 2015–16, primarily but not exclusively refugees from Syria, the overwhelming

1 Pieter C. Emmer, Leo Lucassen: Migration from the Colonies to Western Europe since 1800. In: EGO – European History Online. Available from: http://ieg-ego.eu/en/threads/europe-on-the-road/economic-migration/pieter-c-emmer-leo-lucassen-migration-from-the-colonies-to-western-europe-since-1800#DecolonisationandMigration, accessed 1 July 2017.

majority of whom are professed Muslims. Having in broad terms outlined post-1945 migration patterns within Europe, we shall now move on to make some observations about minorities that are classified as being indigenous to Europe.

Privileged minorities?

While the post-2004 wave of migration from Eastern to Western Europe is one factor in stimulating the growth of atavistic sentiment in Western Europe, it was the migration crisis of 2015–16 that highlighted the cultural gulf that exists between Western Europe and post-communist Europe. Whereas throughout the continent, some welcomed the primarily Syrian refugees and others simply shrugged. A third group, eager to protect indigenous culture from outside and alien influences, demanded that uncontrolled migration be stopped. Although such sentiments exist throughout the continent, this nativist response was particularly marked in post-communist Europe and it reached fever pitch in countries possessed of governments that are particularly concerned with the fate of their ethnic kin in neighbouring states and who are also quick to portray themselves as defenders of 'traditional' values.[2] In so doing, governments in post-communist Europe exhibited a remarkable double standard with regard to attitudes towards migration. For example, the current governments of Hungary, Poland and the Czech Republic are keen to ensure that their citizens have unrestricted access to Western Europe. Yet, these post-communist governments and their supporters are clearly horrified at the prospect of embracing immigrants, who they argue will effectively erode the cultural edifice upon which the titular nation-states for whom they claim to speak have been constructed.[3] According to their own logic of 'cultural self-defence', it could be argued that unrestricted migration of Eastern Europeans to the United Kingdom has the potential to contribute to the erosion of 'traditional British culture'. In their defence, these governing political elites would argue that the cultural similarities between various European peoples are greater than any dissimilarities, therefore the mass migration of Eastern Europeans into rich Western European societies is not a problem for the receiving society. They would also argue that, unlike Muslims, Eastern European migrants do not pose a security threat to the host society. Suffice the say that even casual awareness of 20th-century Europe belies this argument: less than a hundred years ago, indigenous minorities were cast in the same light by assorted (fascistic) nationalist movements throughout the continent.

2 Thomas Faist, Rainer Bauböck Eds.): Diaspora and Transnationalism. Concepts, Theories and Methods. Amsterdam 2010.

3 D. Earnest: The Enfranchisement of Resident Aliens: Variations and Explanations. In: Democratization 22 (2015), No. 5, P. 861–883.

Returning to the main theme of this section, we need now to ask some basic questions about Europe's indigenous minorities. Who are they and what role do they play in the societies that host them? The first thing we must note is that, in the wake of the genocides committed in the Second World War, the forced migrations that took place during and after the war, and the related re-positioning of inter-state borders in Central and Eastern Europe, indigenous minorities are far less numerous today than they were on 31 August 1939.[4] Following the completion of the programme of (internationally sanctioned) forced migrations in 1949, governing elites in communist-ruled Europe claimed that previously existing national questions had been solved. In Western Europe, sub-state nationalist discontents rumbled on, and in two cases, namely Northern Ireland and the Basque Country, civil unrest and armed resistance became an almost everyday occurrence. Since the 1970s, the governance of indigenous minorities in Western Europe (and from the early 1990s, the whole of the continent) has increasingly been governed by the wider impulse towards 'Europeanisation', i.e. the enlargement of today's EU and the enhanced role of the Council of Europe (CoE). This has been driven primarily through accession to the 1995 Framework Convention for the Protection of National Minorities and the associated European Charter for Regional or Minority Languages. It could be argued that this process of 'Europeanisation' was important in the ending armed struggle in both Northern Ireland and the Basque Country.

On the other hand, it is interesting to note that various member states of both the EU and the CoE, such as Greece, France and Bulgaria, have systematically disregarded elements of the very rules to which they have assented, presumably in an effort to maintain 'national integrity' (Greece) or the fiction that in some way the nation-state is 'colour-blind' (France). Such fictions to one side, we find that in Western Europe in recent years, the aspirations of indigenous minority activists and their supporters have been enhanced through a mix of legislative initiatives that have created either decentralised structures, as in the case of the United Kingdom and Spain, or fully-fledged federalism as is the case with Belgium.[5] Even in the once-highly centralised Scandinavian states, forcible assimilation of the Sámi has been replaced with a series of measures providing indigenous people a measure of cultural autonomy coupled with a degree of decentralisation. What unites all of these cases is the reversal of long-standing policies on the part of the centre of assimilation of 'peripheral peoples'. So, in the case of the United Kingdom, British identity is now explicitly portrayed as an over-arching civic identity within which English, Scottish,

4 Stefan Wolff: Ethnic Minorities in Europe. The Basic Facts. 2008. Available from: http://www.stefanwolff.com/files/min-eu.pdf, accessed, 3 July 2017.

5 Marcus Hoppe: Sub-State Nationalism and European Integration. Constructing Identity in the Multi-Level Political Space of Europe. In: Journal of Contemporary European Studies1 (2007), No, 2, P. 13–27, here P. 17–23.

Welsh and (Northern) Irish ethnies are nested. Similarly, in Spain, an over-arching sense of Spanish civic national identity is supposed to be the focus of all whether they be Castilian, Catalan or Basque. Similarly, in Belgium, nigh on a century of cultural and political dominance on the part of the Francophone element of the population was reversed, as much as anything else as part of a wider attempt to head-off Flemish separatism.

This strategy of enhancing the rights of indigenous minorities is part and parcel of the aforementioned Europeanisation process, in which states consent to share and pool sovereignty. The strategy is designed to reduce the salience of the nation-state and, it is hoped, nationalism within the body politic of each of the member states by supplementing existing national identities with some kind of ill-defined European identity. The extent to which this endeavour has been successful is debateable. If it had been accomplished, there would be no point to this chapter. Having said that, the EU in all of its various ancestral guises has clearly been remarkably successful in two areas. The first is in reconciling long-standing enemies to one another and breaking down negative national stereotypes. It may be a hackneyed truism, but above all, the European project as conceived by Monet, Schuman et al, was above all a peace project. Secondly, the EU was until the recent past both a vehicle and the impetus for economic growth and modernisation in Europe.[6]

Small wonder then, that in 1989–1990, as the Iron Curtain was hurled into the dustbin of history, both the emergent political elites and the wider populations of formerly communist countries generally viewed membership of the then European Community (EC) has some kind of holy grail.[7] This is an important point. What mattered here was not detailed knowledge of how the EC worked, or of how liberal democracy functioned and what it meant to live in a modern capitalist economy. What mattered was the symbolism of the endeavour. The EC, later the European Union (EU), was equated with such contested concepts as 'freedom', 'modernity' and 'choice'. It also happened to be where the money was (and still is), which was by no means a minor factor in the post-communist individual and collective calculation.

This is neither the time nor the place to recount the wider process of the eastern enlargement of the EU. It is, however, appropriate to note that as part of the wider accession process, candidate states were expected to achieve myriad policy goals,[8] two of which are of particular concern to this paper. The first was to introduce genuine measures aimed at decentralising what had previously been highly centralised

6 Tim Haughton: Half Full but Also Half Empty. Compliance and the Quality of Democracy in Central and Eastern Europe. In: Political Studies Review 9 (2011), No. 3, P. 323–333.

7 Haughton: Half Full but Also Half Empty (Footnote 7), P. 323–333).

8 European Parliament: Factsheets on the European Union. The Enlargement of the European Union. Available from: https://www.europarl.europa.eu/factsheets/en/sheet/167/the-enlargement-of-the-union, accessed 2 July 2025.

states, whose proclivities towards centralisation certainly preceded the rise of 'really existing socialism'. This goal was viewed as important for a number of reasons. First, it was seen as being virtuous in itself. Second, it was believed that such initiatives would help in the creation of the 'Europe of the Regions', an idea that was very much in vogue in some quarters as the 20th century drew to a close. Third, it was believed that in areas where ethnic minorities were concentrated, such as in Transylvania in Romania, measures of decentralisation might empower the indigenous (Hungarian) minority and help integrate them into the wider fabric of Romanian society. In addition, to return to the CoE treaties highlighted earlier in this section, candidate states were expected not only to adhere and to implement the rules of the organisations that were joining, they were expected to implement minority rights legislation explicitly aimed at reversing decades of assimilationist policies. Again, it was hoped that such policies would promote social cohesion and finally put to bed irredentist and sub-state nationalist claims.[9]

At one level these policies have been successful. For example, residual German minorities, such as that in Opole Silesia in Poland, had to learn that although Germany took its responsibilities as a kin-state seriously, it had abandoned any idea of either moving the Polish-German border or negotiating some kind of special status for the region. On the other hand, residual questions of history that had been taboo were in some instances revived in the early part of the 21st century. For example, the increasingly ethno-nationalist Hungarian Civic Alliance (FIDESZ) administrations in Hungary, although not directly questioning the post-1945 border settlement, came to play an active role with regard to the Hungarian minorities that in 1918–19 had been assigned to modern-day Romania, Slovakia, Serbia and Ukraine.[10] We also heard increasingly strident messages from Poland's nationalist Law and Justice party (PiS) and numerous less powerful, but just as noisy and atavistic, political parties throughout the former communist bloc. In post-communist Europe today, such populism, that was once thought to have been relegated to the margins, has become much more central and socially acceptable. In Western Europe, the debate over the fate of refugees in 2015–16 was vigorous and divided society. In post-communist Europe, the debate was much more one-sided, with post-communist elites and society as a whole largely united in the belief that diversity is a bad thing and that national governments were acting as Christian bulwarks against an alien, criminal and hostile Muslim tide.[11]

The question remains: How did we arrive at this state of affairs? In order to answer that question we must continue with the theme of immigration.

9 Timofey Agarin, Karl Cordell: Minority Rights and Minority Protection in Europe. London 2016, P. 33–57.

10 Faist, Bauböck: Diaspora and Transnationalism (Footnote 2).

11 Agarin, Cordell: Minority Rights (Footnote 10), P. 175–182.

Pity the poor immigrant

In recent years, Europe has witnessed the growth of an amorphous bunch of parties that we can collectively label as 'populist'. They share some basic characteristics, namely that they rail against globalisation and argue that European integration needs to be halted and possibly reversed. They dislike immigrants, particularly recently arrived (Muslim) immigrants, and claim to be anti-elitist. In other words, such parties often claim to be opposed to particular forms of multiculturalism and ethnic diversity. They are also to varying degrees 'Eurosceptic',[12] which is to say, they demand either that political and economic integration comes to a halt or that, as in the case of the Reform UK or France's National Rally (RN), the only sensible choice is withdrawal from the EU. Though coming from different national contexts – for example, the Bulgarian National Movement (VRMO), the Serbian National Party (SRS), the Alternative for Germany (AfD), or the Danish People's Party (DF) – they are united not only by the aforementioned commonalities, but also by nostalgia for a mythical past when the nation-state was just that: a state that encompassed the titular nation. It was also a time when things were generally 'better', and certainly free from predatory 'global elites' and 'immigrant hordes'.

Clearly, immigration plays a significant role in the populist canon and we need to further sharpen our analysis in order to locate the reasons for the rise of this phenomenon. In the wake of Europe's dalliance with fascism, in post-war Western Europe, atavistic and overtly racist parties lost whatever legitimacy they had previously enjoyed and were consigned to the political margins. Populist and nativist ideas that had previously been articulated by fascist parties did not completely disappear, but rather existed in the margins of political discourse. In general 'catch-all' parties of the left and right could dodge such issues without losing support to more radical counterparts.

By the 1970s, however, the combination of migration from former colonies and the importation of 'guest workers', coupled with an economic downturn, gave succour to the dormant spectre of populism. This decade saw the rise of (among others), the National Front in the UK, the Republicans in Germany and the Freedom Party of Austria (FPÖ). While none of these parties, bar the last-named, enjoyed sustained success, they were early indicators of what was to become a broader trend. Discontent with the EU and globalisation is coupled with growing claims that the national fabric of Western European societies is being changed by uncontrolled immigration.

Two events from the last decade gave right-wing populism in Europe an unexpected boost. The first was the destruction of the Libyan state in 2011 and the subsequent lawless vacuum that enabled people smugglers and militias to make fortunes by trad-

12 New Eastern Europe: Euroenthusiast or Eurosceptic? Available from: http://www.neweasterneurope.eu/articles-and-commentary/2303-euroenthusiast-or-eurosceptic, accessed 4 July 2017.

ing on unrealistic expectations of Europe held by the dispossessed people of Africa.[13] Refugees, rather than arriving in some kind of post-Biblical Promised Land, have been received with reactions ranging between sympathy for their plight, grudging acceptance and outright hostility.[14] The second event was the Turkish government's facilitation of the flow of refugees into Europe in 2015. Whatever Ankara's motives, for turning a blind eye to the huge numbers of refugees who crossed over into Greece in 2015/16, the consequences for Europe have been clear. Populist parties have gained support and in general there has been a general hardening of attitudes throughout Europe towards immigration, whether the migrants be Muslim, non-Muslim Africans, or in the case of the United Kingdom from post-communist Europe.

With regard to Western Europe, what has also stimulated resentment of the 'Other' is freedom of movement within the EU. This was vividly illustrated by the result of the UK's 2016 'Brexit' referendum. The 'leave' vote was driven by belief that freedom of movement within the EU has led to parts of the UK allegedly being turned into outposts of foreign countries, for example, Poland, Lithuania and Portugal. Curiously, this resentment of immigrants is sometimes shared by the descendants of migrants: second-generation Britons whose parents settled in the UK and themselves faced a mix of hospitality and hostility. The overall point however is this, that hostility towards migrants in Western Europe is not confined to recently arrived Muslim migrants, but also towards Eastern Europeans, who claim that as they are so culturally similar to Western Europeans, such problems should not exist.

This is an important point, given that populists in post-communist Europe claim that there is but a common, single European culture and heritage (which Syrians, among others, threaten). In order to investigate and de-mythologise this claim, we need first to say a few more words on Eastern European attitudes towards migrants. As the lack of significant public protest of the attitudes of governments throughout post-communist Europe shows, negative attitudes towards immigrants are more mainstream than they are in Western Europe.

One of the great fallacies concerning the collapse of communism was that the newly post-communist states were 'returning to Europe'. As if somehow Marxist-Leninist rule were an alien, quasi-Asiatic imposition and that Karl Marx and his acolytes were intellectually divorced from the European Enlightenment.[15] If we wish to identify the causes of the widespread dislike of the 'Other' that exists in post-communist Europe, we must disregard glib phrases and turn our attention to history.

13 Agarin, Cordell: Minority Rights (Footnote 10), , P. 175–182.

14 Human Rights Watch: Europe's Migration Crisis. Hungary's Xenophobic Anti-Migrant Campaign. Available from: https://www.hrw.org/news/2016/09/13/hungarys-xenophobic-anti-migrant-campaign, accessed 2 July 2017.

15 Beverly Crawford, Arend Lijphart (Eds.): Liberalization and Leninist Legacies: Comparative Perspectives on Democratic Transitions. Berkeley 1997 (Berkeley International and Area Studies 96).

Among others, Stein Rokkan and Seymour Martin Lipset[16] observe that the division of Europe into Eastern and Western parts that followed differing political and socio-economic trajectories historically proceeds southward from the mouth of the Elbe, to Trieste on the Adriatic Sea.[17] The boundary is not fixed, but since the early Middle Ages, it has existed along this somewhat permeable line. The division dates back to changes in agricultural practices, primarily the introduction of the three-field system and the heavy plough in Germanic Europe, which gradually facilitated the production of agricultural surpluses and the growth of embryonic mercantile capitalism. These changes and differences were further re-enforced by the differentiated consequences of the Black Death of 1346–1353, which heralded the decline of feudalism in Western Europe, since it inadvertently gave surviving peasants bargaining power with their feudal overlords. The post-1492 westward economic tilt towards the Americas further re-enforced this division, as did the Reformation, which was largely absent from or defeated in many parts of Eastern Europe. Later factors include the beginnings of industrialisation in Europe, the persistence of empire in the eastern part of the continent, the limited impact the Enlightenment had on the Russian and Ottoman Empires, and the consequently smaller influence of liberalism, and lastly the imposition of Marxism-Leninism in these fundamentally conservative and authoritarian societies after 1945.[18]

In other words, there are differences between and among Europeans that are more deeply rooted than some would like to think. In addition, we need to question the rather dubious assertion that Europe has long been a shining beacon of liberal democracy, when in fact liberal democracy as we understand it was as much the product of Europe's dalliance with authoritarianism in all its guises as it is evidence of the inexorable progressive nature of history. The roots of European authoritarianism are complex and a detailed examination of them is beyond the scope of this chapter. Suffice it to say, they are rooted in religious intolerance, despotic feudalism, uneven and forced industrialisation and varied counter-Enlightenment projects. Like it or not, the consequences of these forces are more apparent in contemporary post-communist Europe than they are in the western part of the continent.

Shocked by its dalliance with the abyss between 1933 and 1945, political elites in Western Europe sought to break free from this rather unenviable legacy after the end of the Second World War, and in so doing, facilitated the partial triumph of the

16 Seymour M. Lipset, Stein Rokkan (Eds.): Party Systems and Voter Alignments. Cross-National Perspectives. New York, London 1967.

17 The author is fully aware of the fact that the German lands straddled this boundary. He is also aware of the fact that, apart from the sovereign territory of the modern German nation-state, the Germans have all but vanished from former areas of settlement east of the River Oder stretching all the way to the Volga, as has their intellectual legacy.

18 Crawford, Lijphart: Liberalization and Leninist Legacies (Footnote 16).

Enlightenment project. That part of Europe that fell under the sway of the Soviet Union was unable to benefit from the European peace project. Quite the opposite – authoritarian and, importantly for our purposes, essentially monocultural societies were created. The German-led genocide of Europe's Jewish population was a major factor in creating this state of affairs, as was the post-war re-drawing of borders and related forced migrations. Surviving minorities such as the Pomaks of Bulgaria and Germans of Upper Silesia were subjected to policies of forced assimilation, whilst others such as the Hungarian minority in Romania were reduced to folkloric status and marginalised. As for the Roma, they continued to be viewed as wholly 'Other' and mostly incorrigible.

Despite various initiatives on the part of the EU, the CoE and assorted civil society activists, the situation of the Roma is little changed. This is due to the aforementioned legacy of authoritarianism, re-enforced by Marxism-Leninism that provides the foundations for the populism that is evinced today by parties such as Law and Justice (PiS) in Poland and FIDESZ in Hungary.[19] It is further fuelled by a narrative of victimhood: in Poland's case the partitions of the 18th century plus the harrowing experience of the Second World War, and in Hungary's case by the Treaty of Trianon that created the post-1918 rump state from the ashes of one half of the Austro-Hungarian Dual Monarchy.

Such narratives of victimhood coupled with an unenviable authoritarian legacy help explain why post-communist countries are fertile territory for those wishing to exercise the politics of grievance. If we wish to understand why such movements came to prominence precisely when they did, we need to examine two other factors: the disputed consequences of globalisation and discontent with the nature and pace of European integration.

The globalisation debate

Globalisation is a concept as slippery as it is contested. What is clear, however, is this: since the late 1980s we have witnessed a telecommunications revolution, a series of radical political upheavals that brought down a variety of barriers, and the growth not only of myriad transnational interactions, but also of a transnational elite.[20] We also witnessed the apparent ideological and political triumph of neo-liberalism, a doctrine that accepts the developments referred to in the afore-

19 Nick Robins-Early: 2017 Will Test The Rise Of Europe's Populist Far-Right. The Huffington Post. Available from: http://www.huffingtonpost.com/entry/europe-populist-far-right_us_587561bce4b03c8a02d3ce90, accessed 1 July 2017.

20 The Economist: Globalisation, 20 June 2009. Available from: http://www.economist.com/node/14031230, accessed 2 July 2017.

mentioned paragraph as virtuous in themselves. The extent to which the majority of society has benefitted from these changes is open to question. Unquestionable, however, is that since the first rumblings of the financial crisis in late 2007, huge numbers of people in Europe and elsewhere have perceived themselves to be the innocent victims of globalisation. From late 2007, unemployment rates shot up throughout Europe, policies of economic austerity were introduced at the behest of a range of international organisations and those who were already the least well off found themselves even worse off than before and with little or no prospect of ever recovering what had been lost.

It was inevitable that a political price would be paid for this mess. The question was who exactly the political beneficiaries would be. In some countries, such as Portugal, Greece and the United Kingdom, explicitly socialist parties initially benefitted from the discontent and disappointment felt. However, in others, even in Sweden, which was previously regarded as a poster-child for European values of tolerance, explicitly right-wing parties that reject globalisation and condemn immigration and immigrants have made greater political capital. Moreover, these parties claim that there is a clear link between globalisation and mass migration. Similarly, they argue that there is a clear and obvious link between globalisation and the financial crisis of 2007–8, with the victims having to bear the greatest costs for a set of circumstances they did not create. Whether or not migrants, who if not victims of globalisation are certainly the victims of war, poverty and (unattainable) rising expectations are at fault for this state of affairs is up for debate. However, for those who feel that their societies and cultures are being hollowed out as a result of unbridled migration as advocated by the globalists, the point is not up for debate at all. It is obvious and the book is closed. Migrants are at fault, the nation-state is unable to combat these globalist forces and the traditional political elites have acquiesced. The populist parties have also identified a collaborator of globalisation and the migrants: the European Union.

The European Union: Unrequited love

Populist parties across the EU have a common set of attitudes towards the EU. First, they see it as remote and undemocratic. Secondly, they argue that European integration has assumed a remorseless logic designed to lead to the creation of a European super-state to which both national sovereignty and national identity will be subordinated. They also argue that the (neo-liberal) policies pursued by the EU and parties that support its endeavours have failed to deal with the consequences of the 2007–8 financial crisis. They are also almost universally opposed to the Euro, which they see as a symbol of failure as well as evidence of the EU's desire to stifle national independence. Lastly, as we have seen, they argue unrestricted migration, as advocated by the EU and pro-EU parties, has serious and overlooked social, economic and cultural costs. It is on this point that we see major divergence between populist parties in Western Europe and their post-communist counterparts.[21]

Populist parties in Western Europe, such as Reform UK and the Dutch Party for Freedom, rail against two broad categories of migrant. The first is those from outside Europe who, it is claimed, have a heritage and shared belief system that is incompatible with European values. They refer primarily but not exclusively to recent Muslim migrants. As evidence they instrumentalise Muslim illiberalism with regard to such matters as same-sex marriage, mixed-sex education, marriage outside of the (Muslim) community, the role of women in society, dress codes for women and the age of consent for heterosexual sex. They also point to the popularity of 'fundamentalist' forms of Islam among sections of the Muslim 'community'. They are careful not to target more established non-European migrants, but the inference is clear: the 'Other' is alien and so a potential (security) threat.[22]

However, the aforementioned parties also have grave reservations about freedom of movement within the EU, a fundamental right that came into operation with the creation of the single market in 2004.[23] Migrants from post-communist Europe are perceived to be problematic precisely because they are portrayed, like their Muslim counterparts, as a drain on scarce resources and a threat to the traditional way of life, by sheer virtue of their presence in number. Western European populist parties therefore make strange bedfellows with their post-communist counterparts, who demand the right of their citizens to move freely within the EU while arguing that Muslim migration in particular and non-white migration in general constitutes both a cultural and security threat. For good measure, post-communist populist parties are usually vociferous in demanding that the rights of co-nationals residing abroad be acknowledged and preserved, as the constant complaints by PiS about apparent restrictions on the Polish community in Germany testify. This example illustrates a more general point, that such parties are anxious to safeguard the rights of their ethnic kin who are citizens of neighbouring states.[24]

The differences that exist between the populist parties in the two parts of the continent bear testimony to a number of things. The first is that although hostility towards the 'Other' exists throughout Europe, it is a somewhat more nuanced

21 Dimiter Toshkov, Elitsa Kortenska: Does Immigration Undermine Public Support for Integration in the European Union? In: Journal of Common Market Studies 53 (2015), No. 4, P. 910–925.

22 Toshkov, Kortenska: Immigration(Footnote 22), P. 910–925.

23 European Parliament: Factsheets on the European Union. Free Movement of Persons. Available from: https://www.europarl.europa.eu/factsheets/en/sheet/147/free-movement-of-persons, accessed 2 July 2025.

24 Enze Han, Joseph O'Mahoney, Christopher Paik: External Kin, Economic Disparity and Minority Ethnic Group Mobilization. In: Conflict Management and Peace Science 31 (2014), No. 1, P. 49–69.

phenomenon in Western Europe and, I would argue, is less deep-seated than in the post-communist part of the continent. Post-communist Europe is more culturally conservative than Western Europe and is home to populations that see themselves as being at a permanent comparative disadvantage. Moreover, their resentment is fuelled by the indifference and occasional hostility they are confronted with when making the journey to Western Europe and the discovery that they are lumped together with people they dislike, i.e. non-white non-European migrants. Moreover, in the post-communist Europe, EU membership is viewed in primarily instrumental terms that are even more marked than in Western Europe. In other words, it is not the peace project conceived by Monet and Schuman that interests them, but rather membership of the EU as a means of promoting economic growth, whilst simultaneously keeping Russia at a respectable distance.

Yet populist parties from east and west nevertheless view immigration and immigrants as an existential problem and the EU as a series of institutions at the root of policies that threaten the integrity of both the nation and the nation-state.[25] What precludes sustained pan-European co-operation between populist parties is the inability to reach an agreement on which immigrants are acceptable and which constitute a threat. This lack of agreement is one factor among many that explains why, despite the fact that migrants greatly outnumber members of indigenous minorities in Europe, the European minority rights regime is unlikely to be extended to migrant communities any time soon. Within this context, populist parties in post-communist Europe that are both anti-immigrant and concerned about the fate of ethnic kin living in neighbouring states should be aware that the continued demonisation of the 'Other' may eventually have catastrophic consequences for the very communities they seek to defend.

Conclusion

In this chapter, I sought to identify the factors responsible for the upsurge in populist sentiment in Europe. I argued that there are three interlinked forces at play: immigration, reactions to globalisation and discontent with the nature and pace of European integration. I also argued that these atavistic sentiments are more mainstream and entrenched in post-communist Europe than they are in Western Europe. This is due to the very different historical trajectories of the two parts of the continent. Lastly, I offer some observations as to what the future may hold.

Populism has experienced a resurgence since 2016. Indeed, the situation remains both fragile and volatile. The future of populism in Europe is dependent upon exogenous as well as endogenous factors. If there are further unbridled waves of

25 Earnest: The Enfranchisement of Resident Aliens (Footnote 3), P. 861–863.

migration then populist parties stand to profit. Similarly, if the apparent economic recovery stalls, populists will gain votes and other forms of support. Mainstream politicians need to be aware of the reasons for the right-wing renaissance and act accordingly. Any deepening pan-European populist co-operation will be dependent upon the confluence of the above-mentioned factors. Such co-operation is hamstrung by mutually contradictory attitudes towards migrants and migration. In addition, Eastern European populists are typically concerned about the fate of ethnic kin living in neighbouring states.[26] It is not unreasonable to assume that the competing and contradictory claims concerning history and ethnic provenance will preclude sustained co-operation between Eastern European populist parties.

Despite these dampening effects on populism in Europe, it is unlikely to wither in the near future. The question then becomes one of how its opponents can work to contain it. Recognition that globalisation and the neo-liberal consensus are more products of ideology than they are statements of fact would be a useful place to start. Doing that would kick off a useful debate and make it easier for practical proposals for change to be taken into account and acted upon.

Globalisation has not benefitted humanity in a uniformly positive manner and the apostles of globalisation need to be cognisant of that fact and prepared to act upon it. With regard to those (in Europe) who have lost out as a result of globalisation and related trends, a useful starting point would be recognition that the views of the less articulate and downright inarticulate should not be dismissed simply because they are not expressed properly. If a large section of society find itself ghettoised it will act accordingly. Secondly, the EU and the promoters of European integration need to take note of the democratic deficit and act to close it. The deficit may be as much apparent as it is real, but the question of how it came about and how it can be solved must nevertheless be addressed. European governments also need to develop policies that support growth and stability in the countries that refugees and economic migrants are currently fleeing. This is not simply an issue of relations with the less-developed world. It is one that concerns inter-state relations within the EU. If young Poles, Hungarians and Lithuanians feel that they have no future at home, they will emigrate. Ultimately, both the societies that export labour and those that import it will suffer a variety of problems. To ignore such facts or to dismiss them as being the province of racists is no solution at all. If Europe is to survive and prosper in the coming decades it needs to define itself in a novel manner that takes the concerns of those attracted to populism more seriously than it currently does.

26 Han, O'Mahoney, Paik: External Kin (Footnote 25), P. 49–69.

Tools and Applications

Tove H. Malloy

European Minority Rights Law: Unilateral Legislation in Favour of Kin-Minorities

Introduction

A number of countries in Europe have adopted legislation or policies that pertain to kin-minorities living outside the territory of the state. While a number of the new democracies in Eastern Europe after 1989 incorporated statements in their constitutions indicating concerns for nationals living outside the 'mother state',[1] ten European countries have taken explicit unilateral action to adopt public law legislation or regulations in favour of kin-minorities outside the 'mother state'.[2] Not all of these actions have extra-territorial reach, nor do all appropriate specific funds. Some address the financial side of minority life. Beneficiaries are mostly individuals, although some pieces of legislation support activities and/or institutions. Most authorise an entity in the mother state to be in charge of implementing the measure, and most make provision for special status of members of minorities in both the home state and the 'mother state'. However, international law does not sanction unilateral legislation as a means to protect minorities. Only in the event that no other measure or mechanism can secure the protection does international law reluctantly sanction legal unilateralism. And in such cases, both parties to the issue must agree and consent. This paper[3] examines nine unilateral measures in force in Europe and puts them in the context of international law.

The international approach to unilateral legislation with extra-territorial reach is quite clear. General principles of customary international law entrust the state where national minorities reside with the task of securing the rights of everybody within its jurisdiction. Preferential treatment of national minorities by their kin-state is considered the exception, unless it is established through bilateral treaties, or as a minimum agreed among the parties involved. The League of Nations system was

1 The Hungarian Constitution (1989), Art. 6; the Romanian Constitution (1991), Art. 7; the Slovenian Constitution (1991), Art. 5; the 'Former Yugoslav Republic of Macedonia' (1991), Art. 49; the Croatian Constitution (1991), Art. 10; the Ukrainian Constitution (1996), Art. 12; the Polish Constitution (1997), Art. 6 and the Slovak Constitution (2001), Art. 7(a).

2 See, Council of Europe: Report on the Preferential Treatment of National Minorities by their Kin-State. Adopted by the Venice Commission, CDL0INF (2001) 19 of 22 October 2001, available from https://www.venice.coe.int/webforms/documents/CDL-INF(2001)019-e.aspx (accessed 1.8.2025).

3 This paper was previously published as an ECMI Working Paper, No. 60, July 2012.

the first European multilateral attempt to provide protection for minorities outside the mother state through bilateral treaties. After the collapse of the League of Nations system and the transfer of international protection of minorities to the United Nations system, bilateralism was no longer specifically promoted but nonetheless carried over as the main approach to kin-minority protection. This approach came under pressure after 1989 and the collapse of Communism when a number of countries adopted unilateral laws on kin-state minorities and compatriots living abroad. The bilateral approach received renewed attention, therefore, as part of the multilateral approach promoted by the international community after 1989.

Bilateral treaties have the advantage that they can procure specific commitments on sensitive issues, while multilateral agreements can only provide for an indirect approach. Furthermore, bilateral treaties are able to directly address the specific characteristics and needs of each national minority as well as of the peculiar historical, political and social context.[4] Bilateral treaties usually contain mutual commitments to respect international norms and principles regarding national minorities. They often incorporate references to soft law provisions, such as the Council of Europe's Parliamentary Assembly's Recommendation no. 1201 (1993) and the CSCE Copenhagen Document (1990), and, by doing so, give them binding effect in their mutual relations.

In 1993, bilateralism received a strong impetus when the EU adopted the so-called *Balladur* initiative, a French proposal for a Pact on Stability in Europe.[5] The Pact aimed to increase stability through the promotion of good neighbourly relations in Eastern Europe, including on questions related to frontiers and minorities, as well as regional cooperation and the strengthening of democratic institutions through cooperation arrangements.[6] As part of its first phase, the Pact on Stability was handed over to the Organization for Security and Co-operation in Europe (OSCE) and eventually adopted by 52 member states in 1995. The OSCE agreement was not identical to the Balladur plan, but contained the same aims together with the principles and commitments earlier agreed to in the CSCE context. It included a list of bilateral treaties, all of which were drawn up outside of the Stabil-

4 See further, Council of Europe: Report on the Preferential Treatment of National Minorities by their Kin-State (Footnote 2); Joseph Marko, Emma Lantschner, Roberta Medda: Protection of National Minorities through Bilateral Agreements in South-Eastern Europe. In: European Yearbook of Minority Issues Online (2001) No. 1, P. 535–561; and Emma Lantschner: Soft jurisprudence im Minderheitenrecht: Standardsetzung und Konfliktbearbeitung durch Kontrollmechanismen bi- und multilateraler Instrumente. Baden-Baden 2009 (Minderheiten und Autonomien 15).

5 French Proposal for a Pact on Stability in Europe, submitted to the summit meeting of the European Council, Copenhagen, 22 June 1993. In: Stockholm International Peace Re-search Institute (Ed.): SIPRI Yearbook 1994, P. 247–249.

6 Pal Dunay, Wolfgang Zellner: The Pact on Stability in Europe – A Diplomatic Episode or a Lasting Success? In: OSCE Yearbook 1995/1996, P. 299–314. Available from: https://ifsh.de/file-CORE/documents/yearbook/english/95_96/OSCE_Yearbook_1995_96.pdf.

ity Pact with the exception of the one between Slovakia and Hungary,[7] as well as a package of cooperative measures financed by the EU.[8] It is estimated that around 100 treaties and agreements were concluded as a result of the Pact. In 2008, the OSCE High Commissioner on National Minorities (HCNM) followed-up with a set of recommendations on inter-state relations in connection with protection of national minorities.[9] The notion of bilateralism as a tool in minority protection was, therefore, clear from 1995 onwards.

Multilateralism

At the multilateral level, specific international agreements have defined the role of states' obligations. In Europe, the Council of Europe's Framework Convention for the Protection of National Minorities (FCNM) is the primary legal document establishing this rule. Article 18 of that Convention provides for bilateral and multilateral agreements to be concluded with other states, in particular neighbouring states, in order to ensure the protection of persons belonging to national minorities. The United Nations (UN) also promotes the stipulation of bilateral and multilateral treaties.[10] In the specific case of national minorities, the HCNM's set of recommendations on bilateralism, referred to as the Bolzano/Bozen Recommendations on National Minorities in Inter-State Relations, mirror the obligations that states have under international law. Thus, the Bolzano/Bozen Recommendations hold that:

> States should refrain from taking unilateral steps, including extending benefits to foreigners on the basis of ethnic, cultural, linguistic, religious or historical ties that have the intention or effect of undermining the principles of territorial integrity. States should not provide direct or indirect support for similar initiatives undertaken by non-State actors.[11]

While the Recommendations do recognise that a state may have an interest – even a constitutionally declared responsibility – to support persons belonging to national minorities residing in other states based on ethnic, cultural, linguistic, religious, historical or any other ties, this does not imply, in any way, a right under international law to exercise jurisdiction over these persons on the territory of another state without the consent of that state. Unilateral legislation with extra-territorial reach is

---

7 Germany concluded a number of treaties with its neighbours between June 1991 and April 1992.

8 Dunay, Zellner: The Pact on Stability in Europe (Footnote 6), P. 300.

9 See OSCE: The Bolzano/Bozen Recommendations on National Minorities in Inter-State Relations & Explanatory Note, June 2008. Available from: http://www.osce.org/hcnm/33633.

10 See resolution of the Human Rights Commission of 22 February 1995, UN Doc. E/CN.4/1995 L. 32.

11 OSCE: The Bolzano/Bozen Recommendations (Footnote 9), Section 10.

therefore only legitimate if it is agreed to by the legal authority of the territory in the external territory or with a legal authority that covers both territories and through which another mode of protection could not be found.

Legal unilateralism

Legal unilateralism is to be distinguished from political unilateralism. The latter is mostly known from the individual acts of states, often military acts, such as the United States' invasion of Grenada in 1983 or the bombing of Libya in 1986. This type of actions does not find any support in international law, and little if any in international relations. It is for this reason that unilateralism has a strong pejorative connotation.[12] Legal unilateralism is not sanctioned by international law either, but it has become increasingly an issue, especially in the areas of international aviation,[13] international trade,[14] international fishing,[15] environmental protection[16] and, as will be discussed in this paper, minority protection.

Legal unilateralism may be defined as expression of the will of one subject of law endowed with legal personality aimed at opposing either a legal order, or exercising sovereign rights, or creating new legal commitments.[17] As such, unilateral action can be tailored to benefit national economic interests over foreign ones, or put national interests before that of the collective interests. While withdrawing from or not signing up to a legal framework may be seen as unilateralism, a more controversial type of legal unilateralism is the imposition one community's values on another community without consent or acquiescence to these values. On this notion, legal unilateralism is 'intrinsically linked to sovereignty, territoriality and jurisdiction.'[18] Legal unilateralism becomes controversial because imposing values on others can cause conflict or tension between states. Legal unilateralism should not be confused with the 'responsibility to protect' or R2P adopted by the UN General Assembly in 2005. R2P is an emerging norm, or set of principles, based on the idea that sovereignty is not a right, but a responsibility. R2P focuses on matters that are relevant to

12 Pierre-Marie Dupuy: The Place and Role of Unilateralism in Contemporary International Law. In: European Journal of International Law 11 (2000) No. 1, P. 19–29, here P. 20.

13 A number of cases on transgression of sovereign airspace have been adjudicated by the International Court of Justice.

14 Most notably within the GATT and WHO systems.

15 The case of Canada's action against a Spanish fishing boat, the *Estai*, in 1995.

16 Unilateral action in environmental protection often occurs in the area of fisheries, either in terms of over-fishing according to quotas or in relation to protection of certain species.

17 Dupuy: The Place and Role of Unilateralism in Contemporary International Law (Footnote 12), P. 20.

18 Philippe Sands: 'Unilateralism', Values, and International Law. In: European Journal of International Law 11 (2000) No. 2, P. 291–302, here P. 293.

minority protection, namely the prevention of genocide, war crimes, crimes against humanity, and ethnic cleansing. But it is clearly a norm, not a law, and it requires multilateral action through the UN Security Council and the General Assembly.[19]

Legal unilateralism is further controversial in the context of international norms on the general obligation of cooperation in solving international problems of an economic, social, cultural, or humanitarian character, as enshrined in Article 1 of the UN Charter.[20] Accordingly, states must engage in dialogue to find a solution to disputes and no state may adopt unilateral measures before first exhausting means of international negotiation. Nevertheless, legal unilateralism has become a stable part of international law, especially in matters of trade. The World Trade Organization (WTO), through the WTO Appellate Body's interpretation of WTO legal provisions, plays a key role in this regard. The WTO does not forbid unilateral regulatory action but it does press states to justify their actions substantively and procedurally or face potential trade sanctions. For example, WTO rules likely permit unilateral regulation of greenhouse gas emissions, especially when a country has engaged in multilateral processes in good faith and these processes have stalemated, but such regulation must be applied in a non-discriminatory manner and meet procedural safeguards of transparency and due process.[21] International law has a critical but delicate role to play in disciplining unilateral action. Therefore, unilateral action is not a one-step dance.

Some argue that unilateral action is better viewed as part of a dynamic process of action and reaction, reassessment and response, in which international law plays an uneasy role as both a check and a potential consolidator.[22] According to this view, "international law needs to discipline (or better stated, provide guidelines for) unilateral action, as part of this dynamic process."[23] This requires a balancing act to avoid, on the one hand, discriminatory and opportunistic policies, and on the other, to avoid impeding needed action. Unilateral action's impact ultimately depends on whether it is persuasive in shaping norms of behaviour. Perceptions of legitimacy determine effectiveness, and if a rule or norm advanced unilaterally is deemed illegitimate, it will spark resistance, including challenges under international law, undermining its effectiveness. Such resistance can spur re-articulations of legal norms and rules as part of a

---

19 Adian Hehir: Chapter 7, The responsibility to protect and international law. In: Philip Cunliffe (Ed.): Critical Perspectives on the Responsibility to Protect: Interrogating Theory, Practice. New York, NY 2011, P. 84–100.

20 Dupuy: The Place and Role of Unilateralism in Contemporary International Law (Footnote 12), P. 22.

21 See Gregory Shaffer, Daniel Bodansky: Transnationalism, Unilateralism and International Law. In: Legal Studies Research Paper Series, Research Paper No. 11-34, P. 8. Available from: http://ssrn.com/abstract=1920470, accessed 23 June 2012.

22 Shaffer, Bodansky: Transnationalism, Unilateralism and International Law (Footnote 21).

23 Shaffer, Bodansky: Transnationalism, Unilateralism and International Law (Footnote 21), P. 8.

recursive process. In contrast, where unilateral action contributes to the forging of a new consensus that results in the adoption and application of common law norms, it can create a transnational legal order, either in the form of international law or more informal institutional settlement. In other words, in this view, legal unilateralism can lead to diverse outcomes both in terms of regression and opportunity.

The key is, however, whether a state has consented to multilateral regimes prior to committing to unilateral action. If a state has consented to a multilateral regime and then subsequently adopts unilateral laws that mirror the provisions of the regime, then the state has not sought to exhaust all options through cooperation. In the case of minority protection in Europe, this would mean that states which have signed and ratified the Council of Europe's FCNM would be required to take the matter up with the Council of Europe first and second with the state where the legislation is going to reach.

European unilateralism

Legal unilateralism in the area of minority protection in Europe is not new. It was largely the reason why the League of Nations collapsed when states party to the bilateral Minority Treaties began to 'defect' and declare that they no longer honoured the requirements enshrined in the treaties.[24] It should be noted that throughout the interwar years, political unilateralism was the policy of the Weimar Republic.[25] After the Second World War and during the Cold War, legal unilateralism was not prevalent. One law without extra-territorial reach was adopted in 1979, by Austria (see below). The proliferation of legal unilateralism began after the adoption of the FCNM in 1995. In this section, unilateral actions will be discussed and put in the perspective of political motivations. While this is not an exhaustive analysis of the political situations surrounding the unilateral actions, it is helpful to outline, however brief, the political motivations, if any.

Austria

The Austrian Federal Law of 25 January 1979 provides for the equation of South Tyroleans with Austrian citizens in certain administrative areas.[26] The law applies to persons of German or Ladin language affiliation who were born in the Province of

24 In 1934, Poland rejected the treaty it had signed with the League of Nations in 1919.

25 Annemarie H. Sammartino: The Impossible Border. Germany and the East, 1914–1922. Ithaca, NY 2010.

26 BGBl. no. 57/1979.

Bolzano in northern Italy, who declared themselves part of the German or Ladin language groups at the latest census in Bolzano, and who do not have Austrian citizenship. It also applies to persons who were not born in the Province of Bolzano but declared themselves to be part of the German or Ladin language groups at a census in the Province of Bolzano and have or had at least one parent of German or Ladin mother tongue. The law provides for certain special rights in the education sector, especially within higher education. The reach of the law is not extra-territorial in so far that the beneficiaries can only enjoy the special rights while in Austria.

The political motivation for the Austrian Law should most likely be seen in the light of the autonomy settlement for the region Trentino / Alto Adige (Trent / South Tyrol) that had been agreed in 1946 through the Gruber-De Gaspari Agreement but which did not see implementation in earnest until after 1972 with the adoption of the New Autonomy Statute. The Autonomy Statute had the main aim of protecting the Austro-German culture and language in the region. However, at the time, the Province of Bolzano (the one of the two provinces in the arrangement) was rather rural and not prosperous. It did not have a university. Young members of the German-speaking minority were left with no choice but to enrol in an Italian university or move to Austria or Germany to enrol in a university. Moreover, at the time there was no international treaty protecting the linguistic and cultural rights of minorities. The FCNM was only adopted in 1995 and came into force in 1998. The Austrian law was, therefore, seen as a necessary step to protect and promote the right to Austro-German culture in South Tyrol.

Italy

An Italian law, Law No. 19 of 9 January 1991, provides for the development of economic activities and international cooperation of the northern Italian region of Friuli-Venezia Giulia, the Province of Belluno and the neighbouring areas.[27] The law appropriated 12 billion Lire for the period 1991–1993 for activities to support the Italian minority in neighbouring Yugoslavia, to be organised in cooperation with Friuli-Venezia Giulia and other institutions. Law No. 73 of 21 March 2001 extended the provisions for the period 2001–2003 to the amount of 29 million Lire (approx. EUR 15,000).[28] According to the 2001 law, the funds would be used

27 Official Gazette no. 17 of 21 January 1991. Cf. European Commission for Democracy through Law (Venice Commission), Legislation on Kin-Minorities, Opinion N°168 / 2001, CDL (2002) 82, Strasbourg, 30 May 2002. Available from: https://www.venice.coe.int/webforms/documents/default.aspx?pdffile=CDL(2002)082-e, accessed 23 June 2012.

28 Official Gazette no. 73 of 28 March 2001. Cf. European Commission for Democracy through Law (Venice Commission), Legislation on Kin-Minorities, Opinion N°168 / 2001, CDL (2002) 82,

through a convention to be stipulated by the Ministry of Foreign Affairs, the Italian Union and the University of Trieste, in consultation with the federation of the associations of exiles from Istria, Fiume or Dalmatia or, at any rate, with the individual associations. The funds were to be used for measures and activities in the fields of education, culture, information, with up to 20% of the annual budget being earmarked for the socio-economic field. Neither of the two laws defines the beneficiaries more specifically but references to activities and institutions indicate that it is not aimed at individual members of the minorities. The laws had extra-territorial reach as the funds were to be used by the Region of Friuli-Venezia Guilia in nearby regions in the former Yugoslavia and later in Slovenia and Croatia.

It is not clear what could have motivated the Italian legislation politically, except that in 1991 neither the FCNM nor the European Charter for Regional and Minority Languages had been adopted. The lack of international instruments could have motivated the Italian authorities. The area of Fruili-Venezia Giulia and Istria has of course a long history of changing borders and the related division of communities and families. The area is also home to a good deal of cultural heritage that can be seen as influencing the identities of groups on either side of the border. Thus, the opening up of Yugoslavia and the sudden access to and ability to cooperate across formerly closed borders no doubt motivated policy makers. The ability to interface and move across the border between Italy and Slovenia, which has long been the home of a small Italian minority, could have been a driving force behind the legislation. Moreover, the proximity of South Tyrol, whose Autonomy Act was becoming a good practice example exactly at that time. Parity between Italian and German speakers in terms of employment in the public sector was reached in 1992.

Slovenia

In 1996, a Slovenian Resolution on the position of autochthonous Slovene minorities in neighbouring countries and the related tasks of state and other institutions in the Republic of Slovenia was adopted.[29] The Resolution applies to autochthonous Slovene minorities that live in the Austrian provinces of Carinthia and Styria, the Italian region of Friuli-Venezia Giulia, the Rába basin area of Hungary, and areas on the Croatian side of the Croatian-Slovenian border, particularly Istria, Gorski Kotar and Medmurje. It provides for financial support for the activities of cultural, educational, sports, research and other institutions and organisations of civil society in Slovenia which cooperate with autochthonous minorities. These

Strasbourg, 30 May 2002. Available from: https://www.venice.coe.int/webforms/documents/default.aspx?pdffile=CDL(2002)082-e, accessed 23 June 2012.

29 Official Gazette of the Republic of Slovenia, No. 35-2280/1996.

institutions are able to include their projects in the annual programmes of work of state bodies of the Republic of Slovenia. The method and scale of financial support provided by the Republic of Slovenia to minority organisations is not indicated in the Resolution, but defined by separate statute and other legal documents. While the Resolution is not a law and thus is not under international law oversight, any statutes or legal documents that might have accompanied it would likely have extra-territorial reach.

There is no indication in the Resolution text that it has been agreed upon by the neighbouring states. Moreover, unlike the Austrian and Italian laws, the Slovenian Resolution was adopted after the FCNM had opened for signature but before it had come into force. The political motivation behind the Resolution should, perhaps, be found in the experiences of turmoil that Slovenes across the Balkans were having due to the break-up of Yugoslavia and the conflict of the mid-1990s. Many Slovenes were living outside Slovenia in other parts of the former Yugoslavia, and due to the splitting up of Yugoslavia, Slovenes were also immigrating to Austria.

Slovakia

The law adopted by the Slovak National Council on 14 February 1997, the Law on Expatriate Slovaks, regulates the status of expatriate Slovaks as well as their rights and duties in the territory of the Slovak Republic.[30] It also defines the process for recognising expatriate Slovak status and the competencies of the different state administration central bodies regarding expatriate Slovaks. In the same manner as the Austrian Law, the Slovak Law provides for special rights of expatriate Slovaks to education in Slovakia as well as a number of other socio-economic advantages. The beneficiaries are individuals, and the law only applies in the territory of the Slovak Republic. The political motivation for the Slovak Law seems different in that it does not have extra-territorial reach, and it does not stipulate any geographic area as to the residence of the beneficiaries, except that they must live outside the Slovak Republic. The relevance of the FCNM, which was not in force at the time, is thus less significant since the beneficiaries of the Slovak Law include the Slovak diaspora. Moreover, the bilateral agreement signed by the Slovak Republic and Hungary two years earlier in 1995, in connection with the Stability Pact for Europe, had regulated the situation of Slovaks in Hungary. The motivation is, therefore, likely to be found internally in domestic politics.

At the time of adoption of the Slovak Law on Expatriate Slovaks, domestic politics in the Slovak Republic had been a bit volatile. Vladimir Mečiar, who came into

30 Law No. 70/1997.

power for the third time in 1994, held a strong grip on power in the young Slovak Republic. Mečiar had been in charge during the break up of Czechoslovakia, which he negotiated directly with Vaclav Klaus, the then prime minister in the Czech part of the country, in 1992. Later he also became responsible for Slovakia's failed attempt to get its application to the European Union approved on the fast track together with Hungary, Poland, Estonia, Slovenia and the Czech Republic. In 1999 and 2004, now out of power, Mečiar ran for the office of President of the Slovak Republic but lost to the opponent. During his term as Prime Minister, Mečiar was seen in Europe as a nationalist authoritarian ruler with undemocratic tendencies due to his purge of the public administration of non-loyal civil servants, including many members of the Hungarian national minority, and he was to a large extent *persona non grata* in other European countries. In 1996, the same year as the Slovak Law on Expatriate Slovaks was adopted, the Mečiar government undertook a vast reorganisation of the districts of Slovakia through the Law Pertaining to the Territorial and Administrative Reorganisation of the Slovak Republic.[31] Unlike, the Law on Expatriate Slovaks, which empowered expatriates if they came to Slovakia, the redistricting legislation was seen largely as an attempt to de-empower the Hungarian minority in those areas where Hungarians constitute large numbers of the population. The Law on Expatriate Slovaks could, therefore, be seen as an attempt by the Mečiar government to boost the Slovak ethnic group domestically.

Greece

In Greece, an April 1998 ministerial decree gave Albanians of Greek origin living and working in Greece the right to identity papers.[32] The validity of the identity card is three years and has the purpose of legalising the stay and work of the beneficiaries. The Decree is not extra-territorial as its jurisdiction pertains only to individuals in the territory of Greece, and it does not grant any entitlements other than the right to work. It is not clear that there is any political motivation for this Decree other than administrative concerns with registration of individuals. After the break up of Yugoslavia and the Soviet bloc, a large number of economic refugees and immigrants from Albania and other formerly communist countries (including Bulgaria, Republic of Macedonia, Romania, Russia, Ukraine, Armenia and Georgia) arrived in Greece, often illegally to seek employment. According to the 2001 census, there were officially 443,550 holders of Albanian citizenship in

31 Collection of Laws of 1996, number 221.

32 Décision ministérielle commune N° 4000/3/10/e des Ministres de l'Intérieur, de le Défense, des Affaires étrangères, du Travail et de l'Ordre public du 15/29 avril 1998 sur les conditions, la durée et la procédure d'octroi de la carte d'identité spéciale aux ressortissants albanais d'origine grecque.

Greece – 60–65% of the total number of immigrants. Greece and Albania signed a Friendship, Cooperation, Good Neighbourliness and Security Agreement on 21 March 1996,[33] and the Decree could well be seen as an outcome of this since it was issued only two years later.

Russia

On 5 March 1999, the Russian State Duma adopted a federal law on the State Policy of the Russian Federation in Respect of Compatriots Abroad.[34] The law is based on the premise that compatriots who are resident abroad are entitled to rely on the Russian Federation's support in exercising their civil, political, social, economic and cultural rights, and in preserving their distinctive identity. The beneficiaries of the law are defined as citizens of the Russian Federation who reside on a permanent basis outside the Russian Federation, who were citizens of the USSR and live in states that were formerly part of the USSR, who have become citizens of those states or become stateless persons, who are expatriates (emigrants) from the Russian state, the Russian republic, the Russian Soviet Federative Socialist Republic, the USSR or the Russian Federation, who had the corresponding citizenship and have become citizens of a foreign state, or who have a residence permit in one of these states or have become stateless persons, as well as the descendants of individuals belonging to the above-mentioned groups, with the exception of descendants of individuals from the titular nation of the foreign state.

The law aims to ensure that Russian compatriots can freely express, preserve and develop their distinct identity and develop their spiritual and intellectual potential, that they can freely establish multifaceted links with the Russian Federation, as well as receive information from the Russian Federation, that they can establish national-cultural autonomy, public associations and mass media and participate in the activities of these institutions, that they can participate in the work of non-governmental organisations at national and international levels and develop mutually beneficial relations between the state of residence and the Russian Federation, as well as exercise their free choice regarding one's place of residence or the right to return to the Russian Federation. Specifically, the law supports compatriots in the field of fundamental human rights, the economic and social field, the field of culture, language and education and the field of information. The law does not refer to appropriations for these many areas but provisions that funding will be allocated

33 See further website of Greek Ministry of Foreign Affairs, http://www2.mfa.gr/www.mfa.gr/en-us/policy/geographic+regions/south-eastern+europe/balkans/bilateral+relations/albania/.

34 Approved by the Federation Council on 17 March 1999 and signed by the President of the Russian Federation on 24 May 1999.

from the federal budget. Funding is to be made available both outside and inside the Russian Federation.

The law has clear extra-territorial reach and there is no indication that the Russian Federation sought approval from specific states in whose territory the law will . By most accounts, the political motivation of the Russian law on compatriots abroad should be seen in the light of the large group of Russians living in Estonia, Latvia and Lithuania and who became minorities in the Baltic states after the break up of the Soviet Union and the independence of these states. With the adoption of stringent citizenship criteria in Estonia and Latvia, many Russians were unable to claim citizenship let alone become naturalised. For these people, the only option in terms of citizenship was to turn to Russia, which issued passports upon request. Over the years, Latvia has loosened the criteria while Estonia maintained the level of strictness. Moreover, in 1998, Estonia adopted for the first time a social integration programme geared towards protecting the culture of the dominant group, the ethnic Estonians. The programme has been renewed several times and is now in its third period. It takes its starting point from the Estonian Constitution's clause on the ethnic Estonian origin of the state and from the outset many believed that its goal was assimilation of Russian speakers.[35] Although Russia became a member of the Council of Europe in 1996 and ratified the FCNM in 1998, a year before they passed the Law on the State Policy of the Russian Federation in Respect of Compatriots Abroad, Estonia's accession to the EU was being negotiated during that period (1997–2002). This likely had some influence on the motivations of the Russian law makers to adopt the law in 1999.

Bulgaria

The Bulgarian Law for Bulgarians Living Outside the Republic of Bulgaria was adopted by the Bulgarian National Assembly on 29 March 2000.[36] It pertains to Bulgarians living outside the Republic of Bulgaria, who have at least one forbear of Bulgarian origin, who have Bulgarian national consciousness, and who stay permanently or continuously on the territory of another country. The aim of the law is to support organisations of Bulgarians outside the Republic of Bulgaria whose activities are directed towards the preservation and development of Bulgarian linguistic, cultural and religious traditions. The law does not refer to appropriations but does provide for material support in the fields of education, language, culture

35 See discussion in Tove H. Malloy: Social cohesion Estonian style: Minority integration through constitutionalized hegemony and fictive pluralism. In: T. Agarin, M. Brosig (Eds.): Minority Integration: Debating Ethnic Diversity in Eastern Europe. Radopi 2009.

36 Prom. SG 30/11 Apr 2000.

and religion, both within Bulgaria and in the country where the individuals of Bulgarian origin are resident. It also facilitates repatriation and return. In addition, the law provides for a National Council for Bulgarians living outside the Republic of Bulgaria, which is a state public body with organisational, coordinating and representative functions. It expresses and coordinates the national interests of Bulgaria with the interests of the Bulgarians living outside Bulgaria. The National Council is funded via the state budget. The territorial reach of the Bulgarian law is somewhat fuzzy in that it does not explicitly mention Bulgarian organisations abroad as beneficiaries but rather refers to the needs of Bulgarians living abroad.

Bulgaria had ratified the FCNM in 1999, a year before, and the political motivation for the Bulgarian law should most likely be seen in the perspective of domestic politics. Based on provisions in its Constitution, Bulgaria has enacted quite liberal laws on citizenship for returnees, and in 1998 it adopted a law on dual citizenship for Bulgarians living outside the country. As a result, many Bulgarians outside of Bulgaria have become citizens and are able to vote in national and local elections. This has become somewhat controversial since Bulgaria became a member of the EU in 2007 because in effect it means that non-EU citizens are voting for the European Parliament. It is estimated that since 2001, thousands of ethnic Bulgarians have applied for and received citizenship, and the Law on Bulgarians Living Outside Bulgaria is generally seen as a supporting law to the citizenship law. Some have argued that it has a strong religious aim – that the Bulgarian government's organisational efforts in this area can be understood as "an attempt to symbolically restore the Bulgarian Exarchate through some modern surrogate, which would institutionalise links with the ethnic Bulgarians abroad."[37] Whether the aim is to increase the voting body or the scope of the Bulgarian Orthodox Church, the law seems to have a domestic purpose mainly.

Hungary

The Hungarian Law on Hungarians Living in Neighbouring Countries, adopted on 19 June 2001 and amended in June 2003, is arguably the best known example of unilateral legislation favouring co-nationals outside the mother state.[38] The beneficiaries of the Hungarian law, also known as the 'Hungarian Status Law', are persons living outside Hungary, who declare themselves to be of Hungarian national-

37 Daniel Smilov, Elena Jileva: The politics of Bulgarian citizenship: National identity, democracy, and other uses. In: Rainer Bauböck, Bernhard Perchinig, Wiebke Sievers (Eds.): Citizenship Policies in the New Europe. Amsterdam 2009, Chapter 7.

38 Act LXII of 2001 on Hungarians Living in Neighbouring Countries, adopted by the Hungarian Parliament on 19 June 2001.

ity, who are not Hungarian citizens, and who have their residence in the Republic of Croatia, Romania, the Republic of Slovenia, the Slovak Republic, Ukraine, or (until 2003) the Federal Republic of Yugoslavia. The aim of the law is to comply with Hungary's responsibilities towards Hungarians living abroad and to support the preservation and development of their manifold relations with Hungary, as prescribed in paragraph (3) of Article 6 of the Constitution of the Republic of Hungary, and to ensure that Hungarians living in neighbouring countries form part of the Hungarian nation as a whole and to promote and preserve their well-being and awareness of national identity within their home country. The purpose of the law is to put Hungarian minorities in the targeted countries in the position to enjoy identical rights in the area of culture that Hungarian citizens do. These rights are described in detail in the legislation. The law does not appropriate any funds specifically but refers to a separate group of appropriations to be made annually by the state budget. The beneficiaries can, on the basis of the establishment of their eligibility apply to a set of public benefit organisations regulated by the Act CLVI of 1997 on Public Benefit Organisations. The jurisdiction of the law is defined as the territory of the Republic of Hungary and the place of residence of the beneficiaries in the neighbouring countries.

The extra-territorial reach of the law is quite clear and has been discussed intensively in the public sphere as well as in the writings of experts.[39] It does not appear that the Hungarian government consulted with the governments of the targeted states during the drafting of the law. Consultations only occurred (eventually) as a result of the public eye. It was reviewed and amended in 2003 due to the ongoing scrutiny that Hungary was subjected to at the time as a candidate country in accession talks with the European Commission.[40]

Much has been written and said about the Hungarian Status Law, its controversial aims and its political motivation. The law was drafted during the first premiership of Viktor Orban, leader of the Hungarian Civic Union Party, Fidesz, which held power from 1998 to 2002. Amendments were made in 2003, only after a new government under Peter Medgyessy came into office. Speculations of Hungary's motive ranged from the symbolic to the urgent and material. For example: that Hungary was still experiencing the trauma of Trianon (the 1920 treaty that legitimised the changes to the territory of Hungary after World War I) and a consequent need for Hungary to make a symbolic reversal of that treaty. Another key factor is that, were Hungary to

39 See, BBC: Hungary 'Status Law' irks its neighbours, 19 June 2001. Available from: http://news.bbc.co.uk/2/hi/world/monitoring/media_reports/1397385.stm; and Osamu Ieda (Ed.): Beyond Sovereignty: From Status Law to Transnational Citizenship? Sapporo 2006 (Slavid Eurasian Studies 9).

40 See, Balázs Vizi: The Evaluation of the 'Status Law' in the European Union. In: Central European Political Science Review5 (2004) 16.

join the EU and eventually the Schengen agreement, many Hungarian co-nationals in Romania would be legally barred from easy access to Hungary.[41] The latter problem has, of course, since become irrelevant as Romania became a member of the EU two years after Hungary. The actual value of the Status Law to Hungarians living outside Hungary remains to be fully assessed. But the law was conceived, drafted, adopted and amended during a time when Hungary was a member of the Council of Europe and had signed and ratified the FCNM (immediately after it was adopted in 1995). The political motivation remains a puzzle, not least because the law was not repealed when the more moderate government of Medgyessy came into power.

Romania

Not surprisingly, the Romanian law concerning Romanians living abroad, adopted by the Romanian Parliament in November 2007, was seen as a reaction to the Hungarian law.[42] The Romanian law replaced the previous "Law Regarding the Support Granted to the Romanian Communities from All Over the World" of 15 July 1998. The 2007 law pertains to persons of Romanian ethnic origin and persons sharing a common Romanian cultural identity, who reside outside Romanian borders. It provisions undefined subsidies in the fields of culture, including cultural heritage, education, language and religion. The subsidies derive both from the annual state budget and private donations. The administration of the law is funded by the Romanian government budget. As to its jurisdiction, the law clearly has extra-territorial reach. However, the law stipulates that it shall be applied without prejudice to the principles of territorial sovereignty, good neighbourliness, reciprocity, *pacta sunt servanda*, respect of human rights and fundamental freedoms and non-discrimination. It states that its implementation will be based, where possible, on the conclusions that arise from agreements and programmes with the states where the beneficiaries reside, on the protocols of the bilateral Joint Commissions, on the basis of reciprocity, and in line with the FCNM, the Venice Commission and the HCNM. The law thus remains within the internationally accepted approach to kin-state relations. Moreover, the law has global reach and thus could be seen as multilateral in that it complies with the international approach. Nevertheless, it was adopted five years after Romania had ratified the FCNM in 2002, thus leaving open the question as to the law's interpretation in European relations.

---

41 Michael Stewart: The Hungarian Status Law: A new European form of Transnational politics? In: Transnational Community Programme, Working Paper, September 2002. Available from: https://scispace.com/pdf/the-hungarian-status-law-a-new-european-form-of-25angml7on.pdf (accessed 1.8.2025).

42 Law No. 299/2007 on the support granted to the Romanians living abroad.

Denmark

On 23 March 2010, the Danish Parliament adopted Bill No L98,[43] which appropriated funds for the Danish minority in Schleswig-Holstein, Germany.[44] The Bill About the South Slesvig Committee and the Subsidies for the Danish Minority in South Slesvig[45] that Lie Within the Minister for Education's Jurisdiction"[46] covers a major part of the subsidies that are appropriated each year to the Danish minority in Schleswig-Holstein.[47] A small number of subsidies for other Danish institutions in Schleswig-Holstein are not covered by this bill.[48] The legislation entered into force on 1 April 2010. Before the adoption of the bill, subsidies for the Danish minority were appropriated through a footnote *[tekstanmærkning]* to the state budget[49] and administered by the Committee Concerning Cultural Issues in South Slesvig.[50] Heretofore, the Danish minority negotiated directly with the members of that Committee as to how funds should be allocated among the various organisations belonging to the minority. The new legislation will continue to be overseen by a committee, the South Slesvig Committee, and a secretariat has been established within the Ministry of Education to which the minority organisations must submit applications for subsidies and specific projects. This Secretariat furthermore enables government oversight, in that the Minister for Education has to pre-review the allocations selected by the Committee.

The aspect of oversight was a key element and likely the political motivation for the adoption of the bill. The Danish authorities have allocated subsidies to the

43 L 98 Forslag til lov om Sydslesvigudvalget og tilskudsordninger på undervisningsministerens område for det danske mindretal i Sydslesvig. Available from: http://www.ft.dk/RIpdf/samling/20091/lovforslag/l98/20091_l98_som_vedtaget.pdf.

44 The Danish authorities have allocated subsidies to this Danish minority since 1920. The northern part of the former Duchy of Slesvig was lost to Prussia in 1864 and returned to Denmark in 1920 as a result of separate referenda in Denmark and Germany. As a result, national kin-state minorities were created in both the northern and the southern regions of the former Duchy.

45 South Slesvig refers to the northern part of the German Land Schleswig-Holstein, which, until 1867, was united with an area north of the Danish-German border and which is now termed North Slesvig by the German minority there, and *Sønderjylland* by the Danish population. Slesvig is the Danish spelling of the German Schleswig.

46 For a full description of the Bill, see Tove H. Malloy: Denmark adopts Unilateral Legislation in favour of Kin-Minority. In: European Yearbook of Minority Issues 9 (2010).

47 In 2009 the amount was DKK 431.5 million (EUR 57.8 million) and in 2010, DKK 435.4 million (EUR 58.4 million).

48 In 2009, this amounted to approx. DKK 70 million (EUR 9.4 million) mainly for the maintenance of the Danish state church in Schleswig-Holstein.

49 See for instance the Danish budget 2009, Paragraph 20, No. 104, Ministry of Education, available from: https://www.retsinformation.dk/eli/ft/200913L00098

50 For more on the Committee, see below.

Danish minority since 1920. Since 1995, the annual subsidies became a budget item approved by the Parliament, albeit in the form of a footnote. The idea of elevating the footnote policies of the Danish Parliament to a legal process began surfacing in 2009: the Danish Auditor General's Office, on the basis of its annual audit of the Ministry of Education, indicated that the amount allocated to South Slesvig was of such a size that it warranted a proper law rather than a footnote. The purpose of the funding was also criticised as being far too broad and lacking operationalisation. Moreover, the scrutiny by the Auditor General's Office criticised the processes by which the funds were allocated. No application process existed, and the funds were allocated according to practice. Thus, no serious assessment of allocations took place, and virtually no conditions were attached to the funding. And lastly, the Committee and the Ministry were criticised by the Auditor General for not following up on the actual use of the funds. Often accounting documentation was missing, and if received, it was seldom reviewed by the Ministry. Thus, there was clearly a feeling in the Auditor General's Office of lack of transparency and democratic openness in connection with the appropriations for the Danish minority in South Slesvig.

The bill's unanimous adoption by the Danish Parliament was hailed by many as a historic day for Denmark and especially for the Danish minority in South Slesvig. The Chairman of the Committee called the event unique not only for Denmark but also for Europe.[51] And he hoped that other countries in Europe would follow the good Danish example.[52] Another member of the Parliament likewise underscored the Danish perspective that the bill could stand as a good European example because it signified a positive story.[53] The positivity of the bill was further highlighted by another member of the Parliament, who argued that it showed the international community that Denmark was able to find mutual solutions to minority issues that did not provoke Germany. In short, there was a general consensus that the bill was good PR for Denmark as well as a broad expectation that the international community would greet the bill with appreciation.[54]

Other than compliance with the state subsidy requirements under EU Community Law, it is not clear whether any international obligations were taken into consideration during the drafting and eventual adoption of the bill. According to the Ministry of Education, Danish norms for administration of subsidies played a vital

51 Siegfried Matlok: Das Folketing hat einstimmig in historischer Stimmung das neue Südschleswig-Gesetz angenommen. Der Nordschleswiger, 24 March 2010.

52 Per Dittrich: Et stort tillykke til Sydslesvig. Flensborg Avis, 24 March 2010.

53 Matlock: Das Folketing hat einstimmig in historischer Stimmung das neue Südschleswig-Gesetz angenommen (Footnote 51), note 22.

54 Jesper Petersen, MP: Mindretallets arbejde anerkendt og sikret. Flensborg Avis, 15 April 2010.

role in the drafting of the legislation.[55] The provider of the subsidies must disburse the funds according to Danish norms, including formulating clear goals for the appropriations, ensuring that the goals are met, making the goals operational and defining clear targets and conditions for the subsidies. The provider must further require timely and accurate reporting by the beneficiaries, and when reporting is received, the provider must review the material and assess whether targets have been met. In addition to ensure adherence to Danish public administration norms, the draft bill was sent for comments to the Danish Ministry of Ecclesiastical Affairs, the Ministry of Interior and Health, the Ministry of Justice and the Ministry of Foreign Affairs.[56] It was felt that, since the Bill had no precedence in Danish law-making, it was necessary to solicit a broad range of comments.

Furthermore, in order to ensure compliance with German legislation, the draft bill was sent to the Danish Embassy in Berlin and the Consulate General in Flensburg. It is not clear how the bill was assessed in these two entities. However, we know from one source in the German Federal Government, that German officials were neither consulted nor informed about the bill or its process.[57] Moreover, at the time, there was no press coverage in German newspapers about the legislation, nor has any been identified later. This may explain why the bill has not raised any interest in European countries with similar kin-state relations.

The bilateral relationship between Denmark and Germany with regard to minorities is based on the so-called Bonn-Copenhagen Declarations,[58] issued in 1955 by both governments. These took the place of a bilateral treaty. Both Denmark and Germany have signed and ratified the FCNM and the Language Charter. Nevertheless, any concerns about Denmark's and Germany's obligations under international law seem to have had little relevance during the drafting period. As the bill went through the obligatory three readings in the Danish Parliament, few objections were raised. Only the authority which had set the entire process in motion, the General Auditor's Office, noted that the bill did not go far enough in reducing the role of the members of the Parliament in the Committee.[59] The motivation behind the drafting and the adoption of the bill appear to be simply the technicalities of good governance of state subsidies for kin-minorities.

---

55 Introduction to the new legislation provided during a seminar at Sandbjerg Gods, Denmark,19–20 April 2010.

56 Interview with official from the Ministry of Education who had been involved in the drafting of the bill, 20 April 2010.

57 Author's interview with official in the German Federal Ministry of the Interior, 23 May 2011.

58 The declarations of intent issued by the German and Danish governments in 1955, the so-called Bonn-Copenhagen Declarations, were non-binding and hold no legal power. They declared the two governments' intentions to protect the other state's kin according to international human rights standards and seek equity in all subsequent measures.

59 Rigsrevisionen er blandt kritikere af et lovforslag om Sydslesvig, P4 Syd, 13 November 2009.

Conclusions

Unilateral action in favour of kin-minorities is not new to Europe. Throughout modern European history, concerns for kin-minorities have been part of the fabric of inter-state politics, and this has contributed to relegating minority issues to the security area of international relations. Prior to the establishment of the United Nations and the emerging human rights regime, irredentism was a prevalent concern in Europe. It was precisely this factor that elevated minority issues to the international arena after the First World War. However, with the emergence of the international human rights regime after the Second World War, and especially with the emergence of the European minority rights regime after 1989, a gradual move from seeing minorities as a security concern to seeing them as a justice concern has basically eliminated the unilateral rhetoric on irredentism. This transformation from a security discourse to a justice discourse is thus a major change in Europe's approach to minority issues and protection.[60] And with this change, unilateral kin-state action has come to be seen as a breach of international law.

Why then do states continue to issue unilateral laws and regulations after the adoption of the FCNM in 1995? Unilateral action prior to 1995 is perhaps understandable, especially in the years running up to the end of the Cold War and immediately after. But some of the strongest unilateral actions, such as the Russian policy on compatriots abroad and the Hungarian Status Law came after 1995, in 1999 and 2001 respectively. This paper has tried to examine these and other initiatives from a political and strategic perspective in order to begin the analysis from an international relations perspective. But more questions need to asked and answered. Does legal bilateralism not work? Does legal multilateralism not work? Is there a tension between bilateralism and multilateralism in minority protection? How does the phenomenon relate to the debate on legal pluralism? Moreover, are there political instruments and fora that could avert unilateral action before it becomes legal? The political motivations behind unilateral action are domestic as well as external. And often they have roots in historical experiences, especially in the case of national minorities. At least this has been indicated in the case of the Hungarian Status Law. A contextual perspective of legal unilateralism is required with regard to inter-state minority politics in Europe to begin answering these questions.

60 Tove H. Malloy: National Minorities in the 21st Century Europe: new discourses, new narratives? In: ECMI Issue Brief, No. 24, December 2010.

Kyriaki Topidi

Dual Citizenship and Minority Protection: Post-Modern Ethos or Cultural Sensitivities?

Introduction[1]

Dual citizenship, as a legal concept, is not designed *per se* to protect minority rights. In other words, it does not belong among the traditional minority protection tools. Autonomy[2] and strong anti-discrimination regulations are the usual instruments. The responsibility for protecting minorities lies, as a general rule, with the state in which the person or group resides. Kin-states, however, often choose to take on the role of representing the concerns of their ethnic co-patriots, ideally taking care not to encroach upon the sovereignty of other states.

It is semantically and legally important to stress that dual citizenship does not grant new rights in the country in which the minorities in question reside. It may do so, however, in the homeland state. It facilitates movement between the country of residence and the 'motherland', carries cultural advantages, such as access to education in the homeland, may carry the potential for higher earnings or social benefits, and in some cases even gives voting rights in the country of ethnic origin. In the country where the minorities reside, however, dual citizenship may be disregarded or, in more extreme cases, lead to the loss of the nationality of the country of residence, as a reaction to the upgraded status of such minorities.

This is in contrast to minority rights, which, as a matter of principle, are not connected to any legal status with a state-entity, nor are they the result of an agreement between states. Additionally, they are not conditioned upon reciprocity between states. They are simply conferred because a person and/or a community is human and part of a minority.[3]

---

1 The present contribution is based on a presentation made in the context of the conference "The Promotion of National Minorities by their 'Mother Countries' in Central and Eastern Europe in the 20th and 21st Century", which took place in Berlin from 9 to 11 November 2016.

2 Understood here as the means to provide not only legal protection for persons belonging to a minority but also the right to dispose of their resources, to experience their national identity and to exercise rights associated with this identity in collective terms. Cf. Iván Halász: Dual Citizenship as an Instrument of the Hungarian Policy Towards the Nation? In: Regio – Minorities, Politics, Society 8 (2005), P. 73–86, here P. 76.

3 Halász: Dual Citizenship (Footnote 2), P. 75.

Why then is dual citizenship of relevance to minority protection? The first reason is that dual citizenship is often used as a tool of *national reintegration*. The term *national reintegration* is difficult to conceptualise: it can signify the symbolic, spiritual and legal bond between groups of people across borders; it can also mean the gathering of all citizens in one territory or even the creation of an enlarged nation-state, for those of more irredentist ideology. Through co-ethnic populations abroad, kinstates mainly use dual citizenship as a strategy to reconnect with their 'external' populations targeting both the repatriation of human but also of physical capital.[4]

The second, more common reason that dual citizenship is relevant, is that it is perceived as a gesture of reparation for past injustices connected with the 'homeland' country, a move aimed at giving persons belonging to minorities the same opportunities as they would have in their homeland. In this context, the most often cited example of Hungary is based on the award of citizenship to persons with ancestry rooted in pre-1920 Hungarian territories, provided they pass a Hungarian language test. [5]

The international legal environment

Article 27 of the International Covenant on Civil and Political Rights grants minority protection rights to all members of an ethnic, religious or linguistic minority, regardless of whether they are citizens of the state.[6] In Europe, however, minority protection is strongly linked to citizenship.[7] For this and other reasons, the question of under what circumstances to grant one or more citizenships/nationalities has become an object of evolving debate in public international law, with implications for minority rights standards.

4 For the political economy implications of dual citizenship, see David Leblang: Harnessing the Diaspora: The Political Economy of Dual Citizenship. Migrant Remittances and Return. February 2013, available at https://personal.lse.ac.uk/RICKARD/david.pdf.

5 See David Owen and Rainer Bauböck: Citizenship as Reparations: Should the victims of historical injustice be offered membership?, 16 February 2025, EUI Global Citizenship Observatory: https://globalcit.eu/citizenship-as-reparations-should-the-victims-of-historical-injustice-be-offered-membership/ .

6 Human Rights Committee: General Comment No. 23 (50) on Article 27/Minority Rights. UN Doc. CCPR/C/21 Rev.1/Add 5, 6 April 1994, here para. 5.1.

7 See Additional Protocol to the European Convention on Human Rights concerning persons belonging to National Minorities, Article 1, which stipulates: "For the purposes of the Convention, the expression 'national minority' refers to a group of persons in a state who: a. reside on the territory of that state and are citizens thereof, [...]." Similarly, the European Charter for Regional or Minority Languages (adopted 5 November 1992) uses the criterion of citizenship in Article 1 to extend protection as follows: "For the purposes of this Charter: a. regional or minority languages means languages that are: I. traditionally used within a given territory of a State by nationals of that State [...]."

The right of the state to determine standards for citizenship has traditionally belonged to the *domaine réservé* (jurisdiction) of states. A generally applicable criterion is the existence of a 'genuine link' or 'genuine connection' between the state and the national in question, as set forth in the *Nottebohm* case.[8] While there is no universally accepted definition of 'genuine link', place of residence over a long period of time, knowledge of the language, and self-sufficiency are commonly used criteria. The 'genuine link' criterion, even when properly defined, however, needs to be used with caution in cases where a citizen acquires an additional (foreign) nationality without a 'genuine link' to the new country: this is not sufficient to show that the individual no longer has a 'genuine link' to their country of origin.

For our purposes, *dual* or *multiple citizenship* is understood as holding the legal status of a citizen in two or more states. The international legal system has for a long time considered the concept to be a systemic 'anomaly', comparable to bigamy, precisely because it challenges the concept of loyalty towards the state, inherent within the concept of citizenship. It has also been interpreted as a direct challenge to state sovereignty. Within a broader process of 'modern national consciousness',[9] citizenship was conceived to embody a sense of community membership, where the citizens are essentially an extension of the state. Traditional mono-dimensional conceptions of national consciousness are, however, clearly challenged by the increased mobility of persons across the world.

The right to citizenship (and conversely the protection from statelessness) received international recognition in the Universal Declaration of Human Rights of 1948.[10] Article 15.1 states: "Everyone has the right to a nationality." Yet while an individual has this right, no specific state has a duty to provide it, which transforms it into a "dubious human right",[11] but one that should be awarded independently of one's national or ethnic affiliation.[12] The European Convention on Nationality of 6 November 1997[13] reiterates in its Article 4 that (a) "everyone has the right to a nationality" and (b) "statelessness shall be avoided". In the same context, the Convention also provides for the possibility of multiple citizenships, reversing the previous 1963 Convention in a realistic attempt to address the needs of immigrant populations and the integration of permanent residents (often members of a minority group). To

8 Reports of Judgments. Advisory Opinions and Orders of the International Court of Justice (ICJ) Reports 1955, P. 4ff (23).

9 Christian Joppke: Citizenship and Immigration. Cambridge, Malden/MA 2010, P. 12.

10 UN Doc. A/RES/217 A (III).

11 Gerard-René De Groot: Staatsangehörigkeitsrecht im Wandel. Berlin 1989. This also explains the non-inclusion of the right in the ICCPR.

12 Article 5 of the International Convention on the Elimination of All Forms of Racial Discrimination of 21 December 1965 prohibiting discrimination on the basis of race covers nationality under (d) (iii).

13 European Treaty Series, No. 166, 1997: https://rm.coe.int/168007f2c8.

clarify, the document does not openly award this possibility but remains neutral. It notes "the desirability of finding appropriate solutions to consequences of multiple nationality and in particular as regards the rights and duties of multiple nationals."

An additional factor points towards the normative tolerance of dual citizenship: the proliferation of instances of recognition of cultural rights and identification. International covenants and declarations recognise cultural rights as human rights. This is relevant because to recognise multiple citizenships is to recognise multiple cultural attachments.[14]

A shift in the perceptions on dual citizenship: A fact of globalisation

The development of the welfare state along with the international recognition of universal human rights has played a role in the gradual 'toleration' of dual citizenship beginning in the 1990s. Academic scholarship on the matter follows two broad directions: some understand citizenship as a path-dependent process that relies on ethnic and civic conceptions of nationality in a given state, while others detach citizenship from its national context and claim post-nationality in a world characterised by globalisation and international human rights norms. This latter view relies considerably on supranational institutions and regionalism away from the particularistic criteria of citizenship and closer to a universal type of 'personhood'.

Within this framework, Weil and Ransen deconstruct the notion of citizenship. To do so, they argue that allegiance is no longer a concept that enjoys exclusivity and perpetual duration. It is indeed possible for one to have multiple allegiances, not necessarily taking the shape of 'competing loyalties'. Likewise, dual citizenship exists independently of security threats and hence such threats represent no longer a valid argument against it. The recent waves of securitization of minority groups combined with a political shift of many states to more conservative visions on citizenship place the latter statement under pressure. Still, international stability has considerably lessened the salience of citizenship for military service purposes, tax purposes or inheritance rules.[15]

More controversial may prove the argument that dual citizenship impedes integration by insisting on the attachment to a foreign culture and language, ultimately also affecting the political identification and participation of dual citizens in their country of residence. In that light, dual citizenship may also be considered a chal-

14 Szabolcs Pogonyi: Dual Citizenship and Sovereignty. In: The Journal of Nationalism and Ethnicity 39 (2011) No. 5, P. 685–704, here P. 690.

15 Joppke: Citizenship and Immigration (Footnote 9). With the exceptions of instances of citizenship as a factor leading to the use of force such as Russia's 2008 invasion of Georgia in order to protect Russians residing in Georgia.

lenge to the equality principle among citizens. Equality requires that each citizen holds the same range of entitlements as others in the same position *(complex equality)*. For example, dual citizenship holders may be entitled to vote in two countries, in violation of the 'one person one vote' principle.

From a policy perspective, multiple citizenship has seen a rise in acceptance due to gender equality in *jus sanguinis* transmission (the right of a newborn child to share the same citizenship as its parents), to integration policies that aim to promote immigrant naturalisation, and to the growing transnational phenomenon of diasporic communities that prove to be valuable economic, political and cultural assets for governments.[16] Any discussion on the normative acceptability of dual citizenship should not leave out the potential economic advantages, especially in cases where emigrants live and work in wealthier countries than the one of their ethnic origin. Scholarship on what is now labeled 'transnational participation' emphasizes, predictably, the impact of dual citizenship not only on the person's sense of belonging and identity but also their political and economic participation. For example, the emerging social category of 'middleman diasporas', who are active as importers of goods and ideas *from* their homelands but who also are important economic actors *within* their homelands are a good illustration in this respect.[17] Given that, diasporic projects cannot be seen as a homogenous entity but rather as tools to make claims that can shift on a case-by-case basis. The implication of a casuistic analysis clearly suggests a corresponding lack of uniformity in the use of law(s) in this area.

Finally, and again from a policy perspective, dual citizenship monitoring has proved challenging to the point of becoming essentially unenforceable, as the lack of extensive data on the phenomenon suggests, due to the difficulty for the states to verify, monitor and control it. For instance, in 2010 the Slovak Citizenship Act was passed, forbidding the holding of dual citizenship as of 2014, in response to the Hungarian legislative initiatives of 2010[18] which made it easier for ethnic Hungarians living outside Hungary to gain citizenship. The Slovak legislation targeting primarily dual citizens of Slovakia and Hungary, is estimated to have resulted in more than 800 Slovak citizenship withdrawals, primarily affecting Slovak nationals of Czech origin.[19] However, the number of Slovak citizens who acquired Hungarian

16 Rainer Bauböck, Vesco Paskalev: Citizenship Deprivation. A Normative Analysis. In: CEPS Paper in Liberty and Security in Europe 82 (2015), here P. 3.

17 Szabolcs Pogonyi: Transborder Kin-minority as Symbolic Resource in Hungary. In: JEMIE 14 (2015) No. 3, P. 73–98, here P. 74–75.

18 On 26 May 2010 the Hungarian National Assembly approved the amendment of Act LV on Hungarian Citizenship of 1993 and introduced a simplified naturalization procedure, extending citizenship to those with Hungarian ancestors.

19 Dagmar Kusa, 'Is the Slovak Citizenship Act unconstitutional? The Constitutional Court leaves the question open', EUI Global Citizenship Observatory, 29 September 2014, https://globalcit.eu/is-the-slovak-citizenship-act-unconstitutional-the-constitutional-court-leaves-the-question-open/.

citizenship after 2011 is around 2000, and these individuals remain unregistered and unaccounted for.[20]

In sum, engagement of states with diaspora and kin-minorities carries both symbolic aspects, which aim to re-conceptualise nationhood, and pragmatic aspects, which relate to economic and/or political considerations and possible gains. Ultimately, trans-border kin-minorities do not appear that different from classical migrant diasporas.

Dual citizenship in Central and Eastern Europe: "Tracing the imprints of a nation's soul"[21]

One of the classic conceptualisations of citizenship describes it as *egalitarian* (a status of full membership for all), *sacred* (involving the sacrifices of citizens for the state), *national* (reflecting a cultural community, a community of language, mores and character at the same time), *democratic* (involving participation in public affairs), *unique* (to the exclusion of all others) and *socially consequential* (expressed in a community of well-being).[22] This model of membership, however, is no longer in tune with the facts of immigration, trans-border minorities or cases of multiple belongings within mixed families. In other words, each person may have more than one 'essential' identity.

Dual citizenship policies in general terms are addressed to external kin populations, either members of a country's diaspora[23] across the world (e.g. Croatia and Poland) or trans-border minorities residing at present on territories that once constituted part of the 'homeland' (e.g. Hungary in the Danube basin, Romania and Moldavia). Gradually, it seems that membership is becoming detached from residence, defying the boundaries of belonging and adopting instead features of a "consequential and ideologically charged distinction between citizens and foreigners".[24]

20 Mónika Ganczer: Hungarians outside Hungary –The Twisted story of dual citizenship in Central and Eastern Europe. In: *VerfBlog*, October 8 2014, available from: http://verfassungsblog.de/hungarians-outside-hungary-twisted-story-dual-citizenship-central-easter-europe.

21 Expression borrowed from Anatol Lieven: The Baltic Revolution. Estonia, Latvia, Lithuania and the path to independence. New Haven 1994, P. 113.

22 Rogers Brubaker: Immigration, Citizenship, and the Nation-state in France and Germany. A comparative historical analysis. In: International Sociology 5 (1990), P. 379–407.

23 According to Takeyuki Tsuda, a diaspora can be defined as "ethnic groups that have been territorially dispersed across different nations because of ethnopolitical persecution or for economic reasons and are united by a sense of attachment to and longing for their country of ethnic origin (the ethnic homeland)". Takeyuki Tsuda (Ed.): Diasporic homecomings. Ethnic return migration in comparative perspective. Stanford 2009, P. 1.

24 Rogers Brubaker: Citizenship and Nationhood in Germany and France. Cambridge/MA1992, P. 31.

Diasporic co-ethnics may therefore be imagined as an integral part of the cultural group of a nation, with dual citizenship used to give shape to this type of 'imagined community'. Germany, Greece, Ireland, Portugal and Spain have all given preferential access to citizenship to ethno-cultural kin without the condition of residence so it is not a rare phenomenon in the countries of Western Europe. For Central and Eastern Europe, the list for non-resident external citizenship is also considerable and includes Bulgaria, North Macedonia, Romania, Croatia, Serbia, Russia, Lithuania and Hungary.

External citizenship policies across the continent share a number of essential characteristics:

a) The identification of beneficiaries is made on ethnic criteria.
b) Cultural support is provided along with political and legal support.
c) The policy has extra-territorial effects.
d) The policy is often implemented without consultation or negotiation with the affected neighbouring states.[25]

Particularly for policies that concern trans-border minorities, there is a recurring argument that they constitute direct assaults on the territorial sovereignty of 'host' states. In fact, as the example of the Hungarian Dual Citizenship Law of 2010 amply demonstrated, such laws may be perceived on one side as the institutionalisation of an ethno-cultural nation and at the same time as an act of aggression against a state's sovereignty.

In more general terms, dual citizenship policies in Central and Eastern Europe include a wide spectrum of political options that range from limited naturalisation rights to full citizenship rights. [26] They are usually motivated by a declared willingness to contribute to more effective minority protection and therefore addressed to external compact kin populations. The opposite paradigm usually holds in Western Europe, where dual citizenship is linked to the integration of permanent residents.

On a comparative basis, dual citizenship is often problematised in Europe on the basis of a binary classification: while dual citizenship policies directed at kin groups are indeed implemented in the West (e.g. Ireland, Spain and Italy), the same projects have been interpreted as nationalist or imperialist in the East of our continent.[27] The real question to debate in this respect is whether this distinction is connected to

25 Rainer Bauböck: The Trade-Offs Between Transnational Citizenship and Political Autonomy. In: T. Faist, P. Kiviston (Eds.): Dual Citizenship in Global Perspective. Basingstoke 2007, P. 69–91.

26 For a recent review focusing on the role of kinstates, in part through extraterritorial citizenship rights, see Zsuzsa Csergö, Kristina Kallas and Tamas Kiss: Kin-State Intervention and the Securitization – Minority Policy Nexus: Hungarians and Russian-speakers in Central and Eastern Europe. In: Journal of Global Security Studies 10 (2025) No. 1 (https://doi.org/10.1093/jogss/ogae035).

27 Szabolcs Pogonyi, Mária M. Kovács, Zsolt Körtvélyesi: The Politics of External Kin-State Citizenship in East Central Europe. Badia Fiesolana 2010 (EUDO Citizenship Observatory 6), P. 10.

a two-speed integration process within Europe and/or to the connected economic cleavages between the two parts of the continent.

Analytically, citizenship acts both as an *object* (access to which is restricted) and an *instrument* of closure (used to draw boundaries). It is worth questioning the degree to which dual citizenship has operated as an instrument for conducting politics of identity, achieving political balances, adjusting demographics or even improving economics. A more pragmatic analysis may indeed reveal other motives than those related to ethno-cultural revival policies. Trans-border minorities often constitute a valuable source of investment or labour (or are perceived to), as already mentioned. Some states in favour of dual citizenship justify their choice on the basis of national interests: emigrants are a source of entrepreneurial human and financial capital. They also reinforce the cultural identity of the 'homeland' and can be used as a political resource to legitimise kin-state elites in times of crisis.[28] Let us briefly consider the Hungarian extension of citizenship to Hungarians living abroad: the law did not bring about any changes to their level of protection as minorities but did have an impact in the process of nation-building. The extension of citizenship affected the composition of the Hungarian polity by forcing law-making processes to react to the newly acquired plurality of the population. Similarly, in the Republic of Moldova, the 2003 Citizenship Law allowing for dual citizenship pushed 40 percent of Moldovans to claim citizenship of Romania, Israel or Russia.

More controversial is the use of dual citizenship to extend citizenship to kin-minorities in neighbouring states or emigrants in order to manipulate electoral results. The 1991 Law on Croatian Citizenship granted citizenship to non-resident Croats, including in Bosnia and Herzegovina where they numbered around 800,000. It was these votes that helped Franjo Tudjman to win elections in 1995 and 2000. Such an 'exchange' was also clear in the case of Victor Orban: his government issued passports to 500,000 ethnic Hungarians who 'rewarded' him by voting in his favour in the 2014 elections. In April 2014, ethnic Hungarian dual citizens residing outside of Hungary cast their vote for the first time in parliamentary elections by voting for Orban's party at the astonishing rate of 95 per cent of extra-territorial votes. The argument against this practice was obvious: external dual citizens, who would not experience the consequences of their vote and the policies enacted, may have determined the result of the elections.

The Lithuanian dual citizenship policy, implemented in 2010 but also later in 2015, and the 2010 Hungarian Dual Citizenship Law appear to be attempts to (re)construct zones of ethno-cultural influence. In the Lithuanian case, the parliament (Seimas) passed a temporary law allowing dual citizenship in exceptional cases only between 15 July 2008 and 12 December 2010, provided that the applicants

28 Myra A. Waterbury: From Irredentism to Diaspora Politics. States and Transborder Ethnic Groups in Eastern Europe. In: Global Migration and Transnational Politics. Working Paper 6 (2009), P. 1.

were Lithuanian citizens prior to 1940 and had fled during Soviet occupation. The award of Lithuanian citizenship also extended to the children and grandchildren of these categories of individuals. Later in 2015, the parliament amended the law further allowing dual citizenship for Lithuanians with 'special merits' (i.e. activities that strengthen the country's statehood, power and authority internationally). The Constitution otherwise generally forbids dual citizenship except in cases defined by law. In 2019, Lithuania held a referendum to amend the Constitution in order to allow dual citizenship with countries of the EU, EEA, NATO and the OECD though retaining prohibition of dual nationality with countries-members to organizations based around the former Soviet Union.

Nevertheless, in some instances, the consequence of dual citizenship provisions has been to grant EU citizenship to a large number of additional persons, in what has been labelled by some commentators a "clandestine"[29] or indirect enlargement of the EU. A paradox that also emerges is that, while some states have allowed external citizenship for their kin-minorities, internally the same states remained critical of other states' policies for their minorities. A typical illustration of this is the case of relations between Croatia and Italy.

The clash between citizenship policies in Moldova and Romania in 1991, which resulted in a flood of applications for Romanian citizenship from Moldovans, was exploited by nationalist parties in Romania leaving Moldova struggling to define itself as a nation with a distinct national identity.[30] The Moldovan Citizenship law granted citizenship to all inhabitants of the republic but dual citizenship only if Moldova had entered into an international agreement with the other country. That was not the case with Romania at that time. At the same time, the1991 Romanian law granted citizenship restoration to Moldovans who held Romanian citizenship and their descendants. Nationalist parties, such as the Greater Romania party, attempted to monopolize the issue with the intent to capture the support of Moldovans that had obtained Romanian citizenship. At the time, the underlying broader political project in the early post-Soviet period was based on the idea of 'two Romanian states'. Following Romania's initiation of negotiations to join the EU, the Romanian passport was particularly sought after since it allowed tax-free transfer of goods between the two countries, including private cars. Romanian passports ultimately became a tradeable good valued between 1,000 and 2,000

29 Benjamin Bidder: Entering the EU through the back door. In: Der Spiegel, 15 July 2010 (https://www.spiegel.de/international/europe/romanian-passports-for-moldovans-entering-the-eu-through-the-back-door-a-706338.html).

30 Constantin Iordachi: Dual Citizenship and Policies toward Kin minorities in East-Central Europe. A Comparison between Hungary, Romania and the Republic of Moldova. In: Zoltán Kántor, Balázs Majtényi, Osamu Ieda, Balázs Vizi, Iván Halász (Eds.): The Hungarian Status Law. Nation Building and/or Minority Protection. Sapporo 2004 (Slavic Eurasian Studies 4), P. 239– 269, here P. 249.

USD at the time.[31] The number of applications for Romanian citizenship climaxed in January 2001, at the moment when Romanian citizens were granted visa-free travel in the Schengen area.

Privileged access to nationality: Violation of non-discrimination or human right?

The ability of certain persons to access nationality on the basis of their ethnicity can be in theoretical terms interpreted by those adopting a formal understanding of equality as 'a suspicious classification' that is in contradiction with the principle of non-discrimination. More liberal interpretations of the concept of equality can reach the opposite conclusion, that as citizenship reflects both a form of association and a means of expression of individual identity, multiple national ties should not be obstructed in the absence of a compelling interest.[32] In that double capacity, dual citizenship does not violate equality as it does not create conditions of inequality within one given polity and does not undermine state solidarities.[33] Instead, if one accepts that by denying an individual citizenship, political rights may be compromised, *a contrario* the acquisition and maintenance of plural citizenship transforms into a value worthy of legal protection.[34]

Such an interpretation enjoys resonance with liberal theories of democracy, which emphasise the territoriality of members of a given society, who are affected by governmental action and who should therefore be able to participate in it. Imposing a renunciation in cases of double citizenship, therefore, appears not only to offend liberal values but also to create barriers between society and polity.[35]

While it is difficult to argue that dual citizenship constitutes a human right as of yet, there are other, more compelling arguments that justify dual citizenship for trans-border minorities. The most powerful of these arguments is that trans-border minorities have never moved, so their minority status is the result of circumstances beyond their control (and will). So while in a migration context, dual citizenship responds more to the need for freedom of movement between two states, for the border-shifting context it signals a gap in the levels of protection of those 'left behind' as a result of territorial changes. In that position, they deserve the opportunity to maintain and reproduce their minority culture and language. The essentialised

31 Iordachi: Dual Citizenship (Footnote 30), P. 250.
32 Peter J. Spiro: Dual Citizenship as human right. In: I-CON 8 (2010) No. 1, P. 111–130, here P. 111.
33 Spiro: Dual Citizenship as human right (Footnote 32), P. 111–112.
34 Spiro: Dual Citizenship as human right (Footnote 32), P. 123–124.
35 Spiro: Dual Citizenship as human right (Footnote 32), P. 124.

choice between being labelled a diaspora as opposed to being identified as a minority, entailing two different levels of protection, seems however highly questionable from a human rights perspective. The Council of Europe and the United Nations have encouraged bilateral approaches between kin-states and states where these groups reside for precisely that reason. A state that hosts a national, linguistic or religious minority has a special duty to protect that group and a citizenship guarantee reflects the minimal level of such protection.

Dual citizenship and European integration: Creating "communities of character"[36]

Central and Eastern Europe abounds with cases of complex demographic circumstances, where the political and the territorial aspects do not match. The geopolitical complications of dual citizenship offer another opportunity to reflect on the direction of the European integration process. More than three decades of political transition and policies of integration into western structures have amply demonstrated that Central and Eastern Europe requires a differentiated analytical approach. Acceptance of dual citizenship cannot eliminate considerations of structural specificities, demographic characteristics, political culture or even international relations. The discursive change surrounding dual citizenship from minority protection to 'nation policy', understood as the description behind the idea of a unified nation shows the willingness of individual countries to extend their normative power beyond their sphere, elevating the issue of dual citizenship from the individual to the regional and global level, while keeping it unambiguously politicised for power gain.

Since the early 1990s, general principles of EU law and the relevant case law have had much to say about the acquisition and loss of citizenship.[37] For the purposes of the present analysis, it is relevant to note that debate is framed not around the 'genuine link' citizenship criterion, but rather around concern for the rule of law and the protection of rights of the individual, especially in cases where the loss of national citizenship entails the loss of EU citizenship.[38] Modern citizenship is indeed modern because it is based on the notion of equality. In this context, the preferred tools for assessing the compatibility of national rules with EU law are the principles of proportionality, equality and legitimate expectations as protective shields against

36 Expression borrowed from Michael Walzer.

37 See for example the Micheletti case (Case C-369/90, judgement of 7 July 1992) finding that member states were required to determine conditions of acquisition and loss of nationality "with due regard to Community law."

38 The protection of EU law does not apply, however, to dual citizens of two EU member states, because in losing one of the two, the individual concerned would not lose EU citizenship.

illiberal choices made by member states.[39] The use of the 'right' family tree in order to obtain citizenship suggests that the concept is drawing closer to becoming an "inherited commodity" rather than an act based on actual identity.[40]

Additionally, and as the example of the 2014 German reform on citizenship illustrates, the 'genuine link' requirement of public international law is not always read by states in consonance with (long) residence requirements. *Ius soli* children, born in Germany but not satisfying the residence conditions (eight years of residence or six years of schooling) have to renounce their third-country nationality by their 23rd birthday, even when residing in another EU member state. This policy collides with the EU principle of free movement because it limits the parents of such children from exercising free movement rights so as not to risk the loss of their children's German citizenship rights.[41] In that respect, there are more voices arguing for the detachment of EU citizenship as a derivative citizenship based on national law status and more towards the acquisition of EU competence in determining the conditions for loss of EU citizenship as a matter of equality of protection.[42]

The instances of extension of citizenship from kin-states to minorities force us also to reflect on the link and interaction between nationalism and Europeanisation. It is interesting to observe how, pre-2004, both an ethno-politicisation process and Europeanisation were exerting dual pressure on states in Central and Eastern Europe. The two parallel processes remain still largely disconnected today. Again taking the Hungarian example, both the side of the government in favour of dual citizenship and the opposition engaged with European integration to justify their case for the law. The former mirrored the concept of borderless Europe, where territorial statehood becomes almost irrelevant, using the slogan "there won't be minorities, only communities", while the latter claimed that the law would displease the European institutions and jeopardise EU membership.[43] At the same time, EU principles of regionalisation, subsidiarity, devolution and protection of minority cultures have been instrumentalised to transform nationalism into post-national statehood while shifting sovereignty to the supra- and sub-state levels in the EU.[44]

Ultimately, the main effect of such use of dual citizenship is to insist further on the link between ethnicity and citizenship, as an expression of an ethno-centric conception of national identity, to be contrasted to the processes of naturalisation

39 Bauböck, Paskalev: Citizenship Deprivation (Footnote 16), P. 28–29.

40 André Liebich: Dual citizenship, no problem? July 16 2010 at http://eudo-citizenship.eu/commentaries/citizenship-forum.

41 Bauböck, Paskalev: Citizenship Deprivation (Footnote 16), P. 30.

42 The argument is made by reference to Grzelczyk v. Centre Public d'aide sociale d'Ottignies-Louvain-la-Neuve, at para. 31.

43 Agnes Batory: Kin-state identity in the European context. Citizenship, nationalism and constitutionalism in Hungary. In: Nations and Nationalism 16 (2010) 1, P. 31–48, here P. 41.

44 Pogonyi: Transborder Kin-minority as Symbolic Resource in Hungary (Footnote 14), P. 92.

of immigrant populations that *de-ethnicise* membership in a political community.[45] This is an evolution that moves clearly away from the arguments that dual citizenship may indeed be the first move towards a post-national constellation. Instead, it may surprisingly achieve the opposite: reinforce the sovereignty of states through the promotion of their interests with the help of trans-border minorities and expatriates. States will continue thus to enjoy a special role in the management of (national) identity. From a minority perspective, the real test remains not how a kin-state treats its co-ethnics but rather how it behaves towards its own minorities internally.

Concluding Remarks

Within Brubaker's famous triangle between a national minority, the external national homeland and the nationalising state, the balance of interests should account for the differing stakes entangled: the individual economic and political interests of citizens, the inter-state ones as they emerge from conflicts and the national ones as represented by state agencies, institutions and/or political parties. Whether pushed by the desire to institutionalise pre-existing cultural ties, the wish to facilitate cross-border travel between the mother country and national minorities, to absorb workforce from the near abroad or even to discourage massive immigration of minorities to the home country, dual citizenship is an interesting socio-political phenomenon that in Central and Eastern Europe has operated more as an instrument to respond to new economic cleavages (perhaps by creating more divisions than it should) within the perspective of European integration. In that frame, citizenship becomes a plural concept that can be analysed from different perspectives adding the dimensions of international organisation involvement but with questionable impact on minority protection, and with the added complications of disturbing legal stabilities in the region. In that sense, it should not be forgotten that the reasons that a state offers dual citizenship to its co-ethnics are not necessarily the same ones for which those concerned will take the offer in the end.

The argument has been made that dual citizenship is not an appropriate instrument for minority protection with neighbouring kin-states.[46] Instead, more political autonomy is preferable within the country of residence, allowing the groups concerned to stay where they are. This option ignores, however, the diversity of objective interests that minorities may have across the border to their kin-state and that range from political participation to economic sustainability, including an 'exit' option in post-conflict contexts. It also does not reflect enough on the

45 Batory: Kin-state identity in the European context (Footnote 43), P. 42.

46 Rainer Bauböck: Stakeholder Citizenship and Transnational Political Participation. A Normative Evaluation of External Voting. In: Fordham Law Review 75 (2007) No.5, P. 2393–2447.

inadequacy of the existing European legal framework to deal with the situation of kin-minorities.

Ultimately, when moving ahead, one must seriously consider dual citizenship as an exercise in interdependence and interactivity between states, especially within the EU's political space. Nationalist citizenship policies not only affect the individual states involved, they also carry the threat of conflicts and uncontrolled immigration in a continent that is more than ever trying to find its way towards meaningful paths of integration and away from fragmentation and 'caste-like' societies.

Helmut Glück

Language and Identity – historical and modern aspects

Language is *conditio humana*

Language is the most important means of communication among humans. In principle at least, the use of language separates humans from all other forms of life. Language is not only used to exchange information. It facilitates social organisation. It also has epistemic and cognitive functions. These functions are concerned with organising thought, and they are key elements of the process of socialisation: language acquisition includes the development of cognitive systems and epistemic orientation. The two are intrinsically linked. And language also has affective functions: we use it to express joy and suffering, enthusiasm and distaste, like and dislike, and a range of far more nuanced emotional reactions. The acquisition of language enables the child to become a social, thinking and feeling person. Günter de Bruyn expresses it like this: "I am unable to think of myself without using my mother tongue".[1] Language is *conditio humana* – the human condition.

The word 'language' has two basic meanings:

(1) Language *in and of itself*, the human faculty of using words in a structured way to communicate, typically spoken aloud but also signed [French: *faculté du langage*]. This faculty is part of the genetic make-up of every person. A number of language-related genes have been identified. This ability to gain language is independent of any specific language.

(2) Individual languages, i.e. the specific use of the human faculty of language in a particular linguistic community, at a particular time and in a particular geographical area [French: *langue*] and its expression in specific acts of communication [French: *parole*]. Udo Lindenberg says of this: "I was not able to convey correctly in English much of what I wanted to say. I had to sing in German [...]".[2]

I shall not elaborate further here on these basic definitions (for further information, see the article 'Sprache' in MLS[3]). However, I will point out that it is quite

---

1 Günter De Bruyn: Dank für den Jacob-Grimm-Preis Deutsche Sprache. In: Helmut Glück, Walter Krämer, Eberhard Schöck (Eds.): Kulturpreis Deutsche Sprache 2006. Ansprachen und Reden. Paderborn 2006, P. 34–40, here P. 35.

2 Udo Lindenberg: Dankesworte. In: Helmut Glück, Walter Krämer, Eberhard Schöck (Eds.): Kulturpreis Deutsche Sprache 2010. Ansprachen und Reden. Paderborn 2010, P. 48–55, here P. 49.

3 Helmut Glück, Michael Rödel (Eds.): Metzler Lexikon Sprache (MLS). 6th edn. Heidelberg 2024, P. 606–608.

possible to acquire more than one 'mother tongue' – one first language. It is possible to have several mother tongues. Where language acquisition successfully includes two languages, a child is in the happy position of being bilingual. If, on the other hand, the process is not so successful, a child can end up with two half-languages [German: *Halbsprachigkeit*].

Definition of *national minority*

In all definitions of the term 'national minority', language, or rather language difference, is a key marker. The terms 'language minority' or 'linguistic minority' are sometimes used to pinpoint the definition. These terms can indicate that a minority group is well integrated into mainstream society, so that the main distinguishing mark is the linguistic difference. The European Bureau for Lesser Used Languages was a non-governmental organisation working in this area between 1982 and 2010. It is, however, highly problematic to describe minority languages as 'lesser used'. Minority languages can in fact be *widely* used languages, often across a border from the area in which the minority lives; examples would be German as spoken by minorities in Belgium and Denmark, and Russian spoken in Estonia and Latvia.

In many countries, legislation uses the terms 'national minority' or 'ethnic minority'. I will not explore here the translation of these terms into other languages (*minorité*, *minornaza*, *men'schinstvo*, etc.). The term 'national minority' is not clearly defined anywhere, yet language is in nearly every case one of its attributed characteristics, for example for the European Council and the OSCE. National minorities generally have clearly defined rights in the education system, in the administration, in the legal system and in other areas of public life. In the main, they are guaranteed the right to maintain their language, their traditions and their institutions. National minorities can be ethnically related to the majority national group of another state; for example, the Szeklers in Romanian Transylvania are ethnic Hungarians, the South Tyroleans in Italy are German-speaking Austrians and the Carinthian Slovenians in Austria are ethnic Slovenians. This paper will focus on these minorities.

Alongside these are national minorities that cannot claim adherence to another state, such as the Friesians in Germany and the Netherlands, the Sorbs in Lusatia and the Kashubians west of Gdansk.

Then there are those minorities that have arisen due to migration. They generally do not enjoy the same rights as indigenous minorities. Modern examples include Turkish and Arabian communities in Germany and Austria, and people originating in the Maghreb who now live in France, Spain and Belgium. History offers examples of migrated minorities that have since become assimilated, e.g. the Czechs in Vienna between 1850 and 1920, and the Ruhr Poles who moved into the German Empire in the late 19th century. This paper will not address minorities that have arisen due to migration.

Languages, dialects, varieties

Describing language as a constituent characteristic of a national minority presents difficulties, since 'language' is a complex issue. We generally think of a language as a fully developed standard spoken and written language, defined by rules and norms in grammar books, textbooks and dictionaries, as it is taught in schools, disseminated via the media, and used in administration, legal systems and government, on the internet and in social networks. Minority languages often display different features from the standard and written languages they are related to. Heinz Kloss[4] coined the phrase 'überdachende *Sprache*' ['umbrella language']. He meant by this the fact that standard and written dialects, sociolects and other language forms work together to develop specific functions, using their own set of rules and norms. In other words, they combine to create an overarching 'umbrella' or 'roof' that embraces members of a language community.

This kind of structure is not essential. Another technique is often used to communicate across language borders: speaking one's own language, but slowly and in a way that focuses on the needs of the listeners, in such a way that even if they have not learned the language, they have some chance of understanding. Einar Haugen calls this technique 'semicommunication'.[5] Semicommunication is used, among many other places, in the overlapping dialect zones within the Romance language area, or in the Silesian border area between Czech and Polish speakers. [6]I have described semicommunication more fully elsewhere.[7] Kurt Braunmüller gives a detailed account for semicommunication between speakers of Scandinavian languages and Low German dialects.[8])

The fact that semicommunication actually works suggests to me that there are differences between hard and soft language boundaries, since "language boundaries

4 Heinz Kloss: Die Entwicklung neuer germanischer Kultursprachen seit 1800. 2nd edn. Düsseldorf, 1978.

5 Einar Haugen: Semicommunication. The Language Gap in Scandinavia. In: Social Inquiry 36 (1966), P. 280–297.

6 Helmut Glück: Deutsch als Fremdsprache in Europa vom Mittelalter bis zur Barockzeit. Berlin, New York 2002, P. 305–311.

7 Helmut Glück: Die Fremdsprache Deutsch im Zeitalter der Aufklärung, der Klassik und der Romantik. Grundzüge der deutschen Sprachgeschichte in Europa. Wiesbaden 2013 (Fremdsprachen in Geschichte und Gegenwart 12), P. 436–439, 466–469.

8 Kurt Braunmüller: Semikommunikation und semiotische Strategien. Bausteine zu einem Modell für die Verständigung im Norden zur Zeit der Hanse. In: Kurt Braunmüller (Ed.): Niederdeutsch und die skandinavischen Sprachen, Vol. II. Tübingen 1995, P. 35–70.

are often not borders, but rather transitional areas in which there are transitional varieties (dialect chains)".[9] Semicommunication works across soft language boundaries but not across hard ones. Soft language boundaries separate genetically related languages, such as Castilian and Catalan. It does not work between languages that have little or no genetic relationship, such as between French and the non-Romance *patois* spoken in the Basque region, Brittany and Alsace. It is generally hard language boundaries that give rise to conflict.

Literacy among the populations of Europe is a relatively new phenomenon, having developed in Central and Western Europe only in the 19th century, and in some countries in Eastern and Southern Europe not until the 20th century. Until then, minority languages were often dialects of a language that developed elsewhere as a standard and written language. The minorities concerned generally lived at the edge of a defined linguistic region, or are even isolated groups that had no connection with the parent language; they therefore tend to have strong dialect features. For them, it is essential to have an 'umbrella' standard spoken and written language.

A key marker of a language is mutual comprehensibility, that is, those using the language are fully understood by others speaking the same language. This implies that if mutual understanding is not present, then we are dealing with different languages. Standard and written languages evolved as tools to ensure mutual comprehensibility over a wide area. This means that they are taught in schools and used in printed materials, in legal proceedings, in the pulpit and by the institutions of government. In France, the French language was ruthlessly imposed after 1789 as the language of the Republic, at the expense of minority languages, which from then on were relegated to the status of *patois*, or vernacular. The norms of standard German were imposed and disseminated from about 1750, to the detriment of South German dialects and Low German. In Italy and Norway, the disputes to establish the 'correct' standard and written language were fought out until the 20th century. The 'rebirth of the nation' acted as midwife to many modern languages in Central and Eastern Europe. A standard and written language does not emerge ready-made. It arises as the result of the work and activity of a society over generations. It has to be imposed, to overcome impediments, and it relies on being used by the instruments of power. It has been quipped that "a language is a dialect with an army and a navy". In other words, it is the level of government support that determines whether a dialect gets elevated to the status of 'language' – not any linguistic feature of the dialect itself.

Standard and written languages are not only tools of communication. They are used to express, in prose and in song, affairs of the heart and longings of the soul. Here, for example, is Friedrich Hölderlin's incomplete *Deutscher Gesang*:

9 MLS (Footnote 3), P. 581.

> *Doch wenn dann sitzt im tiefen Schatten…* [Yet, sitting in the shade…]
> *Am kühlatmenden Bache der deutsche Dichter* [By the cooling stream the German poet]
> *Und singt, wenn er des heilig nüchternen Wassers* [And, having drunk deeply of the blessed sobering water,]
> *Genug getrunken, fernhin lauschend der Stille* [listening to the distant peace,]
> *Den Seelengesang* [sings the soul's song][10]

The word *deutsch* [German] can of course be freely swapped for any other nationality: a Sorbian, Estonian or Ladin poet might just as well sit and sing by this stream, each in his or her own language. This language, in each case, would be the "blessed sobering water" used by the poet to create the "soul's song". The word 'blessed' is here not used in the religious sense, but as a cypher for aesthetic beauty, and the word 'sobering' is a metaphor for a certain style used in literary works. The literary creation that emerges is more than a simple act of communication. It is a soul song, in which the poet gives expression to his innermost feelings in a carefully honed and elevated linguistic form. I would suggest that minority languages are indeed often the vehicle used for soul songs. They are often in a peripheral relationship with the majority language across a geographical border, or are subordinate to the majority language within a state. They are often emotionally charged and loved by their users in a way that standard languages might not be. Günter de Bruyn[11] writes that only persons who love their own language can understand a neighbour's love of *their* own language.

I am certainly not the first person to attribute my interest in language to the love I have for my own language and its literature. In the Foreword to their *Deutsches Wörterbuch [German Dictionary]*, Jacob and Wilhelm Grimm wrote:

> What is the purpose of a dictionary? [...] It sanctifies a language, preserves its treasures, and provides access to it for all. Who can tell how much a dictionary contributes, in that it unobtrusively gives to those who boast that they tackle foreign languages a keener feeling for the value of their own, of its superiority even, and by presenting examples awakens a stronger love for the literature of their mother tongue.[12]

10 Friedrich Beißner (Hg.): Friedrich Hölderlin. Sämtliche Werke. Frankfurt am Main, Wien, Zürich 1961, P. 385.

11 De Bruyn: Dank für den Jacob-Grimm-Preis Deutsche Sprache (Footnote 1), P. 40.

12 Jacob Grimm, Wilhelm Grimm: Vorrede. In: Deutsches Wörterbuch von Jacob und Wilhelm Grimm. Vol. 1. Leipzig 1854, repr. München 1984, P. IV–LXVII, here P. XII f.

Related and unrelated varieties

Dialects are often thought of as provincial forms of speech that are comprehensible to the mainstream society but not culturally valued. This is a misunderstanding. There are standard and written languages that include dialects under their 'umbrella' that do not satisfy the criterion of mutual comprehensibility. An obvious example lies within the German language area: High Alemannic German is rarely understood within Germany. Southern Bavarian in Carinthia also presents insoluble difficulties for some German holiday-makers. By this measure, High German, High Alemannic German and Southern Bavarian would be different (though genetically related) languages.

Not only that, but speakers of 'normal', High German also rarely enjoy mutual understanding with speakers of Low German. Many language researchers, politicians and lawyers consider Low German to be an independent language. It is treated as such in the European Council's Language Charter. In Schleswig-Holstein the authorities are required to process applications and respond to questions presented in Low German, and they are encouraged to respond in Low German if they are able to. The Hamburg city administration accepts applications in Low German and allows Low German to be spoken in the city assembly. So should we see Low German as a minority language at a soft linguistic boundary, or is it simply a dialect of German?

Along the border between Germany and the Netherlands, speakers of western Low German and Low Franconian do not struggle to communicate with each other when using their traditional dialects. But if they were to use their respective standard and written language forms, they would be mutually incomprehensible. So the minority-related problem does not arise at the level of dialect, but it does at the level of standard and written language. The Enlightenment thinker Georg Christoph Lichtenberg (1742–1799) expressed this soft language boundary using arguably unkind framing: "A donkey, it seems to me, is a horse translated into Dutch."[13]

As with Low German, Swiss German and Southern Bavarian are generally incomprehensible to most Germans who speak standard German. Clearly, therefore, the distinction between language and dialect in these cases is very muddied. In fact, we encounter Thümmel's paradox. It states that if one wishes to differentiate between languages, and between a language and its dialects, one must be able to define the conditions under which a system of speech can be called a 'language'. In order to formulate these conditions, it is first necessary to differentiate between languages, and between a language and its dialects – a classic circular argument, in fact.[14]

---

13 Georg Christoph Lichtenberg: Aphorismen. Edited by Kurt Batt. 3rd edn. Frankfurt a. M. 1979, P. 108.

14 MLS (Footnote 3), P. 677.

Some languages are far more mutually comprehensible than High and Low German. A prominent example is given by the languages that derive from a recently extinct language, Serbo-Croat. After the collapse of Yugoslavia in the 1990s, Serbo-Croat evolved into Serbian, Croat, Bosnian (since 2000[15]) and Montenegrin (since 2007). Speakers who are familiar with the differences between the Ikavian, Ekavian and Ijekavian dialects (of the former Serbo-Croat language) bridge any differences between these four new languages with ease. Mutual understanding is assured. These new language borders are soft. I have not studied in detail all linguistic minorities that have arisen through the establishment of newly independent states.

A further example of mutual understanding across language boundaries is provided by *Bokmål* (literally, 'book language'), an official language of Norway, which is also understood by Danes and Swedes. Bokmål is a Norwegianised variety of Danish. Since 1978 there has been a joint *Nordisk språkssekretatiat* [Nordic Language Secretariat], based in Oslo. Its aim is to "preserve and strengthen linguistic cooperation between the Nordic peoples [and] counteract tendencies for their individual languages to become more differentiated one from another."[16] In 1981 the Scandinavian countries signed a reciprocal treaty granting citizens of each country the right to use their mother tongue in each of the other countries, including in exchanges with public bodies.[17] This was made possible thanks to an unofficial hybrid language based on Swedish and *bokmål*, called *fellesskandinavisk* (roughly, 'common Scandinavian'[18]) The previously discussed concept of semicommunication was the facilitating factor here: soft language boundaries were deliberately kept soft. Few people are aware that debates are conducted in each Scandinavian country on the rights of linguistic minorities in other Scandinavian countries.

As we have seen, some minority languages exist under the 'umbrella' of languages that are in the majority on the other side of a state border, while other minority languages exist without benefiting from such an 'umbrella'. The former includes German spoken in Belgium, Denmark, Romania and Southern Tyrol. The latter includes Alemannic German and the Moselle Franconian dialects that remain in Alsace and Lorraine, which are no longer encompassed by standard and written German. They have been maintained in rural areas by the older generation, but they will become extinct in the foreseeable future. They represent a minority that, in the wake of two appalling wars, have lost trust in the majority group and its language

15 Peter Rehder: Bosnisch. In: Nina Janich, Albrecht Greule (Eds.): Sprachkulturen in Europa. Ein internationales Handbuch. Tübingen 2002, P. 12–15.

16 Union of International Associations (UIA): Open Yearbook. Brussels 1998. Available at: https://uia.org/s/or/en/1100050093, accessed 11 February 2025.

17 Cathrine Fabricius-Hansen: Skandinavische Hochsprache und 'Skandinavische Verkehrssprache'. In: Konrad Ehlich, Jakob Ossner, Harro Stammerjohann (Eds.): Hochsprache in Europa. Entstehung, Geltung, Zukunft. Freiburg 2001, P. 111–122, here P. 118.

18 Fabricius-Hansen: Skandinavische Hochsprache (Footnote 17), P. 118.

across the state border.[19] The Swiss journalist Fritz René Allemann described the Alsatians in 1962 as a "minority that no longer wishes to be one."[20]

Luxemburg has followed a different path. Luxemburg too suffered deeply from the German occupation during the Second World War. Around 350,000 people there speak a Moselle Franconian dialect that has evolved, since 1946, into a distinct language. The first orthographic guide for Luxembourgish was published in 1946. Between 1950 and 1977, a Luxembourgish dictionary in five volumes was published, though it had no prescriptive value. In 1999 the spelling conventions were revised. Luxembourgish grammar books have been produced since the 1950s and textbooks since the 1990s. In 1984 a language law was passed: Luxembourgish became an official language alongside French and German, but it was not permitted for use in constitutional or legal documents. In schools it is used when teaching literacy to migrant families, but other than that it is little taught.[21,] The Luxembourgish-speakers have little desire to continue to be seen as a minority. They have managed to establish their own written language, though it is unclear whether it will become a standard language: they have retained French and German as standard and written languages. Their German Belgian neighbours have no desire to adopt Luxembourgish as a written language; they are happy to keep German as the 'umbrella' standard and written language, and they all speak French as a second standard and written language. [22]

Language usage and language rules

In conclusion, I should like briefly to explain the social realities of minority languages. If they enjoy rights as an acknowledged language, then there will be defined regulations about their use in public life. This encompasses all the uses defined under language rights: administration; law, education; the media; workplace safety; road signage; signs in buildings; train stations and airports; and so on. Other issues may well be regulated include where and to what extent a given language can be used in everyday exchanges, such as in shops to label and describe products, on public transport, in banks, in cemeteries, in restaurants or at post offices. Poetry,

19 Dominique Huck: Les enjeux de l'enseignement de l'allemand à l'école primaire en Alsace de 1919 à nos jours. In: Allemagne d'aujourd'hui. Revue d'information et de recherche sur l'Allemagne 216 (2016), P. 165–176.

20 Fritz René Allemann: Die Elsässer. Eine Minderheit, die keine sein will. In: Der Monat 15 (1962) 170, P. 9–16; Vol. 171, P. 32–37.

21 Nico Weber: Letzeburgisch. In: Nina Janich, Albrecht Greule (Eds.): Sprachkulturen in Europa. Ein internationales Handbuch. Tübingen 2002, P. 154–150.

22 Johannes Kramer: Romanisch und Germanisch in Belgien und Luxemburg. Hamburg 2016 (Romanistik in Geschichte und Gegenwart, Supplement to Vol. 22).

song and other traditional activities, recreational facilities and of course, nowadays, the internet and the social networks it carries are not affected by any regulations. In the appendix to this essay is a list of 61 European minority languages used in 2015 as publishing languages by the online Wikipedia encyclopedia.

Minorities who live at soft language boundaries are less in need of legal protection for language rights. They are able to protect themselves by using semicommunication. This, however, is not always used; moreover, soft linguistic boundaries can be hardened for political reasons. This has happened, for example, in Catalonia and in Luxemburg.

Minorities who live at hard language boundaries do need legal protection for language rights. They are able to defend their other rights by becoming bilingual, but this does not protect their right to use their mother tongue. A legal resolution is needed. Sometimes this can be relatively unproblematic, as for instance in Upper Lusatia or the Canton of Grisons. In other cases, the language border can become a cause of perpetual conflict, as for example in Latvia and Estonia.

These conflicts have to be taken seriously – they cannot be dismissed using conciliatory rhetoric. In 21st-century Europe, such conflicts must be addressed by reaching a reliable compromise, one that may be painful on both sides, granting legal protection to the linguistic minority while also preserving the rights of the linguistic majority. Language is *conditio humana*. Compromises of this kind are crucial, because they touch on a human right: the right to use, develop and love one's own language.

Appendix

List of minority languages and dialects that have their own version of the Wikipedia group of internet publications in Western and Central Europe (compilation for Russia is as yet incomplete). In 2015 Wikipedia sites were published in 239 languages worldwide. 61 thereof are spoken and written in Europe, though with widely varying breadth of topics. The abbreviation for the country is given in brackets to show where the language or dialect is (mainly) used.

(1) Alemannic (A, CH, D, F)
(2) Aromunian (RO)
(3) Asturian (E)
(4) Basque (F, E)
(5) Bavarian (A, D, I)
(6) Breton (F)
(7) Catalan (E, F, Andorra)
(8) Lower Sorbian (D)
(9) Emilian (I)

(10) Extremaduran (E)
(11) Franco-Provençal (F, I)
(12) West Friesian (NL)
(13) Ladin (I)
(14) Upper Sorbian (D)
(15) Ischorian (Oblast' Sankt Peterburg, RUS)
(16) Yiddish (B, GB)
(17) Karelian (RUS)
(18) Karpathian Russian (UKR)
(19) Kashubian (PL)
(20) Kildin Sami (RUS)
(21) Cornish (GB)
(22) Corsican (F)
(23) Welsh (GB)
(24) Ladino (Judenspanisch) (GR, BG)
(25) Latgalian (LT)
(26) Ligurian (I)
(27) Limburgish (NL, B, D)
(28) Livonian (Oblast' Sankt Peterburg, RUS)
(29) Lombardian (I)
(30) Manx (GB)
(31) Megleno-Romanian (RO)
(32) Neapolitan (I)
(33) Low Saxon (D)
(34) North Friesian (D)
(35) Northern Sami (N, S, FIN)
(36) Norman (F, GB)
(37) Occitan (F)
(38) Karelian (RUS)
(39) Palatine German (D)
(40) Picardian (F)
(41) Piedmontese (I)
(42) Low German (D)
(43) Pontic Greek (UKR, RUS, GEO)
(44) Ripuarian (D)
(45) Walachian Romani (RO)
(46) Rumansh (CH)
(47) Sardinian (I)
(48) Sassarese (I)
(49) Schemaitian (Schamogitian) (LV)
(50) Silesian (PL)

(51) Lowland Scots (GB)
(52) Zeelandic (NL)
(53) Saterland Friesian (D)
(54) Sicilian (I)
(55) Upper Silesian (PL)
(56) South Sami (N)
(57) Venetian (I)
(58) Walloon (B)
(59) Veps (Oblast' Sankt Peterburg, RUS)
(60) West Flemish (B)
(61) Votic (Oblast' Sankt Peterburg, RUS)

Players

Zoltán Kántor

Kin-state politics. Hungary's kin-state policies, 2010–2018

Kin-state politics has been in the centre of scientific research since at least 1999, when Hungary initiated the law on Hungarians living in the neighbouring states.[1] Although kin-state laws existed before the Hungarian one (i.e. Slovakia, Romania), the Hungarian case reached the interest of scholars working on democracy, citizenship, nationalism and national minorities.[2] We have to find the reason why.

Several reasons can be enumerated, and the answer is probably a combination of these reasons. Not only does Hungary have a huge minority population abroad (around 2.2 million), but Hungary has played an active role in protecting the co-national Hungarians abroad since 1989. Over this period, the Hungarian minorities living in the neighbouring states have been among the most active minorities in Europe when it comes to self-organisation and request of rights. So size complemented with activism is one of the main reasons.

We must also mention that many neighbouring states believe Hungary to have revisionist goals.[3] At the same time, some authors – both politicians and social scientists – have expressed concerns that laws like the Hungarian one may lead to tensions between states, and also at the European level: there was a fear that the spread of kin-state policies could led to tensions across Europe. We should not forget that the debate on the Hungarian status law happened in the time period of EU accession talks. And let's not forget the scientific interest of the scholars, who rapidly observed that a new form of nationalism had appeared.

Kin-state politics is about nationalism. Nationalism, in my understanding, is a neutral concept, and is basically an analytical/descriptive concept, which describes the process of institutionalisation of societies on a national basis. In our case this institutionalisation transcends the borders of the states. Every kin-state policy targets citizens living in other countries. What matters in this case is national belonging: belonging to the same national, linguistic, cultural group as the citizens of the titular majority of the kin-state. This extreme interest in the Hungarian status law and on the Hungarian kin-state initiative can be understood from this perspective.

1 Zoltán Kántor, Balázs Majtényi, Osamu Ieda, Balázs Vizi, Iván Halász (Eds.): The Hungarian Status Law. Nation Building and/or Minority Protection. Sapporo 2004 (Slavic Eurasian Studies 4).

2 Szabolcs Pogonyi: Extra-Territorial Ethnic Politics, Discourses and Identities in Hungary. Basingstoke 2017; Myra A. Waterbury: Between State and Nation: Diaspora Politics and Kin-State Nationalism in Hungary. New York 2010.

3 No official document or statement supports this argument.

Since the Hungarian law was introduced, several other states have adopted similar kin-state laws, and amended citizenship laws making it easier for co-nationals living abroad to acquire citizenship of the kin-state (in certain cases the extension of electoral rights accompanied this). EU-accession talks, EU accession, and increased migration from Eastern and Central Europe towards Western Europe also play a role in understanding the phenomena.[4] The political, cultural, linguistic and national ties between becomes more and more important for the states. Domestic political struggles intensify this. One should also observe that – with a delay of some years – diaspora-policy became similarly important. A kin-state policy and extension of voting rights for co-nationals abroad became the rule, and is no longer the exception.

Struggle for rights, kin-state support for minorities, diaspora policies all are signs that in the Eastern and Central European region, national belonging gets importance.[5] Probably, a quite understudied factor is even more important: the nationalisation policies of the national states. It can be raised only as a hypothesis, but probably national minorities and kin-states would be less active if the nationalising states would approach the requests of the minorities in a more positive way.

There are several countries in which the borders of the state and those of the nation do not coincide. The treatment of this situation constitutes a political task for countries and governments, and they offer very different solutions to the problem. The model of taking responsibility for people belonging to the same nation but living abroad was established in Western Europe in the period after the Second World War (Austria – Italy/South-Tyrol). In the Central European region, supporting compatriots living abroad – either in neighbouring countries (traditional national minorities/communities) or in any other parts of the world (diaspora) – became a norm after the change of regime in 1989. Today it is considered natural that the kin-state provides some kind of assistance to its co-nationals/compatriots living beyond its borders. For twenty years we have been witnesses to these political and academic debates on the "good" relationship between the kin-state, kin-minorities and the nationalising state. Science attempts to understand, to analyse, and to describe the process; politically driven approaches focus on the evaluation of the intentions and outcome of kin-state policies. The mix of these two approaches causes a lot of misunderstanding in the analysis of kin-state policies.

Constitutions, electoral laws, laws on education, and language laws in the Central and Eastern European region all prove that the 'nation' and 'ethnicity' are of cen-

4 The major argument for initiating the Hungarian status laws was to find a solution for when Hungary becomes an EU member, and the neighboring states where kin-Hungarians live would be outside the European Union.

5 The Scottish referendum on independence (and the new Brexit-driven intentions) and the Catalan strive toward independence shows that the issue is also present in other parts of Europe.

tral salience for these newly formed states, both for the titular nation and national minorities. The principle of supporting people belonging to the same nation but living in different (neighbouring or not neighbouring) countries is often included in constitutions.[6] With some rare exceptions, the constitutions of the majority of states located in this region contain the so-called *responsibility clause*. In the period after the regime change, Central and Eastern European Countries supported their compatriots living abroad politically by means of declarations and programs. States have gradually established mechanisms and institutions to operate aid policy. Nevertheless, there is no coherent model for this field; countries are using different solutions, have different objectives and have established different institutions. Relations with nation parts (communities) living abroad depend on the financial possibilities and political priorities of the kin-state as well as the situation of people living abroad. As a basic rule, we differentiate between the support of people living in neighbouring countries and of those living in the diaspora.

Nationalism institutionalises the polity, invoking the nation, and involves a permanent definition and redefinition of boundaries. Since modernity, societies have been institutionalised on a national basis, which is valid for both majorities and minorities. In Europe arguably everyone is nationalised. As Ernest Gellner says, in the modern world, it is impossible not to be nationalist.[7]

One possible approach to national conflicts in Eastern Europe is to stress the parallel and often conflicting processes of nation-building. Once the ideal of the nation becomes important, there does not seem to be any sign that it will lose its significance. Nationalism may be transformed, but it remains an important organisational principle in our world. Nationalist politics are oriented partially on the strengthening of boundaries of the titular/majority nation, and by more or less hostile politics against national minorities. The real explanation for kin-state politics must be sought in the time-period and place of nation-formation in the 19th century, for that is where the importance of national ties is found. A post-communist, present-day approach, especially if it focuses on the political (electoral) interest of the actors, will lead us to only a superficial understanding of kin-state politics.

The Venice Commission, the High Commissioner on Minorities of the Organization for Security and Co-operation in Europe (OSCE), and the Parliamentary Assembly of the Council of Europe – partly as a result of the impact of Hungarian initiatives – consider kin-states' to bear responsibility for compatriots abroad and accept the practical consequences of this.[8] Within Europe, Hungary has the most

6 Irina Culic: State Building and Constitution Writing in Central and Eastern Europe after 1989. In: Regio – Minorities, Politics, Society 6 (2003), P. 38–58.

7 Ernest Gellner: Thought and Change. London, Chicago 1964, P. 16.

8 Zoltán Kántor: A nemzet kérdése a nemzetközi porondon [The Issue of the Nation on the International Arena]. In: Külügyi Szemle 2 (2008), P. 40–57.

complex and most active policy for its communities abroad. This is reflected in its legislation, the institutionalised forums of Hungarian-Hungarian relations, the high-level (ministerial and state secretariat) governmental presence of the Policy for Hungarian Communities Abroad and the aid policy as well (in particular in targeted programs). This is – first of all – because there are large Hungarian communities living in neighbouring countries (they are politically active communities, defining themselves in national terminology and having endeavours for autonomy). Secondly, it is because the Orbán Government (2010 to present) treats the Policy for Hungarian Communities Abroad as a priority.

Kin-state politics encompasses the special status (including citizenship) given to co-nationals living outside the country, political support for kin-minorities bilaterally and internationally, and financial support for the reproduction of language and culture. Kin-state policies might be defined as policies aimed at strengthening the society (community) of the minority. They are much more than kin-minority protection! Such policies attempt to counterbalance the negative effects of nationalising policies of the particular state where minorities live. The major goal of national minorities is to secure the national, cultural and linguistic reproduction of their group. This is similar to the goal of the majorities (titular nations).

Kin-state politics include the goals and financial efforts used to set up a composite system of public administration to manage the kin-state policy. Hungary's kin-state policy is probably one of the most complex, and therefore serves as a good example for analysis. From 1989 until 2010, we can speak in terms of initiatives, the establishing of a system of support, accompanied by intense domestic and international debates. From the year 2010, when Viktor Orbán's FIDESZ-KDNP won the elections, it is more meaningful to speak in terms of the development of an extremely complex public administration system.

The level of principle

The Policy for Hungarian Communities Abroad is Hungary's policy towards Hungarians living in neighbouring countries and other countries of the world. It is aimed at strengthening the relations of the kin-state with Hungarian individuals and communities living abroad to further the prosperity of the unified Hungarian nation. Its objective is to preserve the identity of Hungarian communities living abroad, and to pass this identity on to future generations. The Policy for Hungarian Communities Abroad means nation-building, society-building and institutionalisation.

It is an evident aim for Hungary that, as the kin-state, it has to support the enhancement of ties between the parts of the nation, the unity of Hungarians living in the kin-state and those living abroad and their responsibility towards each other. The Act on the Testimony for National Cohesion (2010) states that:

> Every member and community of the Hungarian nation thrown under the jurisdiction of different states is part of the unified Hungarian nation, the beyond borders unity of which is reality, and is also an important element of Hungarians' personal and community identity.[9]

Actions connected with the Policy for Hungarian Communities Abroad are included in the document *Policy for Hungarian Communities Abroad – Strategic framework for Hungarian communities abroad* (2011).[10] This document systematises Hungary's policy for its nation parts abroad, summarising the strategic aims, leading directives and fields of action both for Hungary's politics and public administration and for Hungarian communities abroad. The *Strategic framework for Hungarian communities abroad* affects every area of Hungarian politics and public administration: due to its horizontal nature, every actor at every level of decision making-and execution has to take it into account.

From the point of view of the reproduction of Hungarians living abroad, the strategy for Hungarian communities abroad considers autonomy the most important objective. This objective is based on the conviction that the long-lasting permanence and prosperity of Hungarians can only be achieved by means of autonomy. Consequently, the short-term aim of the policy for Hungarian communities abroad is society-building. Therefore, *institutionalisation* is a key concept. National reproduction can be realised if the Policy for Hungarian Communities Abroad focuses on areas in which a dense and high-quality network of institutions provides an opportunity for Hungarians to be in contact with the Hungarian language, culture and community throughout their whole life. The aim of the strategic framework is to achieve the numerical growth of Hungarian communities (the number of community members grows, the community is not assimilated, it is characterised by positive population growth and good quality of life), their intellectual growth (the identity of community members is strong, they regard community norms as their own, they have competitive knowledge, they preserve and develop the cultural treasures of the community), economic and legal growth (in the latter case the members of the community are confident in exercising, protecting and – if necessary – expanding their rights).

The Hungarian Diaspora Council adopted the *Hungarian Diaspora Policy – Strategic Directions* document[11] in 2016. The document formulates the priorities and

9 For more details see: https://www.nemzetiregiszter.hu/download/9/93/00000/Nemzeti_osszetartozas_torveny.pdf, accessed 11 February 2025.

10 Hungarian Communities Abroad – Strategic framework for Hungarian communities abroad. State Secretariat for Hungarian Communities Abroad: http://www.nemzetiregiszter.hu/download/9/a2/00000/Magyar%20nemzetpolitika%20A4.pdf (see excerpts in English: https://www.nemzetiregiszter.hu/download/b/12/10000/policy_2013.pdf), accessed 11 February 2025.

11 For more details see: https://bgazrt.hu/wp-content/uploads/2019/03/03-magyar_diaszporapolitika-strat%C3%A9giai-ir%C3%A1nyok.pdf (see excerpts in English: https://www.nemzetiregiszter.hu/download/7/80/30000/diaspora_policy.pdf), accessed 11 February 2025.

strategic path of the Hungarian Government in dealing with the Hungarian diaspora (for Hungary, the diaspora are Hungarians living outside the Carpathian Basin). This is a sign that, even if on the level of principles we speak about a common kin-state policy, for practical and logistical reasons the government technically separates the two large groups of Hungarians.

These two strategies are the guiding documents for the political and public administration of Hungary regarding the Hungarian minorities in the neighbouring states.

The level of legislation

Most European states grant citizenship to their compatriots living abroad by means of a simplified naturalisation procedure, and allows them to participate in the kin-state's elections. Almost every state supports its compatriots living abroad by means of laws similar to status law and various aid budgets connected with it.[12]

Even after the adoption of the amendment to the Hungarian Constitution in 1989, the Basic Law of Hungary stated that "The Republic of Hungary feels responsibility for the fate of Hungarians living beyond its borders, and shall promote the fostering of their links with Hungary". This statement opened a new chapter in the relations between the kin-state and Hungarians living beyond its borders. This responsibility is defined in the Basic Law of Hungary in the following way:

> Bearing in mind that there is one single Hungarian nation that belongs together, Hungary shall bear responsibility for the fate of Hungarians living beyond its borders, shall facilitate the survival and development of their communities, shall support their efforts to preserve their Hungarian identity, the effective use of their individual and collective rights, the establishment of their community self-governments, and their prosperity in their native lands, and shall promote their cooperation with each other and with Hungary.

The Act on Hungarian Citizenship and its amendment adopted in 2010, the status law (2001) and its amendment (2010), and the extension of the right to vote to Hungarian citizens living abroad (2012) all strengthened the ties between Hungary and Hungarians living beyond its borders – either in neighbouring countries or in the diaspora – and transformed the pre-existing cultural ties into a relationship under public law.

12 See: European Commission for Democracy Through Law (Venice Commission): Report on the Preferential Treatment of National Minorities by their Kin-State. Adopted by the Venice Commission at its 48th Plenary Meeting. Venice, 19–20 October 2001.

On 26 May 2010, the National Assembly of Hungary adopted the Amendment to the Act on Hungarian Citizenship. Seven months later, on 1 January 2011, the application of the Act – the simplified naturalisation procedure – began. The amendment states that one can acquire Hungarian citizenship without permanent residence status in Hungary or passing a citizenship test; it is enough to have a command of the Hungarian language and to have one ancestor who was a Hungarian citizen. The amendment of the Act on Citizenship is based on the conception that although Hungarians living abroad are the citizens of other countries, they belong to the same Hungarian nation, regardless of which state they live in. This concept is in line with the position held by Hungarians living in neighbouring countries and in the diaspora.

The new constitution, the amended law on citizenship, and the extension of voting rights to the new citizens accomplished the intentions of the new government regarding the Hungarians living abroad. It is considered by the Hungarian government that the legal framework is proper to support Hungarians living outside the state's borders.

The level of decision-making bodies

Kin-state policy is not only the policy of the kin-state. Hungary states that Hungary supports the claims raised by the Hungarians living abroad. Decisions are taken by legitimate bodies in which the government, the opposition parties, and the representatives of the Hungarian ethnocultural parties are represented. The initiative is in the hand of the government, but decisions are taken in common.

Decisions related to the Policy for Hungarian Communities Abroad are made by the Hungarian National Assembly and Hungarian-Hungarian forums. Earlier, the issues concerning Hungarians abroad were discussed by the Committee on Foreign Affairs of the Hungarian National Assembly (between 2006 and 2010 its name was Committee on Foreign Affairs and Hungarian Communities Abroad). On 1 January 2010 the Committee on National Cohesion[13] was established to focus specifically on the issues of Hungarians abroad. The establishment of the Committee on National Cohesion is an integral part of Hungary's strategy for Hungarian communities abroad. The establishment of the committee has symbolic significance, as the Hungarian Parliament has not had any independent committee exclusively handling questions of Hungarians abroad since the 1989 regime change. Within

13 The Committee on National Cohesion maintains relations with Hungarian political and social organisations abroad, monitors the events of Hungarians living abroad and the work of institutions connected with the Policy for Hungarian Communities Abroad. Since its establishment, it has had several extramural sessions at different venues within the Carpathian Basin.

the framework of the Committee on National Cohesion, the Autonomy Subcommittee was formed to deal with transborder Hungarians' aspirations for autonomy. Besides this, the Foreign Affairs Committee continues to operate and current issues of foreign policy are regularly on its agenda, including issues concerning Hungarian communities abroad. Other questions regarding Hungarians living beyond state borders – like constitutional, budgetary, educational and ecclesiastical issues – are also discussed by other parliamentary committees.

Close relations with Hungarians living abroad, the establishment of dialogue with them and the presentation of their standpoints in the Hungarian Government's decision-making procedures are important elements of the government's Policy for Hungarian Communities Abroad. The Hungarian Standing Conference (Magyar Állandó Értekezlet – MÁÉRT) is the most important Hungarian-Hungarian political forum. After a six-year break, it recommenced its operation on 5 November 2010. The MÁÉRT as an institutionalised forum of dialogue between legitimate Hungarian organisations representing national interests plays an important role in joint thinking and decision-making on issues concerning the Hungarian nation. The MÁÉRT has at least one session every year, and its mid-year work is assisted by different specialised committees. The MÁÉRT consists of representatives of the Hungarian Government, Hungarian parliamentary parties, Hungarian organisations operating outside Hungary with parliamentary or provincial representation, and representatives of the Western Hungarian diaspora. Currently, the Hungarian Standing Conference has four working committees: Committee on Foreign and Legal Affairs, Committee on Education and Culture, Committee on Economy and Local Government, and Diaspora Committee.

The Hungarian Diaspora Council is a forum of Hungarian organisations from all over the world, aiming to support the special needs and interests of Hungarians living in diaspora, and creating an independent representative body for the global Hungarian diaspora. The Hungarian Diaspora Council works in close cooperation with the Hungarian Standing Conference.

The Forum of the Hungarian Representatives of the Carpathian Basin (Kárpát-medencei Magyar Képviselők Fóruma – KMKF) is a forum supplementing the Hungarian Standing Conference with the dimension of parliamentary cooperation. The aim of the body, which was first convened in 2004, is to make cooperation between Hungary's parliamentary parties and the representatives of Hungarian organisations abroad regular and therefore more successful. From 2010, the activity of the KMKF was complemented with a new remit: while MÁÉRT deals with political and governmental communication and sectoral policies, the KMKF focuses on the establishment of long-term strategies, while continuing to deal with parliamentary communication. The KMKF is the forum of Hungarian representatives of neighbouring countries elected at national, provincial or county level and Hungarian members of the European Parliament.

The level of governmental structure

The concept of bearing responsibility for persons belonging to the same nation but living in other countries is present in the governmental structure of several countries. Solutions are different: there are countries in which the department or office dealing with compatriots living abroad operates under the Ministry of Foreign Affairs, while in others it is part of the Parliament, but there also are countries in which it is part of the President's Office.

In Hungary the Secretariat for Hungarians Living Abroad was established in 1990, after the regime change. Two years later it became a body with national competence under the name Office for Hungarians Living Abroad (Határon Túli Magyarok Hivatala – HTMH), under the supervision of the Ministry of Foreign Affairs. During the socialist-liberal government of Gyula Horn, the HTMH was placed under the supervision of the Prime Minister's Office, while from 1998 – under the first, right-wing conservative government of Viktor Orbán – it became part of the Ministry of Foreign Affairs. In 2002 – under the socialist-liberal Medgyessy Government – the HTMH was returned to the Prime Minister's Office again, and in 2006 – during the administrational reform which took place under the socialist-liberal government of Ferenc Gyurcsány – the office was ceased. Between 2007 and 2010 the issues of Hungarian communities abroad belonged to the Department of Affairs of Hungarians Abroad, a department of the State Secretariat for Foreign Relations and Affairs of Hungarians Abroad at the Prime Minister's Office.

The governmental structure established after the 2010 election brought significant changes. The State Secretariat for Hungarian Communities Abroad was established within the Ministry of Public Administration and Justice. With this change, the issue of Hungarians living outside the kin-state was raised to a higher level and became equivalent with any other sectoral policy. Operative policy work is performed by the State Secretariat for Hungarian Communities Abroad.

The State Secretariat for Hungarian Communities Abroad coordinates the Interministerial Committee for Hungarian Communities Abroad (Nemzetpolitikai Tárcaközi Bizottság – NPTB). This committee was established in order to harmonise the activity of different governmental units that touch upon issues of Hungarian communities abroad, based on the principle of mutual responsibility and attention. The president of the committee is the Deputy Prime Minister, while its vice-president is the parliamentary state secretary at the Ministry of Foreign Affairs. The NPTB has a minimum of two sessions per year, but can be convened whenever it is required. The tasks of the committee – among others – are to realise mutual information exchange supporting the government's activity for Hungarians abroad, the coordination and evaluation of tasks concerning this policy, and the harmonisation of other ministries' strategic activity affecting Hungarians abroad. The committee is also responsible for ensuring the most effective possible way of using budgetary resources allocated to targets concerning the Policy for Hungarians Communities Abroad.

No new direction in the field of kin-state politics was formulated after the successive electoral win of FIDESZ-KDNP in 2014.Hungary continued and extended the policy that was begun in 2010. The major changes were:

- increased attention was given to the support of Hungarian entrepreneurs in neighbouring states (materialised in financial support and loans)
- a much greater amount of money was allocated for building and renovating kindergartens in the neighbouring states.

Since 2014 the State Secretariat for Hungarian Communities Abroad continues its work under the Prime Minister's Office.

The level of aid policy

The Bethlen Gábor Fund[14] was established in 2011 as a successor to the Szülőföld Alap [Homeland Fund], managing the financial assistance provided by Hungary for Hungarians living abroad. Its tasks cover three main areas: the payment of aid, the operation of the House of Hungarians (Magyarság Háza) and the Research Institute for Hungarian Communities Abroad.[15] Aid policy was restructured to transfer multicentric and non-transparent financial flows into a centralised, simple and transparent system. Funds are managed by Bethlen Gábor Fund Management Ltd. In 2011 the Hungarian Standing Conference decided to lay emphasis on long-term, predictable and normative aid funding instead of occasional, tender-based payment. It also expanded the scope of institutions of national importance (institutions that play an outstanding role in the preservation of the given Hungarian community, such as educational institutions and cultural associations).

The most important funding category of the Bethlen Gábor Fund is the *Szülőföldön magyarul* – also called educational aid – designated for Hungarian children living abroad and studying in Hungarian-language educational institutions. In 2011 the educational aid was extended to nursery school children as well. In addition, the Bethlen Gábor Fund provides assistance to natural and legal persons, local governments, civil organisations, cultural institutions etc. under an open tender system and decides on the award of individual aids.

Since 2011 Bethlen Gábor Fund Management Ltd. has also been responsible for the realisation of the visitor and educational-methodological centre House of Hungarians (Magyarság Háza). The House of Hungarians operates as a public educa-

14 For more details see: www.bgazrt.hu, accessed 11 February 2025.

15 For more details see: www.npki.hu, accessed 11 February 2025.

tion institution presenting Hungarian communities living abroad. The Research Institute for Hungarian Communities Abroad operates within the organisational framework of Bethlen Gábor Fund Management Ltd. Its primary objective is to conduct research in the field of minorities, to harmonise and encourage research on minorities and Hungarian communities abroad and to process the research findings for further policy implementation.

The level of programs[16]

In order to transform the Policy for Hungarian Communities Abroad into a field policy, several programs have been established. The Hungarian Government enhances the prosperity of Hungarians abroad by means of well-formulated, realisable programs.

Institutions – educational institutions in particular – play a very important role from the point of view of the permanence and prosperity of Hungarian communities abroad. In light of this, the State Secretariat for Hungarian Communities Abroad launched thematic programs in 2012 that target one prioritised field in the particular year (kindergarten, elementary school, vocational school, family entrepreneurs, etc.). The Dr. Szász Pál Scholarship was founded in 2012 to support highly qualified young jurists who have outstanding results in the field of economic law and might contribute to the legal and economic prosperity of Hungarians abroad.

The Határtalanul! (Without Borders!) program aims to provide an opportunity for every Hungarian student studying in public education to make at least one state-funded visit during their studies to Hungarian communities living in neighbouring countries, and to give an opportunity for Hungarian students living abroad to visit Hungary by means of student exchange programs. The Without Borders! program helps young people experience and understand national unity through education.

There are different government projects specifically targeting the Hungarian diaspora in the West. In October 2011, the Hungarian Government launched another initiative, the *Hungarian Register* website, which facilitates direct contact with Hungarians living in different parts of the world. The Kőrösi Csoma Sándor Program[17] aims to develop the Hungarian language skills of diaspora Hungarians, encourage their community activity and strengthen their relations with Hungary. Within the framework of the program, Hungary sends interns to the diaspora to aid Hungarian communities with the preservation of various levels of Hungarian culture, and to foster Hungarian organisations' ties to the motherland.

16 For more details see: https://www.nemzetiregiszter.hu/main-page, accessed 11 February 2025.

17 https://www.nemzetiregiszter.hu/korosi-csoma-program, accessed 11 February 2025.

The objective of the Julianus program[18] is to create a comprehensive register of the Hungarian material heritage located in the diaspora and create broad access to its data. The program presents Hungarian material heritage found in the diaspora territories, and gives an overview of how Hungarian communities living in diaspora have contributed to the universal Hungarian culture. The Mikes Kelemen program[19] focuses on preserving the diaspora's material heritage, collecting its elements in a systematic manner, transferring them to Hungary and making provision for their appropriate utilisation.

These are only some of the most important programs that are managed (in collaboration with professional organisations from abroad) and financed by the Hungarian state. Year by year more and more funds are allocated for the support of Hungarian communities abroad.

Conclusions

Kin-state policies are no longer the exception, but the rule. In recent decades we have observed the growing interest of states in their kin-minorities and diasporas. This interest has been materialised in policies, laws and financial support. Hungary's Policy for Hungarian Communities Abroad integrates into the system of European trends, but has its own peculiarities. Its aim is to support the prosperity of compatriots living abroad and enhance their relations with the kin-state. When it comes to state policies supporting communities living abroad, Hungary is not only one of the most active countries, but is also the country with arguably the most complex state administration designed for the support of co-nationals abroad. This is reflected at the levels of both legislation and decision-making (joint state forums and Hungarian-Hungarian forums established specifically for this purpose). In terms of transforming kin-minority policy into an independent sectoral policy area, Hungary is also on the top, compared with other Central and Eastern European states.

The objective of the harmonised Policy for Hungarian Communities Abroad is to integrate individuals – by means of institutions – into communities, into the nation (in an ethnocultural understanding), and to integrate communities into the political system of the concerned state. Institutionalisation provides a basis for the multilevel national integration of the Hungarian nation:

1. at the level of individuals: strengthening the ties of Hungarians living abroad both with Hungary (citizenship, right to vote) and their own community (institutionalisation)

18 https://www.nemzetiregiszter.hu/julianus-program-en, accessed 11 February 2025.
19 https://www.nemzetiregiszter.hu/mikes-kelemen-program-en, accessed 11 February 2025.

2. at the community level: strengthening the links of Hungarian organisations abroad with the kin-state and – as a community – with their own country (collective recognition and rights, autonomy)
3. the integration of the unified Hungarian nation – integrated both individually and collectively – into the European Union.

Cezary Żołędowski

Polish national minorities in post-Jagiellonian area

Introduction

The aim of the paper is to present the position of Polish national minorities in the countries neighbouring Poland to the east. I will examine the number, location and basic characteristics of the political situation of Poles in Lithuania, Belarus and Ukraine. The choice to examine Polish minorities in these countries reflects the historical political community within the framework of the Polish-Lithuanian Commonwealth which, until the end of the 18th century, was the common state embracing these four nations. The knowledge and evaluation of this former community varies greatly across the societies that have succeeded it. Recent evaluations have been influenced by the historical phenomena that followed the break up of the Commonwealth: long-term subordination to Russia (and then to the Soviet Union), the 19th-century processes from which modern nations emerged in this part of Europe, and conflicts amongst them in the next century (especially the Polish-Ukrainian and Polish-Lithuanian conflicts in the interwar period and during the Second World War). Nevertheless, the former political community of Polish, Lithuanian, Belarusian and Ukrainian lands is the cause of the specificities of national minorities (foreign compatriots) in these countries. This is evident both in the genesis of these minorities and in how they are perceived by the state majorities.

Post-Jagiellonian area – understanding the concept and legitimacy in the study of ethnic relations

The post-Jagiellonian area may, in the most basic sense, be defined as the territories of contemporary Poland, Belarus and Lithuania (more precisely – the area inhabited by Poles, Lithuanians and Belarusians). These three nations have the greatest right to be regarded as successors to the Polish-Lithuanian Commonwealth, officially called the Republic of Two Nations [Polish: *Rzeczpospolita Obojga Narodów*], and unofficially known as First Republic [Polish: *Pierwsza Rzeczpospolita*]. It was established at the end of the 14th century (in accordance with the Polish-Lithuanian agreement in Krewo in 1385), and for almost the next 200 years was ruled by the Jagiellonian dynasty, who bore the title of Polish Kings and Grand Dukes of Lithuania.

Belarusians were not formally part of the titular nation of the Polish-Lithuanian Commonwealth, but even at the beginning of the 19th century, all the inhabitants of the former Grand Duchy of Lithuania (the majority of whom were Belarusians) were called 'Lithuanians'. By contrast, Lithuanians at that time were called Samogitians [Polish: Żmudzini].

Today, the term 'post-Jagiellonian area' should be used primarily in the historical and territorial sense. But in the past, the so-called Jagiellonian idea, which means the restoration of the unity of this area, was of great political significance, even long after the Jagiellonian dynasty had expired (in the 16th century) and even after the collapse of the Polish-Lithuanian State (in the late 18th century).[1] This idea was manifested in the positive evaluation of the past political state community of the Kingdom of Poland and the Grand Duchy of Lithuania, and was expressed in activities aimed at restoring the Polish-Lithuanian community, which also included Belarusians. During the Polish national uprisings against Russia (in 1830 and in 1863) Belarusians and Lithuanians participated in massive numbers, fighting in their small homelands for the resurrection of a common state. Amongst them were not only the nobles and members of other privileged classes, but also the peasants.

The political significance of the Jagiellonian idea began to fade in the last decades of the 19th century,[2] destroyed by the emerging modern nationalism. The fastest and most intense break with the Jagiellonian idea took place in Lithuania. For the Lithuanian national revival (since the 1870s), Polishness had become the greatest enemy. Lying at the core of hostility towards the Poles was the fear of Polonisation. Therefore, Lithuanian nationalism (and in its wake, Lithuanian historiography) denied any positive impact Poland had had on Lithuania. Poland was accused of Polonisation, of weakening Lithuanian elites and Lithuania. The Jagiellonian dynasty (which was a Lithuanian dynasty) was accused of having betrayed Lithuania.[3] This was an understandable defensive position, given Lithuanians desire to survive as a separate nation. But this sort of thinking has damaged current Polish-Lithuanian relations. Only recently (in the past few years) have some Lithuanian historians offered more balanced assessments of Polish-Lithuanian relations.[4]

Belarusian nationalism was much weaker and less anti-Polish than Lithuanian nationalism. But the political dominance of Russia led to a gradual change in how Belarusians saw themselves, beginning with a sense of belonging to the great Slavic Eastern Orthodoxy, and moving towards identifying as a Russian regional group.

---

1 Stanisław Ciesielski, Teresa Kulak, Krystyn Matwijowski (Eds.): Polska – Kresy– Polacy. Szkice historyczne [Poland – Eastern Borderlands – Poles. Historical sketches]. Wrocław 1994, P. 358.

2 Timothy Snyder: Rekonstrukcja narodów. Polska, Ukraina, Litwa, Białoruś 1569–1999 [Reconstruction of nations. Poland, Ukraine, Lithuania, Belarus 1569–1999]. Pogranicze, Sejny 2006, P. 350.

3 Piotr Łossowski: Po tej i po tamtej stronie Niemna. Stosunki polsko-litewskie 1883–1939 [On this side and on the other side of the Niemen River. Polish-Lithuanian relations 1883–1939]. Warszawa 1985, P. 326.

4 Andrzej Rachuba, Jurate Kiaupiene, Zigmantas Kiaupa: Historia Litwy. Dwugłos polsko-litewski [History of Lithuania. Polish-Lithuanian Duet]. Warszawa 2009, P. 388.

It is in Poland that the Jagiellonian ideology lasted the longest. Even after the First World War, it was present in the federal concept of Józef Pilsudski, the most eminent leader of the independence movement at the turn of the 19th and 20th centuries, and since 1918 the first Head of the Polish State. However, this concept was rejected by non-Polish successors of the former Commonwealth, who now placed greater importance on nationalist ideology, and suspected plans to Polonise disputed territories. Today in Poland, the Jagiellonian idea still has a sentimental dimension. It is manifest in a few ways, including a kind of paternalism towards Poland's partners in the East.[5]

It is worth mentioning the Ukrainians. They also comprised a large part of the population of the Polish-Lithuanian Commonwealth, but they never felt – in a significant way – associated with its traditions. Ukrainians were unsuccessful in their attempt to transform the Republic of Two Nations into the Republic of Three Nations. So, the majority of Ukrainians since the 16th century have viewed the Polish-Lithuanian State as an occupying power. But Ukraine is also relevant in that there is a Polish minority in Ukraine, which is also nominally part of the post-Jagiellonian area, albeit in a narrow, territorial sense.

The post-Jagiellonian area is a useful framework for examining national relations within the former Republic of the Two Nations, for two major reasons.

First, research on the national minorities in this area allows us to identify the basic factors that influence the situation of these groups. These factors are, *inter alia:* number and territorial concentration, the economic situation of the background of the majority, the importance of national ideology in the majority group, and social attitudes to their shared past. Of these factors, the most significant was a historical factor, associated with differing evaluations of the common history, including the Polish-Lithuanian Commonwealth. This was particularly evident in Lithuania.[6]

Secondly, the former Commonwealth was responsible for the specific genesis and situation of Polish minorities in the neighbouring countries to the east. Poles in Lithuania, Belarus and Ukraine are not remnants of invaders (despite what we sometimes hear in the political debates in these countries). Poles in these areas are basically indigenous peoples; they are an autochthonous population. They are, in part, the descendants of migrants from ethnographic Poland from the 14th to 18th century. Many of them are also a Polonised local population, especially in Belarus and Lithuania.

5 Marceli Kosman: Mitologia rediviva. Między litwomanią a litwofobią [Rediviva mythology. Between mania and phobia]. In: Marceli Kosman (Ed.): Kultura polityczna w Polsce. Mity i fakty. Tom II [Political culture in Poland. Myths and facts. Vol. II]. Poznań 1999, P. 103–111, here P. 107–108.

6 Cezary Żołędowski: Białorusini i Litwini w Polsce, Polacy na Litwie i Białorusi. Uwarunkowania współczesnych stosunków między większością i mniejszościami narodowymi [Belarusians and Lithuanians in Poland, Poles in Lithuania and Belarus. Determinants of contemporary relations between the majority and minorities]. Warszawa 2003, P. 360.

And indeed, Belarusian and Lithuanian historiography correctly state that the Poles in these countries are, in most cases, Polonised Belarusians and Lithuanians. At the time of the Polish-Lithuanian Commonwealth, the vast majority of local gentry and elites underwent Polonisation (in terms of language, culture and religion – conversion from Orthodoxy to Roman Catholicism). These were gradual and unforced processes, based on the perception of Polish culture and political system as attractive. Polonisation, although to a much lesser extent, also included other social groups, such as the peasants, who were being Polonised even in the first half of the 19th century, despite the efforts of the Russian administration.

Given the complex genesis of Polish minorities in the post-Jagiellonian area, one cannot expect ruling to be made in favour of 're-nationalisation', that is, a return to the 'previous' nationality. Such attempts have been made in these countries, especially in the early 1990s, and they involved questioning the right of the Polish minority to regard themselves as Poles, and limiting the rights of national minorities across the board.

Number and distribution of Poles in post-Jagiellonian area

It is difficult to pinpoint the number of Poles in the area under discussion. It is easier in the case of Lithuania, where Polish-Lithuanian ethnic boundaries are based on distinct cultural differences, but in Belarus and Ukraine these borderlands are less stable and more interlaced. This results in a statistically significant phenomenon of complex ethnic self-awareness, involving different forms of dual, uncertain or labile nationality (so-called 'dormant Poles' or 'sleepy Poles').

The collapse of the Polish-Lithuanian Commonwealthh in 1795 triggered a process of de-Polonisation in the post-Jagiellonian area that continued for over 200 years. Between 1940 and 1941, hundreds of thousands of Poles were deported to remote areas of the Soviet Union, and a similar number lost their lives as a result of the occupation forces and the activities of Ukrainian nationalists. After the end of the Second World War and the cession of Poland's eastern territories to the Soviet Union, there were two waves of repatriation to Poland, in 1944–1948 and 1955–1959, which saw nearly two million people.[7] To Poland were entirely displaced local elites, as Soviet authorities tried to block the repatriation of poorly educated people, who they saw as being more susceptible to denationalisation.

This historical experience, as well as the unification of ethnic policy across the Soviet Union and post-Soviet countries, caused some Poles to hide their nationality

7 Jan Czerniakiewicz: Repatriacja ludności polskiej z ZSRR, 1944–1948 [Repatriation of Poles from the USSR, 1944–1948]. Warszawa 1987, P. 263. Małgorzata Ruchniewicz: Repatriacja ludności polskiej z ZSRR w latach 1955–1959 [Repatriation of Poles from the USSR in 1955–1959]. Warszawa 2000, P. 402.

in order to avoid discrimination, particularly in the education system and the labour market. We may term such people 'hidden Poles'. Such an attitude leads to not participating in culture and native language; most frequently it also leads to denationalisation in the next generation. However, the processes of national assimilation are not limited to 'hidden Poles'. They have a broader character and result from a wider lack of opportunities for participation in Polish canonical culture, which for most Poles in east is now a foreign culture.

The most recent factor in the decline of the Polish population in the east is international migration. After the collapse of the Soviet Union, Polish nationals who had resided there began emigrating to Poland. The scale, however, was still small. The vast majority of the Polish population continued to live in the states of which they are citizens. It was mainly young people from Ukraine and Belarus (for example, students at Polish universities) who emigrated to Poland. Poles from Lithuania emigrated at a high rate to the labour markets in the EU, especially to the United Kingdom.[8] These cases amounted to 'true' emigration, not a return to their previous place of residence.

The official census data show that hundreds of thousand Poles are currently living in Belarus, Lithuania and Ukraine. Their number has decreased in recent years, slightly faster than the general demographic decline in these countries. This is determined by differences in the birth rate, migration, and changes in national identifications. Estimates of 'dormant Poles' and 'hidden Poles' are higher, particularly in Belarus.

In Lithuania the number of Poles recorded in the census is falling – from about 258,000 (7.0% of the population) in 1989 (when it was still part of the Soviet Union) to about 235,000 in 2001 (6.7% of the population), to a little over 200,000 (200,317 – 6.6%) in 2011 and 183,421 in 2021 (6,52%). Polish leaders in Lithuania give a higher estimate of the current figure – most often around 250,000 and are critical of the credibility of the censuses, especially the last one, which was conducted using a representative method.[9] According to the 2011 census, 79% of Poles (and 5.6% of the Lithuanian population overall) speak Polish.

Despite mass repatriation to Poland after 1945, Poles are highly concentrated in the region of Vilnius *[Wilno]*, generally in the territories Poland held before the Second World War. In some municipalities, Poles make up about 80% of the population, for example in Šalčininkai *[Soleczniki]* and Eišiškės *[Ejszyszki]* in the eastern part of the Vilnius region.

8 Tomas Pileckas: Migracje zagraniczne Polaków z Litwy po 1981 roku [Foreign migrations of Poles from Lithuania after 1981]. Warszawa 2016, P. 91. [Unpublished typescript].

9 Antoni Radczenko: Ilu nas faktycznie jest? Krytyczne spojrzenie na spis ludności [How Many of Us Are There? A Critical Look at the Census]. In: Kurier Wileński, 30.04.2021, https://kurierwilenski.lt/2021/04/30/ilu-nas-faktycznie-jest-krytyczne-spojrzenie-na-spis-ludnosci/.

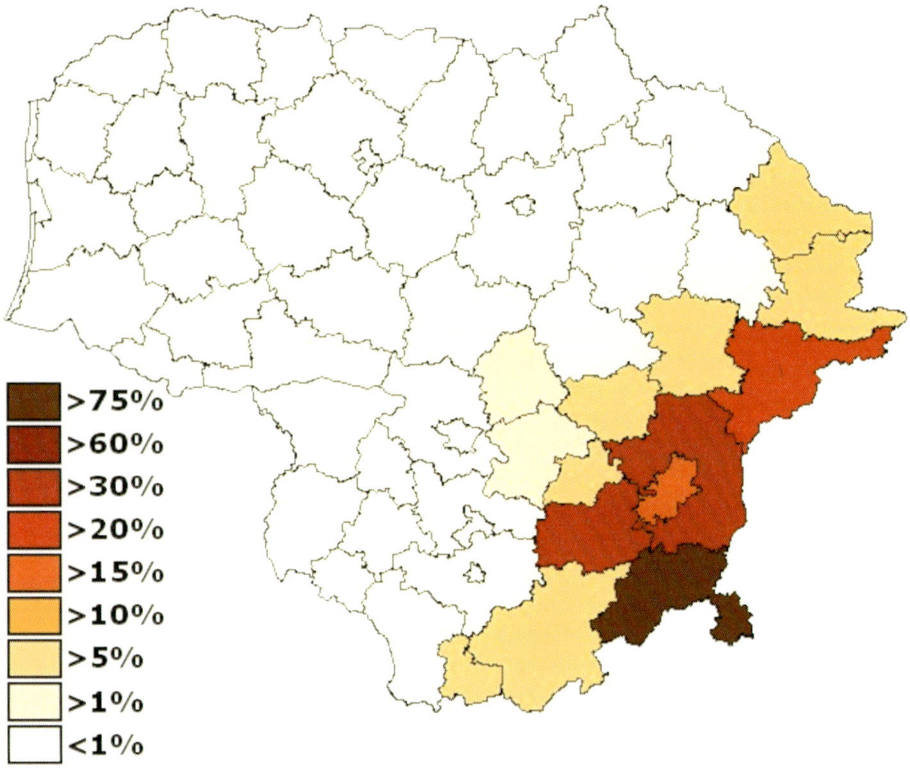

Map 1. Deployment of Poles in Lithuania according to the 2011 census[10]

In Belarus the number of Poles has fallen even faster than in Lithuania. The census gives us the following number of Poles: 1989: 417,720 (4.1% of Belarus's population), 1999: 395,712 (3.9%), 2009: 294,549 (3.1%), 2019: 287,730 (3,1%) Estimates by local leaders of the Polish minority and researchers from Poland are predominantly much higher, between 500,000 and 1,200,000[11], and in the early 1990s they were even higher[12], taking into account people with variable (or uncertain) identification ('dormant Poles'). Only a few of Belarusian Poles speak their mother tongue, far fewer than in Lithuania.

10 https://pl.wikipedia.org/wiki/Polacy_na_Litwie (accessed 15.06.2025).

11 Piotr Eberhardt: Liczebność ludności polskiej na Białorusi na przełomie XX i XXI wieku według danych spisowych [The size of the Polish population in Belarus at the turn of the 20th and 21st centuries according to census data]. In: Studia Migracyjne – Przegląd Polonijny 39 (2013) No. 2.

12 Mikołaj Iwanow, Zdzisław J. Winnicki: Katolicy na terenie byłego ZSRR. Kontrowersje wobec liczebności – szacunki bieżące i potencjalne [Catholics in the Former USSR: Controversy over Numbers – Current and Potential Estimates]. In: Edward Walewander (Ed):, Odrodzenie Kościoła Katolickiego w byłym ZSRR. Studia historyczno-demograficzne [The Rebirth of the Catholic Church in the Former USSR. Historical and Demographic Studies]. Lublin 1993.

The decrease in the number of Poles in Belarus is also the result of a gradual split in the relationship between Catholicism and Polishness. There are about 2 million Catholics and secularized people with Catholic roots in Belarus. In the past, the vast majority of Belarusian Catholics believed themselves to be Poles, despite the fact that they spoke Belarusian. In the public perception, Catholicism was the 'Polish faith' and Orthodoxy was the 'Ruthenian [Rus] faith'[13]. Such a distinction was still clear in Soviet times. Today it is different: the catholic church in Belarus is being Belarusianised and many Roman Catholics have changed their identification to Belarusian. The post-war population living on the border of two nationalities: Polish and Belarusian, using first Belarusian and then Russian, was usually divided by religion, but when they moved to cities, where secularisation processes were advanced, religion also lost its original meaning. The national consciousness of local Catholics became increasingly blurred and undefined. In official declarations, they most often state Belarusian nationality, combining it with citizenship of the country in which they live.[14]

Poles in Belarus are more scattered than they are in Lithuania, but compared to Ukraine, they are still relatively concentrated. Most of them live in the Grodno region, in the north-western part of Belarus along the border with Lithuania, on a piece of territory that belonged to Poland prior to the Second World War. While in 2009 Poles constituted almost 22% of the population of the Grodno region, in the district of Voronava *[Woronowo]* the figure is 81%. In the remaining five Belarusian regions, the participation of Poles is minimal and ranges from 0.2% to 1.3%.

In Ukraine, the number of Poles (according to census data) has decreased the most in relative terms, having dropped by nearly a third – from almost 220,000 in 1989 to less than 150,000 in 2001.[15] The Polish minority is considered an insignificant part of the Ukrainian population (about 0.3%). Only a small portion of it (even less than in Belarus) knows and uses their mother tongue.

There are probably slightly more Poles in Ukraine than official data indicates. A portion of the population (especially in the western areas of Ukraine, which belonged to Poland before the war) are 'hidden Poles'. Some Poles hide their nationality owing to strong Polish-Ukrainian antagonism originating in the last war.[16]

13 Iwona Kobzińska: Wśród 'kościelnych Polaków' [Among the 'Church Poles']. Warszawa 1999.

14 Joanna Dworzecka: Spór o białorutenizację Kościoła katolickiego na Białorusi [The dispute over the Belarusisation of the Catholic Church in Belarus]. In: Collectanea Theologica 86 (2016) No. 2.

15 There are no more recent official data. In subsequent years, no censuses were conducted in Ukraine. The census planned for 2020 was ultimately not conducted.

16 Similarly, in Poland, many Ukrainians hide their nationality. The Ukrainian minority is certainly more numerous than the official figures give (according to census 2011); a little more than 48,000. The 2021 census showed slightly more Ukrainians (almost 80,000, including over 34,000 with dual – Ukrainian and Polish – national identification). This increase is a consequence of the increased influx of migrants from Ukraine to Poland after 2014, many of whom obtained the right

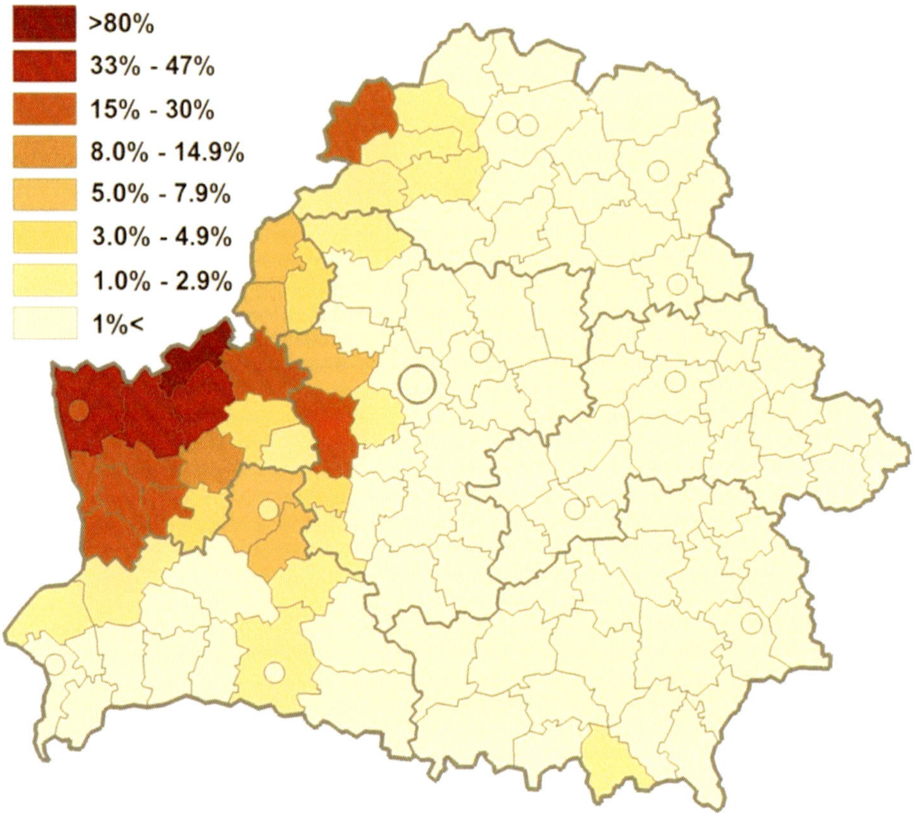

Map 2. Deployment of Poles in Belarus according to the 2009 census[17]

However, the maximum estimates that occasionally appeared in the 1990s, that the number of Poles in Ukraine is even several times higher than the census data, are definitely unreliable. The Ukrainisation of people of Polish origin is caused by similar processes as in Belarus (mainly secularisation and internal migration), the decrease in their numbers is likewise a consequence of emigration (also to Poland). It can be assumed that currently the identification of ethnic Poles with the titular nation in the state (both in the political dimension and cultural identity) is relatively more frequent than in Belarus, among others due to the national mobilisation in Ukraine as a consequence of the open conflict with Russia since 2014.

of residence or naturalization: Wstępne wyniki NSP 2021 w zakresie struktury narodowo-etnicznej oraz języka kontaktów domowych [Preliminary results of the 2021 National Population and Housing Census in terms of national and ethnic structure and language of household contacts]. GUS. Narodowy Spis Powszechny Ludności i Mieszkań [Central Statistical Office. National Census of Population and Housing], Warszawa 2023.

17 https://pl.wikipedia.org/wiki/Polacy_na_Bia%C5%82orusi. (accessed 15.06.2025).

Poles in Ukraine are highly dispersed. According to official records, the highest concentration live in Zhytomyr *[Żytomierz]* region in the middle of Ukraine, but this is only a little over 3.5% of the regional population. More than 1% of Poles (1.6%) still live only in the neighbouring Khmelnitsky *[Chmielnicki]* region. Neither of these regions belonged to Poland before the war. This is important information, because Poles from the pre-war Soviet Ukraine could not be repatriated (being Soviet citizens) to Poland after 1944.

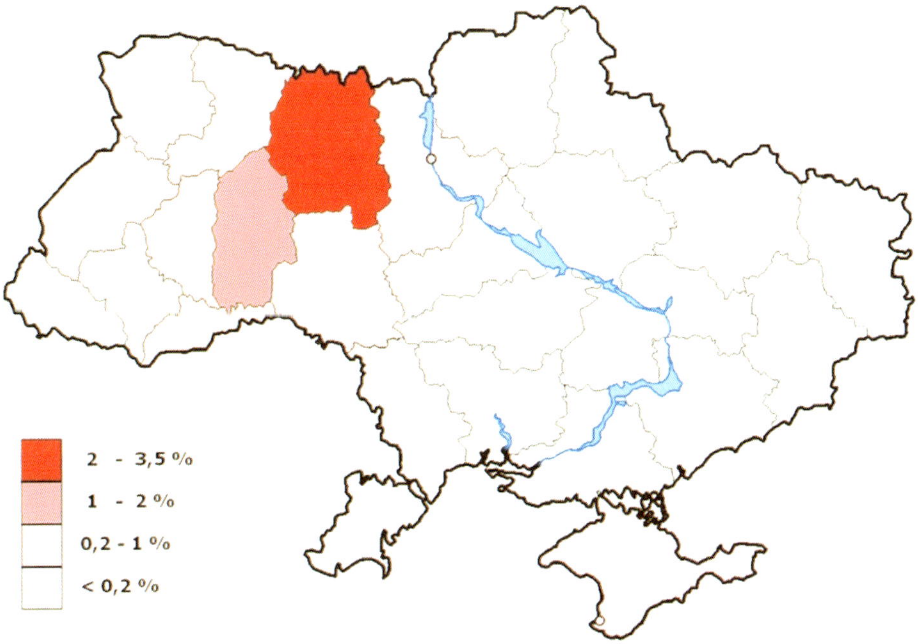

Map 3. Deployment of Poles in Ukraine according to the 2009 census[18]

The situation of Polish minorities in the post-Jagiellonian area

The situation of Poles in the eastern neighbouring countries varies greatly. In terms of the institutionalisation of ethnic life (i.e., ethnic organisations, media and education in the native language, participation in public life) the best situation by far is that of the Poles in Lithuania. Only in this country has the Polish minority developed an education system at the primary and secondary level, its own pluralistic media, numerous non-governmental organisations, and even its own (ethnic) political party – Electoral Action of Poles in Lithuania [*Akcja Wyborcza Polaków na Litwie* – AWPL]. AWPL has representation in the Lithuanian parliament and holds power

18 https://pl.wikipedia.org/wiki/Polacy_na_Ukrainie. (accessed 15.06.2025).

in two county governments (Šalčininkai and Vilnius County). Its leader, Waldemar Tomaszewski, is a member of the European Parliament.

In Belarus and Ukraine, however, there are only a few Polish schools (mostly non-public, financed by Poland) and Polish minorities are far less organised. In this regard, a special situation distinguishes Belarus, where there are two competitive Associations of Poles *[Związek Polaków na Białorusi]*. The first is subordinate to the administrative authorities, while the other is trying to conduct independent activities and maintain contacts in Poland, and is therefore treated by the Belarusian authorities as an anti-establishment opposition group.[19] In Ukraine, owing to the significant territorial dispersion of the Polish minority, Polish organisations have only a local significance. In neither of these countries does the Polish minority participate in an organised way in power at any level.

The highest level of ethnic conflict between the national majority and the Polish minority can be found in Lithuania. This can be explained by the fact that both of these communities – the Lithuanian majority and the Poles in Lithuania – are much more ethnically mobilised than the ethnic majority or Polish minority in Ukraine and Belarus. The ethnic mobilisation of the Polish minority in Lithuania is a response to the denial of their right to Polishness (being treated instead as Polonised Lithuanians, and to a number of anti-Polish policies enacted. While one such policy was instituted by the Conservative Party (of former President Vytautas Landsbergis), other Lithuanian parties have not negated it, and it enjoys significant popular support.

Thus in Lithuania, the majority and the minority pursue conflicting goals. The aim of the Polish minority is to defend itself from Lithuanisation and to maintain the 'Polish character' (in the symbolic and cultural sense) of areas inhabited by Poles. The Lithuanian authorities (and a large part of society) have quite a different aim: the assimilation of Poles, or at least to render their presence in Lithuania 'invisible'. The Polish minority in Lithuania achieved its political and cultural position only through self-determination, and not through support of a foreign homeland or favourable policies implemented by the Lithuanian state. On the contrary – we may rather say that they achieved it in spite of (and in opposition to) Lithuanian policies.

Lithuania, as an EU member state, cannot afford to implement openly discriminatory policy towards minorities. Ukraine and especially Belarus do not have such restrictions. However, it can be assumed that within the EU, the Polish national minority in Lithuania is one of structurally discriminated indigenous national minorities and its situation is clearly worse than that of the Lithuanian minority in Poland.

19 The consequence of this is repression by the Belarusian authorities against the Main Board of the Association of Poles, which they do not recognize. They intensified especially after the presidential elections in Belarus in 2020, which was expressed in the arrests and trials of leading activists, including the Chairwoman of the Association, Angelika Borys.

The following table shows the differences in the level of protection of the rights of the counterpart national minorities in Lithuania and Poland.

Table. Situation of the Polish minority in Lithuania and the Lithuanian minority in Poland (a comparison) [20]

Issue	Poland	Lithuania
Minority language as a local official language	Yes	No
Bilingualism of names in localities inhabited by minority	Yes	No
Official use of original family names	Yes	No
Financing of minority schools compared with other public schools	150%	115%*
Compulsory matriculation exams held in mother tongue	Yes	No
Electoral threshold in force minority parties	No	Yes
State subsidies to the minority media	Yes	No
Using the minority language in public life	No problems	There are problems
Return of collectivised land to members of minorities	No problems	There are problems

* In areas inhabited by the Polish minority, Lithuanian schools receive 110% of standard funding (compared with schools in other parts of Lithuania).

From the point of view of the Polish minority, the most important of these issues in economic terms is return of land that had been collectivised in Soviet times to its pre-war owners. This issue was settled in Lithuania a long time ago, within a few years after regaining independence, but only outside the areas inhabited by Poles. There is clearly bad faith on the part of the authorities in this matter. In the first place, the rights of Polish owners are undermined and contested, even in the most obvious cases. In the second place, the former lands owned by Poles were transferred to Lithuanians who had settled in areas inhabited by the Polish minority – this was allowed for by the so-called Lithuanian law of 'transfer of ownership' from other parts of the country. As a result, the Poles did not regain their property, and their sites have been colonised by outsiders and, in a sense, Lithuanised.

The crucial issues in the sphere of identity are education in the mother tongue, the right to officially use original Polish family names and bilingual signage for place

20 Cezary Żołędowski: Litwini i Polacy – społeczne postawy wobec mniejszości [Lithuanians and Poles – social attitudes towards minorities]. In: Lech Nijakowski (Ed.): Litwini [Lithuanians]. Warszawa 2013, P. 131–149, here P. 149f.

names in localities inhabited by the minority. As with the issue of returning land to the pre-war owners, these issues are the subject of endless dispute between Lithuanian authorities and the Polish minority. For example, representatives of Polish local governments are constantly punished with high fines for displaying bilingual names in places inhabited almost exclusively by Poles. The Lithuanian authorities see these acts as manifestations of populism or even anti-state activities, when in fact it is simply the demand of Polish minority in Lithuania to be given rights similar to those enjoyed by the Lithuanian minority in Poland.

Support for Polish minorities in the post-Jagiellonian area by the Polish state

Assistance given by Poland to Polish minorities in the east (their 'foreign homeland', to use the designation of Rogers Brubaker[21]) is moderate and does not address every aspect of the problems these minorities experience. This support was insufficient to meet the expectations of Poles abroad.

The activities of the foreign homeland directed to the Poles behind the eastern border can be attributed to two essential features.

First, as noted by the researcher Paweł Hut, Poland's attitude to Polish minorities has undergone different phases, moving gradually from 'ethnic solidarity' (organised mainly by NGOs) to 'administrative duty', that is to say, late and relatively limited activities by public institutions.[22]

Secondly, even in the early phases, the greatest support for Poles in the post-Jagiellonian area has always been provided by non-governmental organisations; in particular, the Polish Community *[Wspólnota Polska]* is the largest NGO in the sphere of relations with the Polish diaspora in the world, working in cooperation with the Polish Senate. A considerable role has also been played by organisations of Poles who live in Poland but are originally from the former eastern territories of Poland (the so-called 'East Poles' [Polish: *kresowiacy*]). These organisations have tried mainly to maintain contacts (for example, by arranging for diaspora Poles to visit Poland) and to materially support Poles living in specific areas in the east, their sentimental homelands.

The role of public institutions was limited to promoting NGO activities and supporting young people from the east – as future leaders of Polish minorities – by pro-

21 Rogers Brubaker: Nationalism reframed. Nationhood and the national question in the new Europe. Cambridge 1996, P. 205.

22 Paweł Hut: Polska wobec Polaków w przestrzeni poradzieckiej. Od solidaryzmu etnicznego do obowiązku administracyjnego [Poland towards the Poles in the post-Soviet area. From ethnic solidarity to administrative duty]. Warszawa 2014, P. 357.

viding them with education at Polish universities. This latter goal has been achieved only to a very limited extent. A large proportion of young Poles from the east (especially from Belarus and Ukraine) did not return to their countries after graduation, choosing instead to remain in Poland or emigrate to other EU countries. Government scholarship programmes for Polish youth in the east actually functioned as immigration programmes, which was neither intended nor expected.

The general opinion of Polish leaders outside Poland is that each of the Polish governments since 1989 has prioritised good relations with their neighbouring countries over supporting Polish minorities in these countries. Sacrificing the needs and interests of Polish minorities for the sake of good relations with neighbouring countries is one of the most common accusations against their 'foreign homeland'.

This opinion is not entirely unjust, but it only reflects the one-sided viewpoint of groups that are minorities in their countries and expect support from their foreign homeland. In general, the democratic Polish governments cannot be blamed for disregarding the problems of Polish minorities in the east, including ethnic discrimination against them. The actual options available to the authorities in Warsaw should also be taken into consideration. Polish authorities lack sufficient instruments to exert pressure on neighbouring states' policies towards Polish minorities.

Summary

History continues to be one of the most important factors affecting the contemporary situation of national minorities in the post-Jagiellonian area. Different interpretations of the common past are present in both the framing of history and the social consciousness of nations whose states are located in the area of the former Polish-Lithuanian Commonwealth.

In Poland, the Polish-Lithuanian Commonwealth legacy is valued, in contrast to later relationships with the non-Polish successors to the First Republic, especially in the 20th century. For the eastern neighbours of Poland, the shared past is clearly a greater burden on modern relations, influencing their perception of the presence of Polish minorities and the resulting policy decisions. Historical interpretations most adversely affect the situation of the Polish minority in Lithuania, resulting in relatively high discrimination there. This also influences the Lithuanian government's attitude to other minority groups that reside there. In Belarus and Ukraine, too, the past weighs heavily on contemporary relations with Poland, which in some ways translates into their policies towards the Polish minorities. However, in the case of both these countries, the general condition of democratic institutions and the standards of protection accorded to all national minorities are more important for their national policies.

Martin Klatt

Minority policies – or border policies? A neo-realist interpretation of kin-state policies in the Danish-German "European model" of minority accommodation

This article will analyse kin-state policies towards the two national minorities in the Danish-German border region, the Danish minority in German South Schleswig, and the German minority in Danish North Schleswig. It asks whether kin-state policies reflect minority policies – that is, whether kin-state policies support its kin-minority out of a motivation to demonstrate its interest in a liberal minority regime recognising diversity, or whether kin-state policies reflect neo-realist aims of promoting national interest via the kin-minority abroad. Kin-state policies will be analysed on their aims of active containment of minorities in parallel societies, an active cultural alignment to perceived national values expressed in identity discourses of the kin-state, or in their effort to achieve acceptance of diversity in a border region. When kin-state policies reflect realist aims of national interest, I will use the term *border policies* rather than *minority policies*. The term *minority policies* signifies policies that accept and support both cultural and national diversity as a normative aim to illustrate the border region's history as a border zone under different regional, national and European cultural influences. After presenting the Schleswig case, I will discuss Danish and German kin-state policies over time, analyse the motivations behind them, and conclude with their effect on minority identity and cultural diversity in the region.

The Schleswig case

Schleswig is an example of post-imperial border drawing as a consequence of the evolution of nation states out of feudal, conglomerate empires during the long 19th century. The territories of Schleswig and Holstein were dynastically tied to the Danish crown, which, until 1814, ruled a conglomerate empire in Northern Europe. This arrangement worked well until national awakening in the 19th century. The 1848 revolution resulted in a separatist declaration of independence in Kiel and a national-liberal government in Copenhagen attempting to integrate Schleswig into Denmark proper, separating it from Holstein. Denmark won the first military conflict on Schleswig, with diplomatic help from Sweden, the UK, France, and Russia. When Denmark introduced a joint constitution for the kingdom and Schleswig in

November 1863, Prussia took this as *casus belli* and, together with Austria, declared war on behalf of the German Confederation. After the final Danish defeat in June 1864, Denmark had to cede Schleswig and Holstein to Prussia and Austria; which lost its claims after the war of 1866. Schleswig-Holstein then became a Prussian province in 1867. From the 1880s, a massive policy of discrimination and assimilation was implemented by the Prussian authorities.

When the German *Kaiserreich* surrendered in November 1918, Denmark succeeded in putting the issue of Schleswig on the agenda of the Paris Peace Conference. It was to be resolved by a plebiscite, which was held in two zones on 10 February and 12 March 1920 respectively. The 1920 plebiscite was an attempt to solve the territorial issue of Schleswig. It was a compromise between the Eider Danish project of Denmark as a nation state down to the Eider river, the northern border of the Holy Roman Empire and the German Confederation, and the Schleswig-Holstein movement's claim to integrate both duchies, indivisible, into a German nation state. In practice, it meant dividing a hitherto undivided, socio-economic integrated territory along a line that best reflected national affiliation. This line (today's border) was not drawn coincidentally reflecting local votes. Instead, a Danish expert, folklorist and linguist H. V. Clausen, drew the future borderline around 1900 with national as well as geographical considerations in mind.[1] The terms of the plebiscite were coined primarily by H. P. Hanssen, a newspaper editor and the only Danish member of the German *Reichstag* from 1906 to 1919. An én-bloc vote in plebiscite zone 1 (north of the Clausen line) assured a Danish majority there, while alterations of the Clausen line to the south would have been possible with Danish majorities in parishes immediately to the south; which there were not.[2] Furthermore, 1 January 1900 was a cut-off date: residents who had moved to the plebiscite zone after that date were not allowed to participate. The plebiscite campaigns played on nationality, but also regional identity and rational reasons to vote for either Denmark or Germany were put forward.[3] The result confirmed Clausen's and Hanssen's assessment of the situation: a clear majority of 75% voted for Denmark in zone 1, while 80% voted for Germany in zone 2. Still, about 25% in the north and 20% in the south wished for a different outcome.

To accommodate these dissenters, in line with the post-World War I peace settlement, national minorities were constructed with a high degree of cultural auton-

1 Troels Fink: Den første streg på kortet – Clausen Linjen [Der erste Strich auf der Karte – die Clausen-Linie]. In: Henrik Becker-Christensen (Ed.): Grænsen i 75 år [75 Jahre Grenze]. Aabenraa 1995, P. 11–23.

2 Troels Fink: Da Sønderjylland blev delt [Als Schleswig geteilt wurde], 3 vols. Aabenraa 1979.

3 Nina Jebsen: Als die Menschen gefragt wurden. Eine Propagandaanalyse zu Volksabstimmungen in Europa nach dem Ersten Weltkrieg. Münster 2015; Nina Jebsen and Martin Klatt: The Negotiation of National and Regional Identity During the Schleswig-Plebiscite Following the First World War. In: First World War Studies 5 (2014), P. 181–211.

omy.[4] In numbers, the minorities never managed to mobilise all dissenters in the plebiscite. The German minority's political party, for example, received only between 10–15% of the local vote in national and local elections in the 1920s and 1930s. In South Schleswig, the Danish minority had the challenge of organising a population that was not schooled in speaking Danish and often had a working-class background. They were therefore reluctant to mobilise behind a national-bourgeois leadership.[5] In North Schleswig, many Germans with a working-class background assimilated into Danish culture after the Nazification of the German minority following the Nazi takeover of power in 1933.[6] Nevertheless, some key elements of modern minority accommodation were implemented on both sides of the border: subjective identification, parental decision on whether their children attend a minority school, cultural autonomy with the right to have separate cultural associations, a separate church organisation, and separate schools driven by the minorities themselves (while still operating under the state of residence's school laws).

These principles were not abandoned when the Nazis took power in Germany. After some turbulent years following German surrender in May 1945, they were codified in the separate but reciprocal 1955 Bonn-Copenhagen Declarations. This settlement of minority accommodation produced a narrative of a successful reconciliation process and European model for solving minority conflicts.[7] It is based on subjective identification, cultural autonomy, acceptance of close minority-kin-state relations and kin-state support, political participation by the minorities and an institutionalised minority-majority dialogue including the kin-states. Representatives of the minority and majority have characterised the historic development as a story of

4 Johan Peter Noack: Det danske mindretal i Sydslesvig 1920–1945 [Die dänische Minderheit in Südschleswig], 2 vols. Aabenraa 1989; Henrik Becker-Christensen: Dansk mindretalspolitik i Nordslesvig. Udformningen af den danske politik over for det tyske mindretal 1918–1920 [Dänische Minderheitenpolitik in Nordschleswig. Die Gestaltung der dänischen Politik für die deutsche Minderheit]. Aabenraa 1984; Det tyske mindretal i Nordslesvig 1920–1932 [Die deutsche Minderheit in Nordschlewig], 2 vols. Aabenraa 1990.

5 Matthias Schartl: Rote Fahnen über Flensburg. KPD, linksradikale Milieus und Widerstand im nördlichen Schleswig-Holstein 1919–1945. Flensburg 1999.

6 Martin Klatt: Die Sozialdemokratie in Nordschleswig und die nationale Frage 1918–1922. Kiel, 1995.

7 On the European model narrative, see Jørgen Kühl: Ein Europäisches Modell? Die Schleswigsche Erfahrung und die nationalen Minderheiten. In: Jørgen Kühl, Robert Bohn (Eds.): Ein europäisches Modell? Nationale Minderheiten im deutsch-dänischen Grenzland 1945–2005. Bielefeld 2005, P. 401–507; The Bonn-Copenhagen Declarations of 1955: Background, Context and Impact of the Danish-German Minority Regulations. In: Jørgen Kühl, Marc Weller (Eds.): Minority Policy in Action: The Bonn-Copenhagen Declarations in a European Context 1955–2005. Aabenraa/Flensburg 2005, P. 31–90; Martin Klatt: Von der Abgrenzug zur Grenzüberwindung. Die Minderheiten und die Bonn-Kopenhagener Erklärungen als Wendepunkt der deutsch-dänischen Beziehungen? In: Grenzfriedenshefte 62 (2015), P. 55–64.

progress, "vom Gegeneinander zum Miteinander" or even "Füreinander" – reconciliation from conflict to cooperation.[8]

The principle of individual choice demonstrates a liberal approach to minority policies, but is a challenge, too. It has resulted in fluid minorities, to be understood as un-bordered groups with shifting membership and degrees of affiliation. Membership is not recorded, so the contemporary figures of 15,000 Germans in North Schleswig and 50,000 Danes in South Schleswig are estimates only.[9] Common understandings of national identity as a permanent, stable criteria are challenged in Schleswig, were objective criteria to distinguish "Danes" from "Germans" have been lacking, and where the nationalist narratives never really respected the other side's claim to Schleswig, nor the change of national identification during history.

Financing the minorities' institutions

The core characteristic of the Schleswig model is an institutionalised minority with functional cultural autonomy, with separate kindergartens, schools, church congregations, nursing homes, social services and cultural associations operated by the minorities within the framework of Danish and German legislation.[10] These institutions and associations are financed mostly by public sources, with a combination of federal, state, county and municipal funds from the state of residence, as well as federal, state and NGO funds from the kin-state. The basic principle of this model is equal access to public funds in the state of residence based on the argument that the minority members pay equal taxes, while kin-state support should cover the extra costs of being a minority. These extra costs can be controversial, but the usually accepted argument is that being a minority entails smaller units in schools, extra language training, libraries covering larger geographic areas, cultural associations attracting smaller audiences, and so on.

The reciprocal aspect is sensitive when the balance between state of residence funding and kin-state funding varies considerably between Denmark and Germany. This has been the case for many years, if not since 1920. Overall, Denmark contributes more financially to both minorities than Germany. In 2011, 65% of the Danish minorities' institutions' overall budget were public funds from Denmark.[11] For the minority schools alone, 52% of the Danish minority schools' budget and 83.8%

8 Martin Klatt: Minority Schools Financing in the Danish-German Border Region. In: European Yearbook of Minority Issues 11 (2014), P. 359–375, esp. P. 365; Kühl, Bohn: Ein Europäisches Modell? (Footnote 7).

9 Kühl, Bohn: Ein Europäisches Modell? (Footnote 7), P. 340–352.

10 Klatt: Minority Schools (Footnote 8).

11 Jørgen Kühl: Mindretalsmodel i krise. Flensburg, 2012, P. 15.

of the German minority schools' budget in 2011 were funded by Denmark.[12] This imbalance in the overall financing has not changed since. The budget of the Danish School Association for South Schleswig of 2018 lists the Danish share in the funds of single activities, which ranges from 21.6% (adult education), 46.3% (schools 1st to 10th grade), 61.2 % (high school), 88.5% (dormitory for Danish high school students) to 100% (teaching materials).[13] The German minority's budget for 2019 of 318 million DKK (about 43 million €) was financed by the Danish state (41.5%), Danish municipalities (15.7%), the German federal government (22.3%), the state of Schleswig-Holstein (4.7%) and other sources (15.7%).[14] For 2018, 87% of the German minority's school budget was financed by Denmark.[15]

Kin-state policies

Kin-state policies are often the neglected element of the triad nexus between national minorities, nationalising states and kin-states.[16] On the one side, kin-states and minorities have a legitimate interest in close relations to preserve or fasten linguistic, cultural and social ties. On the other hand, powers have adopted and instrumentalised kin-minorities for their geopolitical goals. The most prominent example is the Sudeten Germans, used by Hitler to get international approval in Munich in 1938 for his strategic plan to dismember Czechoslovakia. Since the end of the Cold War, we have witnessed further attempts to instrumentalise kin-minorities for national or even geopolitical aims. The most violent example in post-World War II Europe is the break-up of Yugoslavia. But Russia has also been accused of using kin-minorities in the newly independent states of the former Soviet Union to maintain geopolitical control of its so-called Near Abroad, even though these groups are far from homogeneous.[17] More recently, Hungary has caused friction by extending citizenship and voting rights to the large communities of ethnic Hungarians in its

12 Sources in Klatt: Minority Schools (Footnote 8), P. 371 (notes 51 and 52).

13 Resultataftale 2019 mellem Dansk Skoleforening for Sydslesvig e.V. og Sydslesvigudvalget, P. 7. https://www.skoleforeningen.org/media/e2qfn2pz/resultataftale-2019.pdf, accessed 4 July 2025.

14 http://www.buecherei.dk/images/Pressearchiv/20180620_SoGibtDieMinderheitDasGeldAus.pdf, accessed 4 July 2019.

15 Bund deutscher Nordschleswiger, Jahresrechnung 2018 der deutschen Volksgruppe in Nordschleswig, provided to the author.

16 Dejan Stjepanović: Claimed Co-Ethnics and Kin-State Citizenship in Southeastern Europe. In: Ethnopolitics 14 (2015), P. 140–158, here P. 140.

17 Among many others, see Martin Klatt: Russians in the "near Abroad", in: RFE/RL Research Report 3 (1994), P. 33–44; Ammon Cheskin, Angela Kachuyevski: The Russian-Speaking Populations in the Post-Soviet Space: Language, Politics and Identity. In: Europe-Asia Studies 71 (2019), P. 1–23.

neighbouring countries,[18] as have Turkey's "neo-Ottomanist" policies in the Balkans and towards kin-minorities in the EU.[19] Similar policies of citizenship extension – Austria towards South Tyrol, and Denmark towards its minority in South Schleswig – have remained largely unnoticed, however.

Kin-state policies in Schleswig – motives and aims

In Schleswig, geopolitical or revisionist aspects of kin-state policies have surfaced periodically, when the German minority worked for a border revision to the north during the interwar yeas, and when Danish nationalists along with the Danish minority campaigned for a revision to the south in the decade following World War II. Otherwise, Germany's and Denmark's kin-state policies were more minority oriented. The motto for Denmark's dominant kin-state policy towards its minority was declared in 1920, when prime minister Niels Neergaard from the liberal Venstre party spoke at the festivities of the reunification of North Schleswig with Denmark. Of the Danish-minded South Schleswigians he said, "they shall not be forgotten". This national commitment to the minority has been reiterated in many forms since, for example in 1999 by then prime minister Poul Nyrup Rasmussen's "as long as you stand by us, we will stand by you".[20]

Being Denmark's only kin-minority, the Danish minority in South Schleswig has enjoyed more focus in Denmark than the German minority in North Schleswig has in Germany. Germany's kin-state policies have not focused on North Schleswig, but the east. This applies to clearly revisionist policies in the interwar years, where Germany accepted the post-WWI western borders in the treaty of Locarno in 1925, but not the eastern borders. It also applies to the post-WWII situation, where West German policies at least until the 1960s were partly influenced by associations representing ethnic Germans driven out of Germany's former eastern provinces and Eastern European countries in general following the Potsdam conference in 1945.[21]

18 Andreea Udrea: The Kin-State Policies of Hungary, Romania, and Serbia in 2015: An Increasingly Centred Approach on Extraterritorial Citizenship. In: European Yearbook of Minority Issues Online 14 (2017), P. 216–230.

19 Nurcan Özgür Baklacioglu: Between Neo-Ottomanist Kin Policy in the Balkans and Transnational Kin Economics in the EU. In: Journal on Ethnopolitics and Minority Issues in Europe: JEMIE 14 (2015), P. 47–72. In Germany, all kinds of bureaucratic tricks were used to prevent president Erdogan from speaking at rallies to attract electoral support within the Turkish community there during the 2017 referendum campaign and the 2018 presidential elections.

20 "Så længe I holder fast i os, holder vi fast i jer!", https://www.graenseforeningen.dk/de-skal-ikke-blive-glemt.html, accessed 10 July 2019.

21 Karl Cordell, Stefan Wolff: Germany as a Kin-State: The Development and Implementation of a Norm-Consistent External Minority Policy Towards Central and Eastern Europe. In: Nationalities Papers 35 (2007) No. 2, P. 289–315.

The West German *Ostpolitik* and unified Germany's policies likewise focused on the German minorities in the east. During the Cold War, policies were about easing emigration for ethnic Germans in Socialist countries. From the 1990s, this was changed into policies that restrict immigration to Germany combined with material support for German minorities, especially in the successor states of the Soviet Union.[22] It was the federal state *(Land)* Schleswig-Holstein, only, who felt obliged to kin-state policies towards the German minority in North Schleswig.

Six clusters of motivation can be identified during the one hundred years of Danish- and German kin-state policies in Schleswig, meandering between liberal minority policies and realist border policies:

- *they shall not be forgotten*
- border revision
- missionary
- beachhead
- neo-liberal
- the *European model.*

All six themes intertwine, and their articulation has reflected general European and global political situations, or more specific Danish-German relations.

Kin-state policy 1: They shall not be forgotten

On the event celebrating North Schleswig's reunion with Denmark, prime minister Niels Neergaard promised the people who voted for Denmark south of the new border that they would not be forgotten, *De skal ikke blive glemt.* Danish kin-state policy in the interwar years, but also after WWII, with the possible exception of the immediate post-war years, can be subsumed under this motto. Cultural support was given to prevent total cultural-linguistic assimilation into the German nation out of a feeling of historical responsibility for the region as former Danish territory. For the German minority, the *they shall not be forgotten* motivation is more regionally based. Government-supported NGOs such as the Schleswig-Holsteiner Bund during the interwar years and its successor the Schleswig-Holsteinischer Heimatbund, together with the social democrat Grenzfriedensbund, the conservative Deutscher Grenzverein and Arbeitsgemeinschaft Deutsches Schleswig after WWII, channelled public funds to the German minority. A special focus was farmland during the agricultural crisis of the 1920s – special funds were set up to prevent land falling into the "wrong" nationality's hands.[23] It was a key aim of these policies to stabilise a national

22 Cordell, Wolff: Germany (Footnote 21).

23 Hans Schultz Hansen: Dansk jord på danske hænder. Foreningen Landeværnet og den nationale

balance achieved in 1920 and prevent the threatening assimilation of minorities into the majority society. With the national balance reversing after the end of WWII, *they shall not be forgotten* became the prime motto for Schleswig-Holstein's support of the remaining German minority in North Schleswig, which had to rebuild their institutions from scratch.

Kin-state policy 2: border revision

Even though the Danish-German border was legitimised by a plebiscite and both countries pledged to implement liberal minority policies, the new border was challenged by different agents, at least from 1920 until 1955. Neither Denmark nor Germany have officially declared their support of their kin-minority to have a border revisionist agenda. Still, kin-state policies of financial subsidies have attempted to secure and stabilise a national minority, an agenda which was not always accepted as genuine by the state of residence. This applies to the interwar years[24] as well as the period after World War II, in effect until today.[25]

Denmark never obtained Germany's official recognition of the border;[26] only the two countries' social-democrat parties agreed to accept it in 1923. The dream of "Denmark to the Eider", a national rebirth of the Danish nation in Schleswig and eventual reunification, remained alive in non-governmental, nationalist associations. These associations channelled public and private funds to South Schleswig and managed to open a Danish school in Schleswig city and in the city of Tönning at the mouth of the Eider. They also supported travelling teachers in the southernmost Schleswig, promoting young people to "rediscover" their Danish-ness.[27] Furthermore, the Danish daily newspaper in South Schleswig, *Flensborg Avis*, was an important instrument in the attempt to maintain and strengthen the Danish element in South Schleswig, aiming at a future re-Danishisation. This was the mission of its editor-in-chief from 1906 to 1940, Ernst Christiansen.[28] When the paper had

jordkamp i Sønderjylland [Dänischer Boden in dänische Hände. Der Verein Landwehr und der nationale Bodenkampf in Schleswig]. Aabenraa 2002.

24 Becker-Christensen: Det Tyske Mindretal (Footnote 4); Noack: Det Danske Mindretal (Footnote 4).

25 Johan Peter Noack: Det Sydslesvigske Grænsespørgsmål 1945–1947 [Die südschleswigsche Grenzfrage], Aabenraa 1991; Det danske mindretal i Sydslesvig 1948–1955 [Die dänische Minderheit in Südschleswig], Aabenraa 1997; Kühl: The Bonn-Copenhagen Declarations (Footnote 7); Klatt: Minority Schools (Footnote 8).

26 Becker-Christensen: Det Tyske Mindretal (Footnote 4), here vol. 2, P. 41–57.

27 Axel Johnsen: Dannevirkemænd og Ejderfolk. Den grænsepolitiske opposition i Danmark 1920–1940 [Danewerksmänner und Eidervolk. Die grenzpolitische Opposition in Dänemark], Flensburg 2005.

28 Martin Klatt: Mobilization in Crisis – Demobilization in Peace: Protagonists of Competing National Movements in Border Regions. In: Studies on National Movements 4 (2019), P. 30, here P. 12.

financial difficulties in the economic crisis of the late 1920s, the Danish state began supporting it directly.[29]

For German kin-state policies, the German minority in Denmark is an interesting case. Even though Germany never formally recognised the border of 1920 in the interwar years, it did not pursue an active policy to revise the border, neither before nor after 1933. Contrary to other German minorities in Europe, the German minority in Denmark was not instrumentalised to revise the Versailles peace order and subsequent loss of territory. For the German minority itself, though, border revision was a core part of their political agenda from 1920.[30] Agitation for a border revision and *"Heim ins Reich"* – homecoming to the Empire, became more open after 1933, especially as Nazi activists in the province of Schleswig-Holstein aggressively demanded the return of North Schleswig to Germany in the so-called Easter Storm of 1933.[31] Berlin stopped these activists quickly, though, and throughout the Nazi period made it clear that it did not want to strain relations with Denmark. A discussion on a revision of the Danish-German border was postponed to after the predicted *Endsieg* (final victory).[32]

Border revision came onto the agenda after the Second World War, but again not as an instrumentalisation of the minority by kin-state policies. The Danish all-party liberation government of May 1945 proclaimed that it supported the right to self-determination and thus did not intend to revise the Danish-German border. The Danish minority, and also nationalists in Denmark, were heavily disappointed and agitated for a border revision to "reunite" all Schleswig with Denmark. We can assume that this movement was supported by the majority of the native residents of South Schleswig in the summer of 1945, and probably until about 1947.[33]

In September 1945, Knut Kristensen became prime minister in Denmark, partly on an agenda of recovering South Schleswig *ad* åre – "in future times", presumably within about a decade. Although this agenda was never backed by a majority in the Danish parliament, it raised hopes in South Schleswig. The plan was to construct a stable Danish-minded population there, so that a future plebiscite in the mid-1950s would result in a Danish majority. This included the build-up of a minority infrastructure, especially schools, which became the dominant element of Danish

29 René Rasmussen: Front og bro. Flensborg Avis i spil mellem Danmark og Tyskland 1930–45 [Front und Brücke. Flensborg Avis im Zusammenspiel zwischen Dänemark und Deutschland], 2 vols.. Flensburg 2005, here Vol. 1, P. 146ff.

30 Becker-Christensen: Det Tyske Mindretal (Footnote 4).

31 Henrik Becker-Christensen: "Nordschleswig Erwache!!!". Det tyske mindretal og nazismen i 1933 [die deutsche Minderheit und der Nazismus]. In: Sønderjyske Årbøger (1998), P. 161–204.

32 Johan Peter Noack: Det tyske mindretal i Nordslesvig under besættelsen [Die deutsche Minderheit in Nordschleswig während der Besatzung]. København 1974.

33 Noack: Det Sydslesvigske (Footnote 25).

kin-state policy in the late 1940s and early 1950s.[34] Somewhat annoyed by continuous Danish meddling in South Schleswig affairs, the UK sent a note to the Danish government in September 1946 proposing a Danish annexation of South Schleswig either without a plebiscite or after a plebiscite, or, as a third option, a population exchange. All options were declined by the Danish government, diminishing the prospects of a future plebiscite.[35] Finally, the border conflict became further appeased with the Kiel Declaration of 1949 (which secured minority rights), and with the establishment of the Federal Republic of (West) Germany in the same year. This institutional stability on the German side combined with the Danish government's reluctance eliminated the option of an immediate plebiscite. The Saarland-option (under French administration with a plebiscite in 1957) was never negotiated, either. Despite this, the continuous Danish moral and financial support to build up a minority infrastructure was perceived as a culture offensive by the Germans, with the end-goal of taking South Schleswig back.

Kin-state policy 3: missionary

Missionary kin-state policies originated in the idea that Schleswig's population in reality belonged to one nation only, in spite of different subjective identification. Regional identification or national indifference[36] were not acceptable. The historical dual identification as German-speaking subjects of the Danish king, which did not pose a problem up to the 19th century, had become obsolete.[37] Indifferent inhabitants of the region were dismissively called the *blakkede* (blurred, but also half-hearted). The 1920 plebiscite had not given a regional (Schleswig) option, but only Denmark or Germany. In consequence, after the plebiscite, dissenters had to join the national minority as a nation state construct,[38] or accept what was supposed to be being "standard" Dane or German. During the interwar years, it was both Danish and German policy to assimilate the *blakkede*, to make a Dane or German out

34 Noack: Det Danske Mindretal (Footnote 25).

35 Noack: Det Sydslesvigske (Footnote 25).

36 Tara Zahra: Imagined Noncommunities: National Indifference as a Category of Analysis. In: Slavic Review 69 (2010), P. 93–119.

37 See among others Steen Bo Frandsen: Holsten i Helstaten. Hertugdømmet inden for og uden for det danske monarki i første halvdel af 1800-tallet [Holstein im Gesamtstaat. Das Herzogtum innnerhalb und außerhalb der dänischen Monarchie in der ersten Hälfte des 19. Jhd.], København 2008; De store tabere i 1864: De nationalliberales glemte modstandere [Die großen Verlierer von 1864: Die vergessenen Gegner der Nationalliberalen]. In: Jes Fabricius Møller, Carsten Jahnke (Eds.): 1864 – og historiens lange skygger [1864 und die langen Schatten der Geschichte). Husum 2011, P. 239–258.

38 Arthur Christiansen: Die Reproduktion der dänischen Minderheit im 21. Jahrhundert zwischen Kultur, Tradition und Gemeinschaftsglauben. Tönning, Lübeck, Marburg 2008.

of every Schleswigian. But the dilemma of indifference is not an issue of the 20th century only; it continues to be a focal issue in minority debates until today.[39]

The background for Danish missionary policies was the narrative of Schleswig as ethnonational Danish territory. This was argued on the base of place names in Schleswig and their linguistic roots, the linguistic history of the territory and the idea of a Danish *folkesind* (folk memory, or mood) in the region's population, independent of linguistic usage or self-perceived national affiliation.[40] German missionary policies were justified by referring to a common Nordic descent and attempts to incorporate Denmark into a greater Pan-Germanic realm, as well as on the medieval union of Schleswig and Holstein under the Danish crown, but with a high degree of guaranteed local autonomy.

German activists and representatives of local government considered the massive Danish investment in schools and teachers after 1945 to be a missionary crusade. Material welfare should transform the region's population to Danish nationals, the widely used term *Speckdänen* (bacon Danes) reflecting the narrative of a true minority and German national traitors who only joined the minority for material reasons. The Danish argument used to justify the material investments into the Danish minority referred to the historical change of national identification over the centuries. Now, the tides had changed again and South Schleswigians were returning to their Danish roots. It was argued that especially the confrontation with the refugees from Germany's eastern provinces had convinced many locals that they really were Danish.[41]

The missionary aspect of Danish support to the minority in South Schleswig has resurfaced at regular intervals. Public and political discourses in Denmark circulate on whether the minority is "genuinely" Danish. Members of the right-wing populist Danish People's Party in particular demand the minority show more loyalty to Denmark in exchange for financial support. They also challenge the minority's liberal approach in recruitment of members and demand more Danish-ness in the way they understand Danish national culture.

Kin-state policy 4: beachhead

Denmark's border policies have focused on securing the 1920 border ever since its implementation. It was political consensus in Denmark to integrate Southern Jutland

39 Klatt: Mobilization (Footnote28); Martin Klatt, Jørgen Kühl: SSW. Die politische Geschichte der dänischen Minderheit 1945–2015. Flensburg 2015; Tobias Haimin Wung-Sung: Beyond the Border: Young Minorities in the Danish-German Borderlands, 1955–71. New York, Oxford 2019.

40 Especially promoted by Claus Eskildsen: Dansk Grænselære [Dänische Grenzlehre]. København 1936.

41 Martin Klatt: Flygtningene og Sydslesvigs danske devægelse 1945–1955 [Die Flüchtlinge und Südschleswigs dänische Bewegung]. Flensburg 2001.

into the kingdom with no special administrative status. This is already highlighted by the historically incorrect term of *Genforeningen*, the reunification of Southern Jutland's northern half with Denmark. Danish border policies meant to cut the economic, cultural and social ties to Schleswig-Holstein after 1920.[42] Regarding Germany, Denmark conducted a policy of diplomatic alingment, especially after the Nazis took power in 1933. The safeguarding of the 1920 border remained a core element of Denmark's policy towards Germany. This policy did not change after World War II. The all-party liberation government agreed that the border should not be moved. In the 1950s and 60s, normal relations were established with the Federal Republic of Germany, but German overtures to make a friendship-and-reconciliation treaty (as Germany did with France) were met with reservations.[43] During these years, and going on into at least the 1990s, Danish kin-state support to the minority in South Schleswig was often justified by a beachhead logic, based on the argument that it is good for Denmark to have some Danes within Germany. The Danish minority was a mediator in Denmark's foreign policy with Germany and it monopolised political contacts between the Danish political parties and German leaders.[44] With Denmark's entry to the European Communities in 1973, but especially with more direct Danish-German political contacts evolving in the 1990s and 2000s,[45] the beachhead argument disappeared in Danish political statements on kin-state policies.

Kin-state policy 5: neo-liberal

In line with a neo-liberal turn in Denmark following the 2001 national elections, a new justification for Danish kin-state policy to its minority in South Schleswig dawned on the horizon. Reflecting the tradition of minority youth to emigrate to Denmark for higher education (often not returning to South Schleswig upon graduation), the minority youth's contribution to the Danish economy was put into focus. This reiterated discourse in Denmark on the continuous need to support a minority living in a rich neighbour country, one which openly claimed a more binational, European identity than a national, exclusive Danish one.[46] At the same time,

42 Morten Andersen: Den følte grænse. Slesvigs deling og genopbygning 1918–1933 [Die gefühlte Grenze. Schleswigs Teilung und Wiederaufbau]. Aabenraa 2008.

43 Martin Klatt: Fra modspil til medspil? Grænseoverskridende samarbejde i Sønderjylland/Schleswig 1945–2005 [Vom Gegeneinander zum Miteinander? Grenzüberschreitende Zusammenarbeit in Sønderjylland/Schleswig]. Aabenraa 2006, here P. 77ff.

44 Martin Klat: Minorities as Secondary Foreign Policy Agents in Peace-Building and Reconciliation? The Case of Denmark and Germany. In: Regional & Federal Studies 27 (2017), P. 239–259.

45 Klatt: Fra modspil (Footnote 43), P. 154ff.

46 See for example Karen-Margrethe Pedersen: Dansk sprog i Sydslesvig [Die dänische Sprache in Südschleswig], 2 vols. Aabenraa 2000; Lars N. Henningsen (Ed.): Sydslesvigs danske historie [Süd-

a financial conflict with the state government of Schleswig-Holstein gave rise to a debate on "real" and "German" members of the minority, or rather parents sending their children to Danish minority schools.[47] This led to a renewed discourse on the justification of Danish state funding of the minority in Denmark.

In 2018, the Danish state supplied the Danish minority with financial support of 456.4 million DKK, about 61 million €.[48] The neo-liberal argument is based on the returns to the Danish state via tax payments of members of the minority who remain in Denmark after finishing higher education and then participate in the labour market, as well as returns to the Danish economy at a time with shortages of qualified labour. Here, it is especially the minority members' command of the German language at native speaker level which is interesting for Danish companies. Germany is still Denmark's largest export market, and the Danes' level of proficiency in German is declining rapidly. A study ordered by the Danish NGO *Grænseforeningen* revealed that the minority thus contributes about 650 million DKK / 87 million € annually to Danish society. The study also revealed university graduates from South Schleswig have a lower unemployment rate than Danish and international university graduates living in Denmark.[49] At a time when national narratives and identification have weakened in the de-facto multicultural societies of today's Denmark and South Schleswig, the neo-liberal motive is an attempt to continuously secure financial support for a minority.

Kin-state policy 6: European model

A key narrative used by both Denmark and Germany to justify their financial support of the borderland minorities has been the story of the European model. This narrative describes the Danish-German border region as exemplary for moving from national conflict to reconciliation and minority accommodation, one that could be followed by other regions with national and minority conflicts.[50] The post-WWII Federal Republic of West Germany needed democracy credit to support its strategy of integration into NATO and the European Communities. It was explicitly im-

schleswigs dänische Geschichte]. Flensburg 2009; Ruaridh Thomas Tarvet: Re-Imagining Sleswig: Language and Identity in the German-Danish Borderlands. Understanding the Regional, National and Transnational Dimensions of Minority Identity. Edinburgh 2018.

47 On the conflict see Kühl: Mindretalsmodel (Footnote 11); Klatt: Minority Schools (Footnote 8).

48 https://kum.dk/kulturpolitik/internationalt-kultursamarbejde/sydslesvigudvalget/tilskudsordninger/tilskud-2018/driftstilskud-og-resultataftaler-2018/, accessed 1 July 2019.

49 Moos-Bjerre & Lange: Sydslesvigs bidrag til Danmark [Südschleswigs Beitrag für Dänemark]. København 2017.

50 Most important: Kühl, Bohn: Ein Europäisches Modell (Footnote 7). More critical: Kühl: Mindretalsmodel (Footnote 11) and Klatt: Abgrenzung (Footnote 7).

portant to demonstrate that Germany was able to conduct and implement liberal minority policies; this was the key factor for the pressure placed on the suppressive Schleswig-Holstein state government to pursue a liberal minority policy in the 1950s.[51] The European model narrative was advocated by Denmark and Germany when the so-called Copenhagen Criteria for acceptance of Central and Eastern European countries into the EU were compiled in 1993. To manifest the perceived success story, Denmark and Germany established the European Centre for Minority Issues (ECMI) in Flensburg in 1996.[52] Both countries have supported an initiative to apply for the status of UNESCO Cultural World Heritage for the model to preserve national, cultural and linguistic diversity in the Danish-German Borderlands, which was rejected in 2021. This narrative has not prevented the Schleswig-Holstein government from unilaterally cutting funding to the Danish minority schools in 2010,[53] nor from decisively altering the prevalent imbalance in financial support of minority institutions. It reflects the continuous self-interest of both countries to present Schleswig and its minorities as a success story, neglecting the challenges to adapt the frozen structures of contained national minorities into a more liberal approach that accepts the cultural diversity of Schleswig as a border zone with inhabitants of multi-contextual cultural, national, regional and local allegiances.

Impact of kin-state policies on minority identity

Having scrutinised the motivations behind kin-state policies, I will now turn to kin-state policy's impact on minority identity. The connection with the kin-state is central to minority identification in Schleswig and both minorities express the importance of close cultural contact and exchange with the kin-state. On the other hand, both minorities commit to social integration into the state of residence's society, avoiding so-called parallel societies. Neither contemporary nor historical socioeconomic data indicates any significant differences between minority and majority populations in Schleswig. Social integration, however, facilitates social assimilation. The German language's role as a driver of upward social mobility explains the linguistic changes in the region, with the retreat of the spoken Danish language in the 18th and 19th century.[54] Organisation in the labour movement led to cultural

51 Thomas Loxtermann: Das deutsch-dänische Grenzgebiet als Modell nationalstaatlicher Minderheitenpolitik? Die Minderheitenfrage in Schleswig von den Bonn-Kopenhagener Erklärungen von 1955 bis zum Beitritt Dänemarks zur EWG 1973. Münster 2004.

52 Land Schleswig-Holstein: Minderheiten und Volksgruppenpolitik in der 18. Legislaturperiode. Minderheitenbericht 2017. Kiel 2017, P. 19.

53 Klatt: Minority Schools (Footnote 8); Kühl: Mindretalsmodel (Footnote 11).

54 Martin Klatt: Mobile Regions: Competitive Regional Concepts (Not Only) in the Danish-German Border Region. In: Dorte Jagetic Andersen, Martin Klatt, Marie Sandberg (Eds.): The Border

assimilation of large parts of the originally Danish working class in Flensburg in the late 19th century.[55] On the other hand, Nazification of the German minority resulted in the German North Schleswig workers' assimilation into Danish culture. The collapse of Germany in 1945 induced a massive wish to change nationality in South Schleswig. It is obvious today that the Danish minority has "survived" by recruiting families who do not necessarily have long genealogical connections with Danish-ness or Schleswig.

Kin-state policies have played an important role in these developments, attempting to maintain distinct cultural and linguistic minority identities. To explain the success and continuous existence of national minorities in an open border region within the EU, Arthur Christiansen has applied the model of *nation state construct.*[56] This simply means the construct of a nation state within the state by a Danish elite (from Denmark and from within the minority) with norm-setting and autonomous institutions, creating a mini-Denmark or mini-Germany that enables minority members to live as Danes in Germany or Germans in Denmark. This institutional framework educates young minority members to be Danes or Germans; under this framework, losing a child to the regular, public school system is considered a failure of the mission. Likewise, working for a minority institution is more than a job, it is a call. This agenda produces discourses on neo-colonialism, implying conflicts between immigrated *rigsdanskere*, Danes from the kingdom, and South Schleswigian minority members.

These discourses challenge the concept of the minority as a segregated, parallel society that reflects the culture and values of the kin-state rather than the state of residence, and highlight how minorities are socially integrated as Schleswigians. Minorities' self-perception, but also their identity as perceived by the majority population, is fluid and diverse. Identity is, of course, multi-contextual and cannot be determined as a Danish/German binary. It is more an issue of how minorities deal with the dilemma of pressure for clear, binary identification and social reality in a borderland. Recently, especially youth in the minorities have been more proactive in claiming that their Danish-ness or German-ness does not negate the other national culture in the borderland. This has been confirmed in a recent study on minority identification in Schleswig, which revealed that minority members identify more strongly with the other borderland minority than with either their respective kin-state or the state of

---

Multiple. The Practice of Borders between Public Policy and Everyday Life in a Re-Scaling Europe. Aldershot 2012, P. 55–76; Hans Schultz Hansen: Danskheden I Sydslesvig 1840–1918 [Das Dänentum in Südschleswig]. Flensburg 1990.

55 Martin Klatt: Fliessende Grenzen in einer Grenzstadt. Sprache, Kultur, gesellschaftlicher Status und nationale Identität im Flensburg des langen 19. Jahrhunderts. In: Christophe Duhamelle, Andreas Kossert, Bernhard Struck (Eds.): Grenzregionen. Ein europäischer Vergleich vom 18. bis zum 20. Jahrhundert, Frankfurt, New York 2007; Hansen: Danskheden (Footnote 54).

56 Christiansen: Reproduktion (Footnote 38).

residence population.[57] This form of minority identity can be labelled European or Schleswigian, but with a different connotation than that of the 18th and 19th century Schleswigians. It could also be labelled national indifference, but kin-state policies have resulted in a population that is in fact not indifferent to nationality, but rather caught in a dilemma of kin-state and state of residence expectations of how nationality should be expressed. This raises questions about whether the concept of *national minority* is able to accommodate national cultural diversity in borderlands, as it puts humans into boxes framed according to the rather exclusive idea of nationality as it has evolved from 19th-century nationalism. Jørgen Kühl therefore invented the term *post-national minority* to describe the minorities of contemporary Schleswig.[58]

Conclusion: Kin-state policy interests in conflict with social reality of 21st century minorities in appeased borderlands in a united Europe

The above reflects that kin-state policies in the Danish-German borderland have predominantly reflected the national interests of the Danish and German kin-states. They have resulted in a sustainable system of non-territorial autonomy, providing both minorities with their own independent school system and a wide range of other cultural and social organisations and institutions. The latter serve minority elite's interest in having a nation state construct to recruit and form the minority in their interest, according to perceptions of what it means to be a Dane or a German transferred from the kin-states. When Denmark and Germany were forced into an alliance during the Cold War, both countries had an overall interest in appeasement of the borderland and preventing any challenge to the position of the border. Furthermore, a stable national balance was perceived as decisive for a peaceful border. Especially Germany needed to demonstrate its capability to implement a liberal minority regime to convince its allies that its newly acquired democratic political culture was in earnest. Kin-state policies were border policies: claims for a border revision were to be avoided by accommodating the minorities. The collective right to self-determination was replaced by the individual right to self-determination, safeguarded in cultural autonomy. This meant in practice stabilising the minorities as parallel societies, appeased by generous kin-state support. Since then, recurring identity debates within and outside the minorities have demonstrated their binational character, their social integration and increasingly their active commitment as political agents for all of society, from a cross-border perspective. The minorities

57 Tarvet: Re-Imagining (Footnote 46).

58 Jørgen Kühl: "Ihr seid nicht vergessen worden". Königliche Neujahrsgrüße 2001–2017 und Vorstellungen von der dänischen Minderheit in Südschleswig. In: Jørgen Kühl (Ed.): Klaar Kiming. Festschrift für Thomas Steensen. Bredstedt/Bräist 2018, P. 110–116, esp. P. 111.

have become what Border Studies scholar Oscar Martinez defines as transnational borderlanders,[59] borderland residents with proficiency in both states' languages and adaptability to both cultural settings, taking advantage of the opportunities of economic and social life in two countries.

Such a scenario is unintended by the respective kin-state policies as well as the self-perception expressed in the bylaws of the minority institutions and associations, where kin-state policies and support is meant to protect minorities from assimilation into majority culture. Rather than providing a framework for borderland diversity, kin-state policies seek to cement a status quo of a borderland with a clear, stable national balance and clearly identifiable minorities segregated from the majority population.

59 Oscar J. Martinez: Border People. Life and Society in the U.S.-Mexico Borderlands. Tucson, London 1994.

Gerald Volkmer

Germany and the German national minorities in Central and Eastern Europe

Introduction

Germany belongs to the group of European states that, as a 'mother country' (kin-state), are associated with 'their own' minorities (kin-minorities) living abroad. Like Russia, Poland, Austria, Hungary, Romania, and Slovakia, Germany is also intertwined with their kin-minorities through a shared history, ethnic, linguistic or other cultural ties. The German minorities are promoted and supported by the German Government in agreement with the respective country in which they live. In contrast to other kin-states, 'minority issues' and 'minority policy' are not a topic of daily politics for Germany. They rarely find their way into political debates or the wider public discourse. This is part because there are no longer large German minorities in other European states, and the national minorities living in Germany are generally quite small. The four groups recognised as national minorities in Germany – the Danish minority, the ethnic Frisian minority, the Sorbian population, and the German Sinti and Roma – together add up to around a quarter of a million people. Altogether, they constitute around 0.3 percent of the population of Germany.[1] The German minorities in East-Central and South-Eastern Europe and in the states of the former Soviet Union number around one million in total, and are also rarely taken note of by the German public. This is partly because their numbers are small compared to the 84 million inhabitants of Germany itself, but also because they are spread across around two dozen countries.[2] This essay will focus on the German minorities living in East-Central and South-Eastern Europe and in the states of the former Soviet Union, and on the support they receive from Germany. This primarily means the ethnic German groups with 'national minority' status, which provides them with protection under the Framework Convention for the Protection of National Minorities of the Council of Europe.[3] The region

1 Sonja Wolf: Zur sozialen und politischen Lage der anerkannten nationalen Minderheiten in Deutschland. In: Aus Politik und Zeitgeschichte 67 (2017) No. 11–12, P. 16–22.

2 Gerald Volkmer: Deutsche Minderheiten im Ausland. In: Aus Politik und Zeitgeschichte 67 (2017) No.11–12, P. 38–46.

3 cf. on the concept of 'minorities', Rainer Hofmann: Minderheitenschutz in Europa: Entwicklung und aktueller Stand. In: Aus Politik und Zeitgeschichte 67 (2017) No. 11–12, P. 9–15. See also

we are focusing on includes minority population groups who speak German as a mother tongue or who accept German as a minority or identity language. This identifying factor is true not only for standard German, but also for dialects of German. It is, however, difficult to distinguish between people who speak German as a mother tongue and people who don't, but who claim to be ethnic Germans (in legal terms, for example, as an ethnic or national group). We shall consider both these categories here. When determining the groups to be treated, the criterion of 'autochthony' is decisive. This criterion underlies the standards of the Framework Convention and the Language Charter of the Council of Europe, but has not yet been given a binding definition under international law.[4] In his foundational work on the worldwide status of the German language, the sociolinguist Ulrich Ammon recommends the definition proposed by Romanian German theologian and minority-politician Paul Philippi (1923–2018):

> 'Minority groups are autochthonous at least if their existence is older than the state to which they currently belong. Above all, older than the state, which, on the basis of the majority of one of the ethnic groups present in the territory, has declared itself as the nation state of precisely this one ethnic group.'[5]

The words 'at least' indicate that this narrow definition can also be extended to apply, for example, German populations living in Russia.[6]

This essay will therefore start by outlining the history of the Germans in Eastern Europe. In history and cultural studies, the term 'Eastern Europe' has become established as a general term embracing the regions of East, East-Central, and South-Eastern Europe. The essay will then describe the current situation of German minorities in East-Central and South-Eastern Europe and in the states of the former Soviet Union. In conclusion, it will examine the ways in which the Federal Republic of Germany offers support to German minorities living in Eastern Europe.

Georg Kneer: Nationalstaat, Migration und Minderheiten. Ein Beitrag zur Soziogenese von ethnischen Minoritäten. In: Armin Nassehi (Ed.): Nation, Ethnie, Minderheit. Beiträge zur Aktualität ethnischer Konflikte. Georg Weber zum 65. Geburtstag. Köln, Weimar, Wien 1997, P. 85–102.

4 Christoph Pan, Beate Sibylle Pfeil, Paul Videsott (Eds.): Die Volksgruppen in Europa. Handbuch der europäischen Volksgruppen vol. 1. 2nd edn, Wien, Berlin 2016, S. 224–225. cf. Stefan Oeter: Die Entwicklung der europäischen Sprachenvielfalt und die Rolle der Minderheiten. Der völkerrechtliche und nationale Schutz. In: Christoph Bergner, Matthias Weber (Eds.): Aussiedler- und Minderheitenpolitik in Deutschland. Bilanz und Perspektiven. München 2009 (Schriften des Bundesinstituts für Kultur und Geschichte der Deutschen im östlichen Europa 38), P. 151–175.

5 Ulrich Ammon: Die Stellung der deutschen Sprache in der Welt. Berlin 2015, P. 255–260.

6 Ammon therefore suggests also including in this definition minority groups that established themselves in a different non-German-speaking country than the one they currently live in, such as the Danube Swabians and the Russian Germans, who now live as a separate group in North and South American countries: Ammon: Stellung (Footnote 5), P. 148–154, 255–260.

The history of Germans in Eastern Europe

The history of Germans in East-Central and South-Eastern Europe begins in the High Middle Ages. Around the turn of the first millennium AD, the eastern border of the German-speaking area of Europe ran along the Elbe and Saale rivers and the Bohemian Forest, and largely corresponded to the eastern border of the Holy Roman Empire. To the east of this line lived West Slavic tribes and the Magyars. From the 11th century onwards, the dukes and kings of Poland, Bohemia and Hungary settled German-speaking farmers and craftsmen for the purpose of developing their lands. The expansion of the dominions of the Roman-German kings and emperors to the east and the strong population growth in West-Central Europe accelerated this migration process, which is also known as the 'medieval German eastward settlement'.[7] By the time this migratory movement finished in the late 14th century, new German populations had been established in Mecklenburg, Brandenburg, Pomerania, Upper Saxony, Silesia, East and West Prussia, in the Baltics, in Bohemia, in Moravia, in Upper Hungary (modern Slovakia), and in Transylvania; in these regions they variously were the majority population, had self-governing territories, or were the established local elites.[8]

Plagues and wars combined to halt the migratory movement, but it started up again in the 18th century, under the influence of Prussian kings, Habsburg emperors and Russian Tsars, and continued until the middle of the 19th century. These more recent German groups established themselves in the southern Baltic region (e.g. in East and West Prussia), in the Danube region (e.g. Bačka/Bácska and Banat), to the north of the arc of the Carpathians (e.g. Galicia and Bukovina), in the Volga region, and to the north of the Black Sea.[9] The growth of nationalist movements in Eastern Europe in the 19th century led people who spoke dialects of German – and people who defined themselves by their status in law, their social position, and their religious affiliation – to describe themselves as 'German'. Germans living in the Russian Empire and in the Hungarian part of the Habsburg Monarchy were by the

7 A fundamental reference on the history of Germans living in Eastern Europe is Sabine Doering, Matthias Weber (Eds.): Online-Lexikon zur Kultur und Geschichte der Deutschen im östlichen Europa (http://ome-lexikon.uni-oldenburg.de). cf. Matthias Weber: Deutsche Minderheiten in der europäischen Siedlungsgeschichte. In: Christoph Bergner, Matthias Weber (Eds.): Aussiedler- und Minderheitenpolitik in Deutschland. Bilanz und Perspektiven. München 2009 (Schriften des Bundesinstituts für Kultur und Geschichte der Deutschen im östlichen Europa 38), P. 33–45.

8 Konrad Gündisch: Deutsche. In: Harald Roth (Ed.): Studienhandbuch Östliches Europa, vol. 1. 2nd edn, Köln, Weimar, Wien 2009, P. 463–471. cf. Hermann Scheuringer: Einst privilegiert, dann geächtet, nun wieder geschätzt oder nur genutzt? Status und Perspektiven des Deutschen in Ostmittel- und Südosteuropa. In: Jahrbuch des Bundesinstituts für Kultur und Geschichte der Deutschen im östlichen Europa 26 (2018), P. 11–33, here P. 11–13.

9 Gündisch: Deutsche (Footnote 8), P. 463–471.

1870s being described as a 'national minority group' and were subjected to a strong policy of Russification and Magyarisation.[10]

When the Austro-Hungarian Empire collapsed at the end of the First World War, Germans living in many of the crown lands of the former Austrian part of the empire became minority groups in the new nation-states that emerged.[11] The same fate befell the Germans who lived in those parts of the eastern provinces of the Prussian kingdom, which had to be ceded to Poland by the Treaty of Versailles in 1919.[12] The new world of states established after the First World War between the Baltic and the Adriatic encompassed a multitude of German minorities. Around 1930, over 3.3 million Germans were living in Czechoslovakia; in Poland there were 741,000 people whose mother tongue was German, and more than a million who claimed 'German nationality'; and almost 200,000 Germans lived in the three Baltic states of Estonia, Latvia, and Lithuania. In Hungary 551,211 people listed German as their mother tongue in the 1920 census, and in Greater Romania in 1930, a total of 745,421 people declared themselves to have 'German nationality'. The German minority population in Yugoslavia at that time numbered around 500,000. Including all the groups of Germans living in the Soviet Union, the German minorities living in Eastern Europe amounted to around 8.5 million people in total. As a result, public interest in 'German expatriates' grew rapidly in the Weimar Republic. Revisionist organisations, in particular, campaigned for Germany to develop a protective relationship with Germans living in areas adjacent to the Reich that had been part of Germany prior to the Versailles treaty.[13] The political representatives of the German minorities in East-Central and South-Eastern Europe sought to improve the situation of these Germans during the interwar period, including by establishing a dedicated Europe-wide association, the Association of German Minorities in Europe *(Verband der deutschen Minderheiten in Europa)*. When German minorities were involved in confrontations with political parties of majority populations, they were often seen as representatives of the defunct Habsburg Empire or the defeated Germany and subjected to harassment. This fed a sense among German expatriates,

10 Günter Schödl: Am Rande des Reiches, am Rande der Nation: Deutsche im Königreich Ungarn (1867–1914/18). In: Günter Schödl (Ed.): Deutsche Geschichte im Osten Europas: Land an der Donau. Berlin 1995, P. 359–454.

11 Friedrich Prinz: Auf dem Weg in die Moderne. In: Friedrich Prinz (Ed.): Deutsche Geschichte im Osten Europas: Böhmen und Mähren. Berlin 1993, P. 379–396.

12 Jochen Oltmer: Deutsche Zuwanderer aus den nach dem Ersten Weltkrieg abgetretenen Gebieten in Deutschland. In: Klaus J. Bade (Ed.): Enzyklopädie Migration in Europa. Vom 17. Jahrhundert bis zur Gegenwart. 2nd edn, Paderborn 2013, P. 525–529.

13 Cornelia Eisler: Minderheiten als volkskundliches Kompetenzfeld? Das Konzept des ‚Grenz- und Auslandsdeutschtums' in der Weimarer Republik. In: Cornelia Eisler, Silke Göttsch-Elten (Eds.): Minderheiten im Europa der Zwischenkriegszeit. Wissenschaftliche Konzeptionen, mediale Vermittlung, politische Funktion. Münster 2017, P. 43–65.

especially the younger generation, that they had to rely on help from Germany for any improvement in their situation.[14]

Conscious of these sentiments, the political elites in East-Central and South-Eastern European countries feared for the integrity of their multi-ethnic states; in order to protect them from collapse, they further limited the political participation of minority groups. The negative spiral of mutual distrust, and the deteriorating situation for German minorities, laid the foundations for new and radical developments among the younger generation of politicians. After 1933 these newer politicians developed a close network of relationships with the National Socialist forces in the German Reich. Within a few years, the two sides had succeeded in bringing the political and social structures of the Germans in East-Central and South-East Europe into line with Berlin, destroying the historically established parties and associations of the German minorities. From then on, the younger generation of politicians, who were influenced by National Socialism, put – under orders from Berlin – the German minorities fully at the service of the Second World War, which was criminally started and waged by Germany.[15]

Shortly after the start of the Second World War, it became clear that Hitler was less interested in improving the situation of the German populations in their host countries than in using them as an instrument to further his war aims. Between 1939 and 1941, around one million Germans, belonging to small population groups considered unviable by the Nazis, were forced to leave their homes and to move to areas that Germany had occupied and then annexed in the East. In August 1941, shortly after the German invasion of the Soviet Union, Moscow issued a blanket declaration that the German minority population living in the Soviet Union were 'national enemies'. Up to a million Germans were deported to the Asian east of the Soviet Union during 1941–42, and remained there until 1955 in forced labour camps, where a high proportion of them died. They were forbidden to return to the areas in which they had formerly been settled.[16] This decade of forced migrations reached its peak between 1944 and 1946, when around 4 to 5 million Germans fled the Red Army, and then around twice that number were expelled from the new Polish 'western regions', Czechoslovakia, Hungary, and Yugoslavia. Before 1939 there were more than 18 million Germans living east of the Oder and Neisse rivers, the modern German-Polish border, and up to 2 million of these died as a result of war, flight,

14 cf. Weber: Deutsche Minderheiten (Footnote 7), P. 39–41.

15 Gündisch: Deutsche (Footnote 8), P. 468–471. cf. Weber: Deutsche Minderheiten (Footnote 7), P. 40.

16 cf. Alfred Eisfeld: Vom Stolperstein zur Brücke – Die Deutschen in Russland. In: Christoph Bergner, Matthias Weber (Eds.): Aussiedler- und Minderheitenpolitik in Deutschland. Bilanz und Perspektiven. München 2009 (Schriften des Bundesinstituts für Kultur und Geschichte der Deutschen im östlichen Europa 38), P. 79–85.

expulsion, or deportation. By 1950, about 12 million had reached the territory of the Federal Republic of Germany and the GDR, and about 400,000 Austria.[17]

Around 1950, there were still over 4 million Germans living principally in Polish Upper Silesia, Slovakian Spiš/Zips, Hungary, Romania, and in the Asian parts of the Soviet Union. They were persistently treated as fascists and endured political and social discrimination and, along with the rest of the population, were subject to the restrictive exit regulations of the communist dictatorships. German educational and cultural institutions were forbidden; only Romania permitted a very limited amount of German-language teaching and cultural activity, provided it conformed to criteria laid down by the regime. The often-prominent role of Germans in cultural and economic life before the war was turned into its opposite, with Germans categorised as 'class enemies' and therefore a 'group hostile to the regime' according to communist ideology. The German minorities were further intimidated by Stalinist terror measures and were kept under extra close observation by the communist secret services, especially any with relatives in the German Federal Republic.[18] In the 1960s, especially, a spirit of détente developed, and a significantly increased number of ethnic Germans emigrated to the German Federal Republic under the policy of 'family reunification' *(Familienzusammenführung)*, which entitled this group to German citizenship. As periods of political thawing were replaced in several countries by periods of greater repression, Germans who had remained in the Eastern Bloc began losing hope that their situation would improve. Trust between the Germans and their home countries shattered. This was seen most clearly in the late 1980s and after the political turning point *(die Wende)* of 1989, when the lifting of travel restrictions enabled German minorities to leave their homes, driven almost by panic. This is clearly highlighted in the statistics on ethnic German 'resettlers' *(Aussiedler)*. (Those who arrived after 1 January 1993 were designated 'late resettlers' *[Spätaussiedler]*.) Between 1950 and 2015, 2,375,602 Germans migrated into the Federal Republic of Germany from the (former) Soviet Union. During those same years, a total of 430,323 Germans left Romania. The second largest group of resettlers, from Poland, migrated principally during the 1980s, when 632,803 people left their homes out of the total of 1,445,201 who emigrated during 1950 to 2015. Notably fewer resettlers came from

17 Mathias Beer: Flucht und Vertreibung der Deutschen. Voraussetzungen, Verlauf, Folgen. München 2011 (Beck'sche Reihe 1933). cf. Bayerische Landeszentrale für politische Bildungsarbeit (Ed.): Flucht und Vertreibung. München 2021 (Einsichten und Perspektiven, Themenheft 1/2021). cf. Klaus J. Bade, Jochen Oltmer: Einführung. Aussiedlerzuwanderung und Aussiedlerintegration. Historische Entwicklung und aktuelle Probleme. In: Klaus J. Bade, Jochen Oltmer (Eds.): Aussiedler: deutsche Einwanderer aus Osteuropa. 2nd edn, Göttingen 2003, P. 9–54, here P. 18–19.

18 Karl Cordell, Stefan Wolff: Germany as a Kin-State: The Development and Implementation of a Norm-Consistent External Minority Policy towards Central and Eastern Europe. In: Nationalities Papers 35 (2007) No. 2, P. 289–315, here P. 296–297. cf. Weber: Deutsche Minderheiten (Footnote 7), P. 35–42.

Czechoslovakia and Yugoslavia: 104,627 and 90,370 respectively, between 1950 and 2015. Of these German migrants, the greatest number arrived between 1950 and 1969, respectively 76,094 and 78,625. It was the Germans from Hungary who felt most strongly the link with their home country. After their expulsion they made persistent efforts to return to their homes in Hungary, and of a population of 21,419 German resettlers from Hungary, only 2,825 emigrated after 1989 – by some margin the smallest group of ethnic German resettlers between 1950 and 2015.[19]

Altogether, then, the records show that between 1950 and 2015, a total of 4,523,170 resettlers and late resettlers settled in the Federal Republic of Germany.[20]

The current situation of German minorities in East-Central and South-Eastern Europe and in the states of the former Soviet Union

At the start of the 2020s, around 650,000 Germans were living in the states of the former Soviet Union and around 400,000 Germans in East-Central and South-Eastern Europe. The largest European population groups are in Poland (between 148,000 and 300,000), Hungary (between 132,000 and 186,000), and Romania (about 23,000); we shall now examine these more closely. Some 40,000 Germans are spread across Estonia, Latvia, Lithuania, the Czech Republic, Slovakia, Slovenia, Croatia, Bosnia and Herzegovina, and Serbia. All except these last two states are members of the European Union.[21] In almost all of these states, the ethnic Ger-

19 Gündisch: Deutsche (Footnote 8), P. 463–471. cf. Ágnes Tóth: Rückkehr nach Ungarn 1946–1950. Erlebnisberichte ungarndeutscher Vertriebener. Aus dem Ungarischen übersetzt von Andreas Schmidt-Schweizer. München 2012 (Schriften des Bundesinstituts für Kultur und Geschichte der Deutschen im östlichen Europa 43).

20 Some further 55,626 emigrants arrived from countries not mentioned here by name. Between 125,000 and 150,000 Germans migrated to the German Democratic Republic after 1950, principally during the 1950s and 1960s; they were designated as *Übersiedler* (emigrant). Jannis Panagiotidis: Aussiedler/Spätaussiedler. In: Online-Lexikon zur Kultur und Geschichte der Deutschen im östlichen Europa, 2015. URL: ome-lexikon.uni-oldenburg.de/p32717 (accessed 31.08.2020). cf. Bundeszentrale für politische Bildung (Ed.): (Spät-)Aussiedler in der Migrationsgesellschaft. Bonn 2019 (Informationen zur politischen Bildung 340, No. 2/2019). cf. Jürgen Hensen: Zur Geschichte der Aussiedler- und Spätaussiedleraufnahme. In: Christoph Bergner, Matthias Weber (Eds.): Aussiedler- und Minderheitenpolitik in Deutschland. Bilanz und Perspektiven. München 2009 (Schriften des Bundesinstituts für Kultur und Geschichte der Deutschen im östlichen Europa 38), P. 47–61. cf. Bade, Oltmer: Aussiedlerzuwanderung und Aussiedlerintegration (Footnote 17), P. 20–39.

21 On the German minorities in the European Union, which are not examined here, see Gerald Volkmer: Die deutschsprachigen Minderheiten in der Europäischen Union. In: Oxford German Studies 48 (2019) No. 1, P. 17–53. In 1989 the German Foreign Ministry commissioned a survey of German-speaking expatriate minorities: Joachim Born, Sylvia Dickgießer: Deutschsprachige Minderheiten. Ein Überblick über den Stand der Forschung für 27 Länder. Mannheim 1989. A booklet

man groups have the 'national minority' status that gives them protection under the Framework Convention for the Protection of National Minorities of the Council of Europe.

The German minority in Poland

The German population in Poland constitutes the largest recognised 'national minority' and in demographic terms it is the most significant German minority group in East-Central and South-Eastern Europe.[22] On the 1930 census, 741,000 Polish citizens declared that they spoke German as their mother tongue, and a little over one million claimed to belong to the 'German national' group in Poland.[23] The 2011 census shows 147,814 people claiming to belong to the German minority population.[24] Most of this group live in the former East German territories, especially in Silesia, East Pomerania, and southern East Prussia. A considerably larger proportion of this minority German population lives in Upper Silesia than in the other regions. Until the political *Wende* in the late 1980s, the communist regime in Poland officially denied that there was a German minority, and the use of the German language was strictly forbidden.[25] German action groups in Poland were only

published in 2016 by the German Interior Ministry offers an overview of the current state of German minorities in East-Central, Eastern and South-Eastern Europe, in the successor states to the Soviet Union, and in Denmark: Bundesministerium des Innern (Ed.): Deutsche Minderheiten stellen sich vor. Berlin 2016, 3., rev. edn. 2018. cf. Stiftung Verbundenheit mit den Deutschen im Ausland (Ed.): Memorandum. Deutsche Minderheiten und Deutschsprachige Gemeinschaften in der Welt als Bürgerdiplomaten einer werte- und interessengeleiteten Außenpolitik Deutschlands stärken. Bayreuth 2025. cf. on the language situation of Germans in Eastern Europe: Christoph Bergner, Hans Zehetmair (Eds.): Deutsch als Identitätssprache der deutschen Minderheiten. München 2014 (Argumente und Materialien zum Zeitgeschehen 92). cf. on the promotion of the German language: Goethe-Institut (Ed.): Das Goethe-Institut fördert deutsche Minderheiten. München 2011.

22 The Polish Act of 6 January 2005 on National and Ethnic Minorities and on the Regional Languages, in Article 2 Paragraph 2, defines the concept of a 'national minority' and includes in this category nine groups, one of which is the minority German population. It also defines four 'ethnic minorities': Roma, Rusyns, Tatars and Karaims: Maria Dziekonska, Mieczyslaw Dziekonski: Nationale Minderheiten in Osteuropa am Beispiel von Polen und Ungarn. In: Gilbert Gornig, Angel Manuel Rafael (Eds.): Minderheitenschutz. Eine interdisziplinäre Betrachtung. Minority Protection. An Interdisciplinary View. Marburg 2013, P. 149–197, here P. 162.

23 Maria Katarzyna Lasatowicz, Tobias Weger: Polen. In: Ludwig M. Eichinger, Albrecht Plewnia, Claudia Maria Riehl (Eds.): Handbuch der deutschen Sprachminderheiten in Mittel- und Osteuropa. Tübingen 2008, P. 147–158, here P. 148–152.

24 Pan, Pfeil, Videsott: Die Volksgruppen in Europa (Footnote 4), P. 155–158.

25 Further on the period 1945–1989: Thomas Urban: Deutsche in Polen. Geschichte und Gegenwart einer Minderheit. 2nd edn München 1994, P. 66–100. The Polish government's regulation meant that one could even be prosecuted for having a private collection of books in German. Born, Dickgießer: Deutschsprachige Minderheiten (Footnote 21), P. 166–167.

able to become official associations following the 1989 free elections, although they had existed illegally since 1982.[26]

In today's Poland, most local associations of German people are organised as 'German friendship groups', and on the regional level of voivodeships they take the form of 'social and cultural associations'.[27] In 2015, there were a total of 330 German minority organisations within the voivodeship of Oppeln/Opole in Upper Silesia, and a further 132 in the Upper Silesian voivodeship of Silesia/Śląskie. In southern East Prussia (in the voivodeship Ermland-Masuren/Warmińsko-Mazurskie) there are 26 such organisations.[28] These latter groups serve communities that are more widely scattered, so they are not as tightly organised as those in Upper Silesia.[29] It is only in the voivodeship of Opole that the German minority amounts to almost 10 per cent of the population.[30] The umbrella organisation for these associations, the League of German Social and Cultural Associations in Poland (*Verband der deutschen sozial-kulturellen Gesellschaften in Polen*, VdG), has its headquarters in Opole. It was able to send several deputies to the Polish parliament in the 1990s and still has one there today. In the Opole voivodeship, the organisation has representatives on a number of district and local councils; in 2016 its members provided 1 deputy marshal, 3 district commissioners, 1 deputy district commissioner, 7 representatives to the Opole voivodeship parliament, and 26 mayors.[31]

Because of the Polish Act on National and Ethnic Minorities and on Regional Languages, the municipalities are entitled to put up local place-name signs in two languages if Germans make up more than 20 per cent of the local population (provided the municipal parliaments and Ministry of the Interior agree). Almost two dozen municipalities have accordingly been able to use German as a secondary local language and put up bilingual signs.[32] The communities in the neighbourhood of

26 Carsten Eichenberger: Die Deutschen in Polen. Von der verleugneten Minderheit zur anerkannten Volksgruppe. Augsburg 1994, P. 70–134.

27 For further information on the local involvement of the associations: Katharina Schuchardt: Zwischen Berufsfeld und Identitätsangebot. Zum Selbstverständnis der deutschen Minderheit im heutigen Opole/Oppeln. Münster 2018, P. 98–122.

28 BMI: Deutsche Minderheiten (Footnote 21), P. 41–42.

29 cf. Andrzej Sakson: Die deutsche Minderheit in Pommern, im Ermland und in Masuren. In: Felicitas Drobek (Ed.): Polen in Deutschland – Deutsche in Polen. Referate der Tagung des Johannes-Künzig-Instituts für ostdeutsche Volkskunde vom 12./13. Juni 1997. Freiburg 1999, P. 145–154.

30 Jan Puhl: Ein Loch in der Geschichte. Im Oppelner Land lebt die größte deutsche Minderheit Ostmitteleuropas. In: Annette Großbongardt, Uwe Klußmann, Norbert F. Pötzl (Eds.): Die Deutschen im Osten Europas. Eroberer, Siedler, Vertriebene. Bonn 2011, P. 280–290, here P. 281.

31 Lech M. Nijakowski: Die Politik des polnischen Staates gegenüber den nationalen und ethnischen Minderheiten. In: Polen-Analysen 177 (2016), P. 2–19. cf. Ammon: Die Stellung der deutschen Sprache (Footnote 5), P. 326.

32 Till Scholtz-Knobloch: Die deutsche Minderheit in Oberschlesien. Selbstreflexion und politisch-soziale Situation unter besonderer Berücksichtigung des so genannten 'Oppelner Schlesiens' (Westoberschlesiens). Görlitz 2002, P. 75–78. cf. Ammon: Die Stellung der deutschen Sprache

the city of Opole lost this right on 1 January 2017, when a decree from the Polish government altered the local administrative boundaries and they lost their independence, being integrated into the territory of Opole. People affected by this change consider it to breach Article 16 of the European Framework Convention for the Protection of National Minorities.[33]

The VdG estimates that the German minority population in Poland now numbers between 300,000 and 350,000 people.[34] It argues that the 2011 census was not accurate, since it did not take into consideration the fact that many of those surveyed hold dual Polish and German citizenship.[35] Many members of the German minority, moreover, declared themselves to be Silesian: this included 809,000 people, of whom 362,000 explicitly did not declare themselves as Polish.[36] Their dual citizenship enables many members of the German minority to work in German-speaking countries, and thus to consolidate their German language.[37] Few ethnic Germans in Poland speak German with mother-tongue fluency, however, as there are still relatively few German-language schools compared to the size of the German-minority population: until 1990, it was strictly forbidden to teach German either as a mother tongue or as a foreign language in the German-minority settlement areas.[38] Only following the friendship treaty between Germany and Poland in 1991 was the German language permitted in private or in public. In 2013, six schools in the Opole voivodeship offered bilingual education, and German as a mother-tongue subject; half the school's teaching was in German and half in Polish. In the 588

(Footnote 5), P. 326. cf. Schuchardt: Zwischen Berufsfeld und Identitätsangebot (Footnote 27), P. 204–205.

33 Bernard Gaida: Die Perspektiven der Minderheitenrechte in Polen. In: Frank Spengler, Bence Bauer (Eds.): Zur Situation der deutschen Minderheit in der Mitte Europas. Tagungsband der Konferenzen „Die Deutschen in Westungarn" der Konrad-Adenauer-Stiftung und der Landesselbstverwaltung der Ungarndeutschen am 19. Januar 2017 in Sopron/Ödenburg, Ungarn sowie „Zur Situation der deutschen Minderheit in der Mitte Europas" der Konrad-Adenauer-Stiftung und der Landsmannschaft der Donauschwaben in Kroatien am 7. September 2017 in Osijek/Essegg, Kroatien. Budapest 2017, P. 37–40.

34 BMI: Deutsche Minderheiten (Footnote 21), P. 41. cf. Cordell, Wolff: Germany as a Kin-State (Footnote 18), P. 303–304.

35 Till Scholtz-Knobloch: Die deutsche Minderheit in Oberschlesien (Footnote 32), P. 69–72. cf. Otto Luchterhandt: Nationale Minderheiten und Loyalität. Köln 1997, P. 102–103.

36 Eugeniusz Kłosek: Zwischen Deutschland und Polen. Über die ethnische Grenzgebiet-Identifikation der Schlesier und ihre Erforschung. In: Felicitas Drobek (Ed.): Polen in Deutschland – Deutsche in Polen. Referate der Tagung des Johannes-Künzig-Instituts für ostdeutsche Volkskunde vom 12./13. Juni 1997. Freiburg 1999, pp. 155–164. cf. Haus der Deutsch-Polnischen Zusammenarbeit (Ed.): Die Deutschen in Polen. Artikel aus der deutschen und polnischen Presse aus den Jahren 1989–2010. Opole 2010, P. 95–98. cf. Ammon: Die Stellung der deutschen Sprache (Footnote 5), P. 321–322.

37 On the identities of the more recent generations: Schuchardt: Zwischen Berufsfeld und Identitätsangebot (Footnote 27), P. 215–309.

38 Lasatowicz, Weger: Polen (Footnote 23), P. 156–158.

other schools, of which 410 are in the Opole voivodeship, all subjects were taught in Polish and the subject 'German as a minority language'[39] was taught for three lessons per week.[40] The Committee of Experts of the European Charter for Regional or Minority Languages of the Council of Europe assessed this level of provision to be inadequate in terms of both learning and practising a mother tongue.[41]

On 4 February 2022, the Polish government dramatically reduced the amount of mother-tongue German teaching to one lesson per week, in order to pressure the German government to increase the amount of mother-tongue teaching of Polish in Germany. However, decisions on the German educational curriculum rest with the *Land* government, not the federal government. This decision by the Polish government affects only children in the German minority, not those in other minority groups. The government further imposed a measure prohibiting any combining of lessons teaching German as mother tongue with German as a foreign language. In response, language lessons outside regular school hours were set up, under state supervision. The Polish government then also reduced their financial support for school teaching provided under local authorities by around 10 million euros. This latest measure too affected only the German minority, who – together with observers in other countries – see it and the other onslaughts on the German population by the Polish government as contrary to the European Charter for Regional or Minority Languages.[42] These measures were cancelled by the Tusk government in 2024.

As with the teaching of German as a mother tongue, the variety of media available to the German minority is not proportionate to the size of the population. There is no German-language daily paper, though there are high-circulation weekly papers. Most prominently, there is the VdG periodical, *Wochenblatt.pl*, published twice a month with the insert *Oberschlesische Stimme (The Voice of Upper Silesia)*. The weekly paper *Heimat (Homeland)* is circulated as an insert in the Polish-language regional paper for Opole. There are also a number of German newsletters produced by German minority groups, and periodicals with German-language sections. The VdG publishes a yearbook and organises not only specialist conferences on the history and culture of Germans in Poland, but also major events such as the German

39 Altogether, 40,000 schoolchildren follow classes in 'German as mother tongue': BMI: Deutsche Minderheiten (Footnote 21), P. 43.

40 Bernard Gaida: Auf der Suche nach Lösungen: Polen. In: Christoph Bergner, Hans Zehetmair (Eds.): Deutsch als Identitätssprache der deutschen Minderheiten. München 2014 (Argumente und Materialien zum Zeitgeschehen 92), P. 47–50.

41 Lasatowicz, Weger: Polen (Footnote 23), P. 147–158. cf. Ammon: Die Stellung der deutschen Sprache (Footnote 5), P. 323–335. cf. Bernard Gaida: Vom Stolperstein zur Brücke – Die deutsche Minderheit in Oberschlesien. In: Christoph Bergner, Matthias Weber (Eds.): Aussiedler- und Minderheitenpolitik in Deutschland. Bilanz und Perspektiven. München 2009 (Schriften des Bundesinstituts für Kultur und Geschichte der Deutschen im östlichen Europa 38), P. 91–99.

42 https://www.aussiedlerbeauftragte.de/SharedDocs/kurzmeldungen/Webs/AUSB/DE/2022/01–03/20220210-polen.html (accessed 22.11.2022).

minority culture festival that takes place every three years in the Breslau/Wrocław 'Jahrhunderthalle'. There are a few short programmes in German on the radio, and the *Schlesien Journal (Silesian Journal)* is broadcast three times a week for 11 minutes on television (2017 figures).[43]

The VdG has identified that the greatest challenges faced by the German minority in Poland are, first, to maintain the German language and its Upper Silesian dialect,[44] and second, to strengthen the rights of minorities in Poland. Especially because it has been legal since 1990, there is a certain shift back to using the German language, at least as a second mother tongue alongside Polish, but this depends on whether the Polish educational authorities stipulate that German should be taught to the level of mother-tongue fluency.[45]

The German minority in Hungary

When Hungary lost about two thirds of its territory at the Peace Treaty of Trianon in 1920, around a quarter of the Germans who had lived in the Hungarian part of the Habsburg Monarchy before the war remained living in the new Hungarian state. In the 1941 census, 477,057 people declared that German was their mother tongue, and 303,419 that they belong to the German minority (within the 1920 borders of Hungary).[46] This discrepancy highlights the fact that, since the 19th century, Hungarian Germans have tended to identify with the Hungarian state and the 'Hungarian nation'. Nevertheless, around half of the Hungarian Germans (c. 220,000) were expelled after the Second World War. Those who remained in the country lived mainly around Budapest and in the south and west, and were subjected to a consistent policy of assimilation by the Hungarian state.[47] It was not until the 1970s

43 BMI: Deutsche Minderheiten (Footnote 21), P. 44. cf. Ammon: Die Stellung der deutschen Sprache (Footnote 5), P. 325.

44 Schuchardt: Zwischen Berufsfeld und Identitätsangebot (Footnote 27), P. 189–204.

45 BMI: Deutsche Minderheiten (Footnote 21), P. 45. cf. Ammon: Die Stellung der deutschen Sprache (Footnote 5), P. 327.

46 Gerhard Seewann: Geschichte der Deutschen in Ungarn. vol. 2: 1860 bis 2006. Marburg 2012 (Studien zur Ostmitteleuropaforschung 24/I–II), P. 283.

47 John C. Swanson: Fassbare Zugehörigkeit. Deutschsein im Ungarn des 20. Jahrhunderts. Regensburg 2020 (Veröffentlichungen des Instituts für deutsche Kultur und Geschichte Südosteuropas (IKGS) an der Ludwig-Maximilians-Universität München 140), P. 77–89. cf. Elisabeth Knipf-Komlósi, Marta Müller: Zwischen Vitalität und Aufgabe. Dynamische Aspekte in der Sprache der deutschen Minderheit in Ungarn. In: Jahrbuch des Bundesinstituts für Kultur und Geschichte der Deutschen im östlichen Europa 26 (2018), P. 51–67, here P. 54–56. cf. Ágnes Tóth: Deutsche in Ungarn 1950–1970. Die deutsche Minderheit zwischen Stalinismus und Kádár-Regime. Berlin, Boston 2025 (Schriften zur Kultur und Geschichte der Deutschen im östlichen Europa 90), P. 99–435.

and 1980s that the Hungarian German minority were able to develop a cultural life of their own.[48] In the 2011 census, the 131,951 Hungarian citizens who declared themselves to be part of the German minority included only 38,248 who declared German to be their mother tongue. Some further 32,000 people claimed to speak German as a mother tongue but did not claim to be part of the German minority. Hungarian German organisations therefore assume that there are between 164,000 and 186,000 Germans respectively German speakers in Hungary.[49]

During the communist era, permission was granted in 1955 to establish a 'Cultural association for German workers in Hungary' *(Kulturverband der deutschen Werktätigen in Ungarn)*. Its room to manoeuvre varied, depending on the current orientation of the Communist Party. Following the political changes in 1989, its name was changed to 'Association of Hungarian Germans' *(Verband der Ungarndeutschen)*, and it developed the 'Self-administration of the Hungarian Germans' *(Landesselbstverwaltung der Ungarndeutschen)*, the organisational framework for national minorities in Hungary on the basis of the Hungarian Minorities Law, which came into force in 1993.[50] Hungarian Germans thus benefited from the minority-friendly policy pursued by Hungary after the political changes of 1989 in order to improve the situation of Hungarian minorities abroad.[51] Accordingly, the representative bodies of the Hungarian Germans at national, regional and local level are the 'self-administrations', which represent the political, economic, social and cultural interests of

48 Further to the history of Hungarian Germans between 1918 and 1989: Seewann: Geschichte der Deutschen in Ungarn (Footnote 46), P. 188–406. cf. Scheuringer: Status und Perspektiven des Deutschen (Footnote 8), P. 21–23.

49 Knipf-Komlósi, Müller: Dynamische Aspekte in der Sprache der deutschen Minderheit in Ungarn (Footnote 47), P. 52. cf. BMI: Deutsche Minderheiten (Footnote 21), P. 75, 79–81. Christoph Pan reports that following the 2011 census there were 185,696 'Germans' in Hungary: Pan, Pfeil, Videsott: Die Volksgruppen in Europa (Footnote 4), P. 208–210. The German Federal Government Commissioner for Matters Related to Ethnic German Resettlers and National Minorities gives the same figure: Bernd Fabritius (Ed.): Tätigkeitsbericht des Beauftragten der Bundesregierung für Aussiedlerfragen und nationale Minderheiten. Zweites Amtsjahr, April 2019 – April 2020. Berlin 2020, P. 30, 53.

50 Tóth: Deutsche in Ungarn 1950–1970 (Footnote 47), P. 437–529.The 1993 Hungarian law for the Protection of National Minorities uses the historically established term 'nationalities' for indigenous ethnic minorities, and thus also for Hungarian Germans. According to this law, minority groups that have been living on Hungary's territory for at least one hundred years can be recognised as indigenous national minorities. Dziekonska, Dziekonski: Nationale Minderheiten in Osteuropa am Beispiel von Polen und Ungarn (Footnote 22), P. 176–184. cf. Koloman Brenner: Ausbau der kulturellen Autonomie der Ungarndeutschen. In: Frank Spengler, Gabriele Baumann (Eds.): Integration von religiösen und ethnischen Minderheiten im Osten Europas. Symposium der Konrad-Adenauer-Stiftung und des Rates der Deutschen in der Ukraine am 13. September 2016 in Uschhorod/Ungwar. Budapest 2016, P. 17–39, here P. 18–26.

51 Ralf Thomas Göllner: Ungarns Minderheitenpolitik von 1990 bis 2014. Minderheiten in Ungarn, Magyaren in den Nachbarstaaten. In: Herbert Küpper, Zsolt K. Lengyel, Hermann Scheuringer (Eds.): Ungarn 1989–2014. Eine Bilanz nach 25 Jahren. Regensburg 2015, P. 77–117.

the German minority in 13 districts and more than 400 towns and municipalities.[52] Hungarian Germans are represented in the Hungarian parliament by a 'speaker' who has the right to speak, but not to vote. Most Hungarian German localities have bilingual place-name signs.[53]

The self-governing bodies of the Hungarian Germans are responsible for more than 40 educational and cultural institutions, of which nine are supra-regional. The Association of Hungarian German Authors and Artists *(Verband Ungarndeutscher Autoren und Künstler)* is highly significant in the development of a regional German-language literary scene. The first priority for the Hungarian German self-governing bodies is to establish modern educational provision in mother-tongue German, because since the Second World War Hungarian has become the language of most families, often alongside standard or dialect German.[54] This change to Hungarian was slowed and to some extent reversed when, from the end of the 1970s, German-language education was once again fostered. German is taught as a 'mother tongue', 'minority language' or 'second language' with conscious reference to the ethnic identity of the Hungarian Germans at 28 bilingual primary schools and ten bilingual grammar schools, which the self-governing bodies of the Hungarian Germans are responsible. German language and literature, history, 'minority studies',[55] geography and some mathematics and biology lessons are taught in German. The principal centres for Hungarian German education are the Valeria-Koch School Centre in Fünfkirchen/Pécs, the Friedrich-Schiller Grammar School in Werischwar/Pilisvörösvár, the Budapest German Nationality Grammar School, and the Educational Centre in Frankenstadt/Baja.[56]

Most schools, however (there are around 280), teach all subjects in Hungarian and then also 'German language' for five lessons per week.[57] There are also German-language pre-schools, and German-language degree programmes at Hungarian universities and colleges, including four degree programmes for 'German as a minority

52 Seewann: Geschichte der Deutschen in Ungarn (Footnote 46), P. 403–406.

53 BMI: Deutsche Minderheiten (Footnote 21), P. 75.

54 Knipf-Komlósi, Müller: Dynamische Aspekte in der Sprache der deutschen Minderheit in Ungarn (Footnote 47), P. 56–59.

55 See the textbook recently published for this subject: Nóra Rutsch, Gerhard Seewann: Geschichte der Deutschen in Ungarn für die 9.–12. Klasse. Pécs/Fünfkirchen 2014.

56 Knipf-Komlósi, Müller: Dynamische Aspekte in der Sprache der deutschen Minderheit in Ungarn (Footnote 47), P. 64–66. cf. BMI: Deutsche Minderheiten (Footnote 21), P. 76.

57 Ibolya Hock-Englender: Das Sprachbildungsangebot für die deutsche Minderheit in Ungarn. In: Christoph Bergner, Hans Zehetmair (Eds.): Deutsch als Identitätssprache der deutschen Minderheiten. München 2014 (Argumente und Materialien zum Zeitgeschehen 92), P. 51–55. cf. Elisabeth Knipf-Komlósi: Ungarn. In: Ludwig M. Eichinger, Albrecht Plewnia, Claudia Maria Riehl (Eds.): Handbuch der deutschen Sprachminderheiten in Mittel- und Osteuropa. Tübingen 2008, P. 267–281.

language'.[58] German-language education receives important support by virtue of neighbouring countries that are part of the German-speaking area. The prospect of working in a German-speaking company in Hungary, Germany or Austria increases the attractiveness of German language lessons.

The status of the German language in Hungary is boosted by well-established German studies in universities and by German-language periodicals.[59] The *Neue Zeitung*, published weekly in Budapest, and the bi-monthly *Sonntagsblatt* are mainly aimed at the Hungarian German population; the *Budapester Zeitung*, on the other hand, is aimed at all German-speaking groups living in Hungary, including employees from Germany and Austria. The Hungarian Broadcasting Corporation broadcasts for two hours daily on two medium-wave frequencies to national minorities, and Radio Pécs/*Funkhaus Fünfkirchen* broadcasts for two hours daily to Hungarian Germans; one TV station broadcasts one hour-long programme a week in German.[60] Although these media offerings contribute to the consolidation of German language skills among Hungarian Germans, they will not be able to fully compensate for the constant decline in speakers of the Danube-Swabian dialects, as is the case in neighbouring countries. Nevertheless, linguists have observed a sustained revitalisation of the German language and culture among the Hungarian Germans, which – according to the self-governing bodies – should be stabilised through the considerable development of German-language educational institutions and a modern school system.[61]

The German minority in Romania

Compared to other states in East-Central and South-Eastern Europe, development in Romania after the war followed a somewhat different path. The relationship with Germany was not so heavily burdened by history, and Romania is not an immediate neighbour to the German-speaking countries, so the Romanian German minorities did not suffer expulsion. Nevertheless, the population (745,000 in 1930) fell by half between 1939 and 1949. In 1940, Germans living in Bukovina, Bessarabia, and Dobruja were resettled by Nazi Germany to the newly annexed eastern provinces of

58 Ammon: Die Stellung der deutschen Sprache (Footnote 5), P. 337–338.

59 Scheuringer: Status und Perspektiven des Deutschen (Footnote 8), P. 22.

60 Knipf-Komlósi, Müller: Dynamische Aspekte in der Sprache der deutschen Minderheit in Ungarn (Footnote 47), P. 53–54. cf. Brenner: Ausbau der kulturellen Autonomie der Ungarndeutschen (Footnote 50), P. 30–32.

61 Knipf-Komlósi, Müller: Dynamische Aspekte in der Sprache der deutschen Minderheit in Ungarn (Footnote 47), P. 66–67. cf. Ammon: Die Stellung der deutschen Sprache (Footnote 5), P. 334–341. cf. BMI: Deutsche Minderheiten (Footnote 21), P. 81.

the Reich. Most of the men serving in German military units who belonged to the Banat Swabian and Transylvanian Saxon populations that had remained in Romania were unable to return to Romania after the war, as was the case for a large number of the 70,000 younger Germans deported in 1945 by the Soviet Union to forced labour camps. The Romanian Germans were subjected to much discrimination of various kinds under the communist regime, and as a result the longing to emigrate grew year by year.[62] From the 1950s on, and especially after 1978, the communist regime allowed a small but growing number of Romanian Germans to 'buy' permission to emigrate to the Federal Republic of Germany each year. The dam broke after the end of the Ceaușescu-dictatorship in December 1989, and 111,150 Germans emigrated from Romania during the following 12 months alone. In the 2022 census, there were still 22,907 people in Romania declaring that they were of 'German nationality',[63] and 15,943 said they spoke German as their mother tongue. The main areas of German settlement are in Transylvania and the Banat. There are still some Germans living in the north-west of Romania (district of Satu-Mare), in southern Bukovina, and in the Romanian towns east and south of the Carpathians, especially Bucharest. In all localities, the German minority only makes up a small proportion of the population and does not reach the 20 per cent share required for bilingual place-name signs in any municipality or town. Nevertheless, several municipal parliaments have decided to make their town signs bilingual, e.g. Hermannstadt/Sibiu, the centre of the Transylvanian Saxon population.[64]

The political organisation of Romanian Germans is the Democratic Forum of Germans in Romania (*Demokratisches Forum der Deutschen in Rumänien*, DFDR). There

62 On the historical background, see: Harald Roth: Die deutsche Minderheit. Geschichte und Gegenwart. In: Durchblick. Politik und Gesellschaft in Rumänien. Osteuropa (2019), vol. 6–8, P. 63–72. During the later 1970s and the 1980s especially, the Ceaușescu-regime exercised a policy of assimilation towards national minorities: Born, Dickgießer: Deutschsprachige Minderheiten (Footnote 21), P. 177–178. cf. Cristian Cercel: Romanian Germans after the Second World War: Transnational History, Transnational Memory. In: Jahrbuch des Bundesinstituts für Kultur und Geschichte der Deutschen im östlichen Europa 24 (2016), P. 357–379, here P. 362–366. cf. James Koranyi: Migrating Memories. Romanian Germans in Modern Europe. Cambridge 2022 (New Studies in European History), P. 173–214.

63 Quo vadis, deutsche Minderheit? Volkszählung und Minderheiten: Ein Blick auf Sprache und Bildung. In: Allgemeine Deutsche Zeitung für Rumänien, 13. Januar 2023. In the 2011 census, 36,042 people in Romania declared their 'German nationality' and 27,019 stated that they spoke German as their mother tongue: Pan, Pfeil, Videsott: Die Volksgruppen in Europa (Footnote 4), P. 162–165.

64 Johanna Bottesch: Rumänien. In: Ludwig M. Eichinger, Albrecht Plewnia, Claudia Maria Riehl (Eds.): Handbuch der deutschen Sprachminderheiten in Mittel- und Osteuropa. Tübingen 2008, P. 331–344. cf. BMI: Deutsche Minderheiten (Footnote 21), P. 49–51. cf. Sergiu Constantin: Romanian Minority Politics and Policies in a European Context. In: Enikő Dácz (Ed.): Minderheitenfragen in Ungarn und in den Nachbarländern im 20. und 21. Jahrhundert. Baden-Baden 2013 (Andrássy Studien zur Europaforschung 8), P. 341–362.

are regional forums in the areas listed above, which are in turn subdivided into local forums. As with all recognised national minorities in Romania, Romanian Germans have one representative in parliament, and the DFDR is also represented by 7 mayors, 12 deputy mayors, over 150 town councillors, and several district councillors. The Transylvanian Saxons make up only 1.6 per cent of the population of their political and cultural centre Hermannstadt/Sibiu (147,000), but since the year 2000, the DFDR has held an absolute majority on the town council and the position of mayor. In 2014, the long-serving mayor of Hermannstadt/Sibiu and chairman of the DFDR, Klaus Johannis, was elected President of Romania (re-elected in 2019)[65] and was succeeded as mayor by Astrid Fodor, also member of the DFDR.

Another speciality is the Romanian German school system. Although it was nationalised after the Second World War and was subjected to severe restrictions, it was able to reorganise itself in the 1950s in accordance with the requirements of the communist regime. The traditional schools that used German as the teaching language – some of which were able to award the German Language Diploma of the German Standing Conference of the Ministers of Education and Cultural Affairs *(Deutsches Sprachdiplom der Kultusministerkonferenz)* – enjoyed an excellent reputation among Romanians and members of the Hungarian minority, so they were not forced to close following the mass emigration of Romanian Germans in the early 1990s. As a result, for Romanian Germans there has been a close match between national affiliation and the use of German as a mother tongue.[66] This changed after the turn of the millennium, as is demonstrated in the results of the 2011 and 2022 censuses. Together with the incidence of bilingualism, which shows that Romanian Germans are increasingly tending towards using the majority language, this suggests that the situation in Romania is becoming similar to that in the other countries examined above.[67] During 2014–2015, however, across Romania 17,000 schoolchildren attended the 84 mother-tongue German-language schools, of which some

65 Benjamin Józsa: Zur Lage der deutschen Minderheit in Rumänien. In: Frank Spengler, Bence Bauer (Eds.): Zur Situation der deutschen Minderheit in der Mitte Europas. Tagungsband der Konferenzen „Die Deutschen in Westungarn" der Konrad-Adenauer-Stiftung und der Landesselbstverwaltung der Ungarndeutschen am 19. Januar 2017 in Sopron/Ödenburg, Ungarn sowie „Zur Situation der deutschen Minderheit in der Mitte Europas" der Konrad-Adenauer-Stiftung und der Landsmannschaft der Donauschwaben in Kroatien am 7. September 2017 in Osijek/Essegg, Kroatien. Budapest 2017, P. 29–31.

66 Scheuringer: Status und Perspektiven des Deutschen (Footnote 8), P. 23–25. cf. Cristian Cercel: Romania and the Quest for European Identity. Philo-Germanism without Germans. London, New York 2019.

67 Christiane Cosmatu: Die deutsche Minderheit in Rumänien. In: Frank Spengler, Gabriele Baumann (Eds.): Integration von religiösen und ethnischen Minderheiten im Osten Europas. Symposium der Konrad-Adenauer-Stiftung und des Rates der Deutschen in der Ukraine am 13. September 2016 in Uschhorod/Ungwar. Budapest 2016, P. 40–44. cf. Ammon: Die Stellung der deutschen Sprache (Footnote 5), P. 341–349.

20 are grammar schools or secondary sections, and in which nearly all subjects are taught in German (Romanian as the state language is always taught as a main subject). A notable feature is the school subject 'History and traditions of the German minority in Romania', a clear sign that the mother-tongue German education system is designed to reinforce German identity.[68] Seven Romanian universities also offer a number of German-language degree programmes, and graduates have the prospect of well-paid jobs in the economy. However, this has led to an acute shortage of qualified German-speaking teachers, which is alleviated by a salary subsidy paid by the German government.[69]

German is also used as the official language in the Evangelical (Lutheran) Church of the Augsburg Confession, of which around a third of Romanian Germans are members, and which maintains several German-language cultural institutions, especially in its core region of Transylvania. There is also a German National Theatre in Temeswar/Timişoara, a German department in the National Theatre in Hermannstadt/Sibiu, a German-language research institute for humanities in the Romanian Academy in Hermannstadt, and the German-language publishing house 'Kriterion-Verlag' in Bucharest.[70] After the Second World War, the diverse German-language press in Romania was banned, although some German-language periodicals, such as the daily paper *Neuer Weg*, were established in order to promote the communist regime. From 1992, *Neuer Weg* was renamed *Allgemeine Deutsche Zeitung für Rumänien*, and it is now the only German-language daily newspaper in Eastern Europe, alongside three weekly German newspapers in Romania.[71] There are a further forty or more German-language periodical publications, such as association and church newsletters. Six Romanian radio stations broadcast German-language programmes, and the national TV station broadcasts two short German programmes each week.[72]

The German minority population in Romania is ageing fast, which is the principal reason for its falling numbers, so the German-language cultural institutions, media and school system are dependent for their future on continuing interest among the majority population in the German language and German culture.

68 Hannelore Baier, Martin Bottesch, Dieter Nowak, Alfred Wiecken, Winfried Ziegler: Geschichte und Traditionen der deutschen Minderheit in Rumänien. Lehrbuch für die 6. und 7. Klasse der Schulen mit deutscher Unterrichtssprache. Mediaş 2004.

69 BMI: Deutsche Minderheiten (Footnote 21), P. 47–48. See: Deutschland unterstützt erneut die Förderung von Lehrkräften im deutschsprachigen Schulwesen in Rumänien. In: Allgemeine Deutsche Zeitung für Rumänien, 3 September 2022. cf. Cordell, Wolff: Germany as a Kin-State (Footnote 18), P. 304–305.

70 BMI: Deutsche Minderheiten (Footnote 21), P. 48.

71 Annett Müller: Abschied in Raten. Vom Neuen Weg zur Allgemeinen Deutschen Zeitung für Rumänien. Der Wandel der Zeitung nach der massenhaften Auswanderung der Deutschen aus Rumänien. Hermannstadt 2002, P. 40–121.

72 Bottesch: Rumänien (Footnote 64), P. 331–348.

The German minorities in the states of the former Soviet Union

At the start of the 2020s, around 650,000 Germans were living in the states of the former Soviet Union, principally in the Russian Federation (c. 400,000), Kazakhstan (182,000) and Ukraine (33,000), with a further 30,000 Germans living in Belarus, the Moldavian Republic, Georgia, Armenia, Azerbaijan, Kyrgyzstan, Tajikistan, Turkmenistan, and Uzbekistan.[73]

The main area of German settlement in Russia is in Siberia, which goes back to the deportation of Russian Germans there in 1941. The population is therefore very scattered among areas that are generally very distant from each other. The number of people in the German-minority population derives from the census, which follows the pattern used in Soviet times and uses 'nationality' in the sense of origin, and mother tongue as criteria. Soviet passports include a note of national affiliation, and this practice has become among Russian Germans – who had few other ways to identify themselves as a community – a strong identity-forming effect. Following a failed attempt to re-establish the prewar Volga German Autonomous Republic, in 1996 the Federal German National Cultural Autonomy *(Föderale deutsche nationale Kulturautonomie)* was established to represent the interests of Russian Germans, though the lack of financial support from the state means that this representative body is only able to fulfil a fraction of its functions. Although its chairman belongs to the board of the Council for Relations between National Groups alongside the president of the Russian Federation, the Russian German population exerts very little influence on Moscow's political decisions, and does not even have a representative in the Duma. Their situation has become dramatically more difficult since the start of Russia's full-scale invasion of Ukraine. A distinctive feature of the legal position of the Russian Germans is that the legal standards that were established in Moscow in the 1990s and were favourable to them have not been properly implemented. The association 'Renaissance' *(Wiedergeburt)* was established in 1989 to foster efforts to re-establish their autonomous national territory. In 1991 the International Association for German Culture (*Internationale Verband der deutschen Kultur*, IVDK) was also established as an interest group for Russian German community centres, which carries out numerous cultural and educational projects, in particular to maintain the cultural heritage and to retain – or in some cases revive – knowledge of the German language. Language skills had been largely eroded because, following the Second World War, the state banned the use of the German language. In the 2010 census, 42,421 people declared that German was their mother tongue. This represents 10.78 per cent of those who claim to belong to the German minority in Rus-

73 Fabritius: Tätigkeitsbericht des Beauftragten 2019–2020 (Footnote 49), P. 21–29, 53. cf. BMI: Deutsche Minderheiten (Footnote 21), P. 7.

sia. In 2009, an ethnosociological survey found that only 30.6 per cent of Russian Germans speak German as a mother tongue. Projects coordinated by the Russian German Youth Association *(Jugendring)* therefore lay particular emphasis on language acquisition in childhood. Because the language skills of so many Russian German schoolchildren are so poor, recent years have seen the extra subject 'German as mother tongue' offered in some Russian schools developed into a wider programme, available to all children, teaching German as a foreign language. Communication between the extremely widely scattered Russian German population groups is now conducted over the internet and through the only nationally distributed German-language weekly paper, the *Moskauer Deutsche Zeitung*.[74]

A sister publication appears as the *Deutsche Allgemeine Zeitung* in Almaty in Kazakhstan. The only weekly German-language newspaper in post-Soviet Central Asia, it was established in 1966 as the voice of the nearly one million strong German population in Kazakhstan. Aside from a few villages colonised by Germans before the First World War, this population arose from the deportation of Russian Germans into this Soviet Republic in 1941. Political and economic conditions in the Central Asian republics in the early 1990s were especially difficult, so that a far higher proportion of the Germans living in the region sought to emigrate than in Russia.

Those who remained have joined forces in the Association of Kazakh German Social Organisations – Renaissance *(Assoziation der gesellschaftlichen Vereinigungen der Deutschen Kasachstans, AgVDK – Wiedergeburt)*, whose 20 member organisations are mainly active in the north and east of the country. The AgVDK belongs to the 'Assembly of the People of Kazakhstan', a constitutional body that enables the more than 130 ethnic groups in the country to participate in political life. It elects 9 of the 107 members of the Kazakh lower house of parliament. The German group emphasises its claim to act as a bridge between Kazakhstan and Germany, especially in terms of the economy, through the activity of the German-Kazakh Association of Entrepreneurs *(Deutsch-Kasachische Assoziation der Unternehmer)*. The government of Kazakhstan shares this view, and in collaboration with the German government it fosters German cultural institutions such as the German Theatre in Almaty and German-language media (radio programmes). The German House *(Deutsches Haus)* in Almaty is especially active in coordinating the cultural, social, and economic activities of the German minority. These activities are focused, as in the other post-

74 Nina Berend, Claudia Maria Riehl: Russland. In: Ludwig M. Eichinger, Albrecht Plewnia, Claudia Maria Riehl (Eds.): Handbuch der deutschen Sprachminderheiten in Mittel- und Osteuropa. Tübingen 2008, P. 19–33. cf. Eisfeld: Vom Stolperstein zur Brücke (Footnote 16), P. 85–89. cf. Cordell, Wolff: Germany as a Kin-State (Footnote 18), P. 302–303. cf. György Dalos: Geschichte der Russlanddeutschen. Von Katharina der Großen bis zur Gegenwart. München 2014.

Soviet republics, on maintaining and reviving German-language skills and on securing the German population's cultural heritage.[75]

This is also the case for the German minority in Ukraine. At the start of the 2020s, some 33,000 Germans were living in Ukraine, mostly in the east and south of the country, and were recognised as a 'national minority'. As it did in Russia, the organisation *Wiedergeburt* established around 60 German community centres. Approximately 140 German associations and organisations, including two supra-regional theatre and singing groups, were coordinated and represented by the umbrella organisation Council of the Germans in Ukraine *(Rat der Deutschen der Ukraine).* Larger German groups also lived in Odessa, Kyiv and in Transcarpathia, on the border with Hungary. As in Kazakhstan, the transmission of German as mother tongue is only happening through language courses offered by the relevant community centre, often in the context of Sunday schools or in collaboration with the Goethe Institute. State schools only teach German as a second foreign language, and this is available in 52 per cent of Ukrainian schools.[76]

The German minority populations were hit hard by the annexation of Crimea in 2014, by the fighting in Luhansk and Donezk, and especially in 2022 by the full-scale invasion of Ukraine by Russia, since their settlement areas are principally in the conflict areas in the east and south of the country. Large numbers of people from the German minority have fled Ukraine to seek shelter in Germany. Many of these migrants are no longer expecting to return to their homes and have applied to be 'late resettlers' *(Spätaussiedler)* to Germany. The German government has therefore set up a hardship case process in which such resettlers can be assessed verbally at the Friedland transit camp, to check that they meet the conditions for late resettlers of the Federal Law on Expelled Persons (*Bundesvertriebenengesetz*, BVFG), and do not need to wait to be assessed in their home country (Ukraine).[77] The German government also gives support to a crisis centre established by the Council of the Germans in Ukraine, which offers various forms of help to members of the German minority still living in Ukraine.[78]

75 These activities are carried out in particular with the support of the Goethe Institute's language teaching centres in Almaty: Goethe-Institut: Das Goethe-Institut fördert deutsche Minderheiten (Footnote 21), P. 11, 14–15. cf. Berend, Riehl: Russland (Footnote 74), P. 19–33.

76 Olga Hvozdyak: Ukraine. In: Ludwig M. Eichinger, Albrecht Plewnia, Claudia Maria Riehl (Eds.): Handbuch der deutschen Sprachminderheiten in Mittel- und Osteuropa. Tübingen 2008, P. 85–103. cf. Peter Hilkes: Migrationsverläufe: Aussiedlerzuwanderung aus der Ukraine. In: Klaus J. Bade, Jochen Oltmer (Eds.): Aussiedler: deutsche Einwanderer aus Osteuropa. 2nd edn, Göttingen 2003, P. 55–79.

77 https://www.aussiedlerbeauftragte.de/SharedDocs/kurzmeldungen/Webs/AUSB/DE/2022/01–03/20220311-haertefallverfahren-ukraine.html (accessed 11.03.2022).

78 https://www.aussiedlerbeauftragte.de/SharedDocs/kurzmeldungen/Webs/AUSB/DE/2022/04–06/20220517-dt-minderheit-ukraine.html (accessed 17.05.2022).

The promotion of German minorities living in Eastern Europe by the Federal Republic of Germany

The greatest challenges faced by most of the German minorities are their diminishing numbers (due to the mass expulsion or emigration of their members) and the loss of their language in the years following the Second World War. These minority populations also often endure intergenerational conflicts caused by differing attitudes to a possible emigration to Germany and issues arising from their relationship with the majority population or with maintaining their customs. Nevertheless, the German minority groups, especially in Russia, Poland, Hungary and Romania, have been able to consolidate their community life, which is now largely supported by a younger generation. Following the political change in 1989, there was a significant improvement in the framework conditions for the political, cultural, social, and economic development of the minority communities. This was to some extent enabled by the European Council's Agreements on Minorities, but also by the growing openness on the part of majority populations to consider the needs of the German minority populations (though this varies from country to country).[79] Since national minorities are principally defined by their language, most German minorities face the question of whether they will succeed in maintaining or reviving the use of the mother tongue. Given the small numbers in these minority populations, it is understood that the prospect of ongoing survival is dependent on certain framework conditions. Policies in their home countries (and also in Germany) therefore need to have a positive attitude to minority populations and German-language school systems, media outputs, and cultural institutions.[80]

The legal context

At the European level, there are a number of international law agreements on protecting and maintaining national minority groups and their languages. These are examined in greater detail elsewhere in this collected volume and will therefore be described only briefly here.[81] The Organization for Security and Cooperation in Europe (OSCE), in its 1990 Copenhagen Declaration, agreed to provisions on the

79 Pan, Pfeil, Videsott: Die Volksgruppen in Europa (Footnote 4), P. 71–218. cf. Vladimir Wakounig: Interethnische Beziehungen zwischen Minderheit und Mehrheit. Ein (Macht-) Verhältnis auf gleicher Augenhöhe? In: Enikő Dácz (Ed.): Minderheitenfragen in Ungarn und in den Nachbarländern im 20. und 21. Jahrhundert. Baden-Baden 2013 (Andrássy Studien zur Europaforschung 8), P. 239–258.

80 Cosmatu: Die deutsche Minderheit in Rumänien (Footnote 67), P. 41.

81 Hofmann: Minderheitenschutz in Europa (Footnote 3), P. 9–12.

protection of minorities, and in 1992 it established the Office of the High Commissioner on National Minorities, which has its headquarters in The Hague.

Minorities living in member states of the Council of Europe are protected by the 1995 Framework Convention for the Protection of National Minorities. This prohibits discrimination towards anyone for their membership of a national minority, and any efforts to assimilate them against their will. Member states are moreover required to defend the legal freedoms of national minorities and to offer them all the support they need. They must report every five years to the Council of Europe. The 1992 European Charter for Regional or Minority Languages is also relevant here. It takes as its starting point the inalienable right of each person to use their own regional or minority language both in private and in public. According to the Charter, minority and regional languages traditionally spoken in one of the signatory states are to be protected and fostered as an endangered aspect of European cultural heritage. This must be reported on every three years to the Council of Europe. The two agreements mentioned above came into force in 1998.[82]

Bilateral treaties between Germany and its neighbours to the east provide further legal frameworks.[83] Germany has made agreements with several of its neighbour states in Eastern Europe, designated as 'Agreement on [good neighbourliness and] friendly cooperation [and partnership in Europe]', including with Poland (1991), Hungary (1992), Romania (1992), and Czechoslovakia (1992), which enable the German government to promote German minorities. Numerous other states have made similar agreements, creating a close network of such treaties across Europe.[84] The 1991 agreement between Germany and Poland, for example, explicitly confirms

---

82 Liv Jaeckel: Der Minderheitenschutz im Völkerrecht – ein System im Werden. In: Frank-Lothar Kroll, Matthias Niedobitek (Eds.): Vertreibung und Minderheitenschutz in Europa. Berlin 2005, P. 174–180. cf. Christoph Schnellbach: Internationalisierung des Minderheitenrechts. In: Enikő Dácz (Ed.): Minderheitenfragen in Ungarn und in den Nachbarländern im 20. und 21. Jahrhundert. Baden-Baden 2013 (Andrássy Studien zur Europaforschung 8), P. 13–28. cf. Günther Rautz: Die europäische Dimension von Minderheitenrechten. In: Enikő Dácz (Ed.): Minderheitenfragen in Ungarn und in den Nachbarländern im 20. und 21. Jahrhundert. Baden-Baden 2013 (Andrássy Studien zur Europaforschung 8), P. 29–44.

83 On the protection to be offered by 'kin states': Pan, Pfeil, Videsott: Die Volksgruppen in Europa (Footnote 4), P. 311–324. cf. Peter Hilpold, Christoph Perathoner: Die Schutzfunktion des Mutterstaates im Minderheitenrecht (The 'kin-state'). Eine völkerrechtliche und europarechtliche Untersuchung unter besonderer Berücksichtigung der Schutzfunktion Österreichs gegenüber der deutsch- und ladinischsprachigen Volksgruppe in Südtirol sowie der Diskussion um das ungarische Statusgesetz. Berlin 2006.

84 In 2008, there were 186 comparable bilateral agreements in Europe. There is a comprehensive examination of the many bilateral agreements that address the protection of minorities in: Björn Arp: International Norms and Standards for the Protection of National Minorities. Bilateral and Multilateral Texts with Commentary. Leiden, Boston 2008, P. 217–495. cf. Cordell, Wolff: Germany as a Kin-State (Footnote 18), P. 309.

that the parties to the treaty are required to 'enable and facilitate' (Art. 21) the lives of the German minority in Poland (and those of Poles living in Germany).[85]

The treaties, agreements and declarations between Germany and other states mentioned above provide for annual planning meetings and round-table discussions between representatives of the relevant governments, or bilateral government commissions, for the purpose of supporting German minorities.[86] The 'Protocol on the gradual restoration of statehood for the Russian Germans' *(Protokoll zur stufenweisen Wiederherstellung der Staatlichkeit der Russlanddeutschen)* signed between Germany and Russia in 1992 forms the basis for the activities of the German-Russian Government Commission for the Affairs of the Russian Germans, which met with the participation of the self-organising bodies of the Russian Germans.[87]

The political context and the objectives of the promotion policy

German minority policy is based on the Federal Republic of Germany's solidarity with the German minorities in East-Central and South-Eastern Europe, and in the states of the former Soviet Union. The Federal Republic views their support for German minorities abroad as a voluntary commitment. This results from the special historical and moral responsibility for those people who, due to their belonging to German minorities in Eastern Europe, became the object of National Socialist 'Ostpolitik' and victims of Germany's resettlement campaigns, for example in the Baltic states and South-East Europe, which they had to leave in 1939–1940. This sense of solidarity was further reinforced by the fact that the German minorities were, after the Second World War, collectively taken into detention and subjected to associated acts of repression simply because of their German ethnicity, on account of the crimes of the Nazi regime. The consequences of this repression last until the present day, in that the German minority communities are suffering from disintegration as a result of flight, expulsion, and deportation, and because of the suppression of their language use and cultural practices by the communist regimes after 1945, which led to further loss of their mother-tongue. Acknowledgement

85 Jaeckel: Der Minderheitenschutz im Völkerrecht (Footnote 82), P. 180–181.

86 cf. Bergner, Zehetmair: Deutsch als Identitätssprache (Footnote 21), P. 71–74. cf. Matthias Weber: Minderheitenfragen als Thema aktueller Kulturpolitik. In: Cornelia Eisler, Silke Göttsch-Elten (Eds.): Minderheiten im Europa der Zwischenkriegszeit. Wissenschaftliche Konzeptionen, mediale Vermittlung, politische Funktion. Münster 2017, P. 33–42.

87 The commission's work was suspended in 2022: Natalie Pawlik (Ed.): Tätigkeitsbericht der Beauftragten der Bundesregierung für Aussiedlerfragen und nationale Minderheiten. April 2022 – Mai 2025. Berlin 2025, P. 33. cf. the review 'Zwischenstaatliche Erklärungen und Vereinbarungen der Bundesregierung betreffend die Belange der deutschen Minderheiten' in: Bergner, Weber (Eds.): Aussiedler- und Minderheitenpolitik in Deutschland (Footnote 4), P. 254–260.

of responsibility for the above-mentioned traumatic events and the desire to offer compensation for injustice and oppression have led to political conditions in which the German government offers support for German minorities abroad. In this context, the German government is committed to the principle of agreement with the respective countries in which the minorities live. The government lays great store by acknowledging that Germany and the home countries of the minorities are jointly responsible for the existence of the German minority populations. So, for example, they work to ensure that the support available benefits not only the German minority population, but also that country's majority population in the settlement areas of the German minorities.[88]

Beyond coping with the consequences of the war, the German government also aims to establish structures and partnerships in Europe designed to secure peace. It views the German minorities, not only as bicultural links, but also as carriers of partnership relationships. Germany's historical and political responsibility is understood explicitly to include fostering the regional culture in the former home areas of the German population groups, some of whom had, since the Middle Ages, been engaged in mutual exchanges with their neighbours and built up a rich and varied cultural heritage. In this context, the support is no longer – as it often was before the turn of the millennium – mainly aiming to improve living conditions and economic aspects. Instead, the support offered now focuses on fostering self-help in order to enable the German minorities to control and manage their own lives and circumstances. Help is therefore offered in particular in strengthening cultural identity, improving language skills, and establishing efficient self-organising bodies. One especially important objective is to sustain German-language school systems and German-language courses in the community centres where the German-minority population groups meet. When members of German minorities succeed in improving or recovering their German-language skills, they are in a better position to realise their desire for a more clearly defined identity; they are moreover able to use their multilingualism not only to improve their own life chances but also to serve as a bridge between the local majority population and Germany. A further purpose for the German government in providing com-

88 Cordell, Wolff: Germany as a Kin-State (Footnote 18), P. 296–297, 309–310. cf. Christoph Bergner: Thesen zur Fachtagung „Zwei Jahrzehnte Politik für Aussiedler und nationale Minderheiten – Bilanz und Perspektiven". In: Christoph Bergner, Matthias Weber (Eds.): Aussiedler- und Minderheitenpolitik in Deutschland. Bilanz und Perspektiven. München 2009 (Schriften des Bundesinstituts für Kultur und Geschichte der Deutschen im östlichen Europa 38), P. 23–30, here P. 24–25. cf. Christoph Bergner: Revitalisierung der deutschen Sprache als Identitätssprache. Sprachbildungsarbeit für die deutschen Minderheiten im Rahmen der deutschen Hilfenpolitik. In: Christoph Bergner, Hans Zehetmair (Eds.): Deutsch als Identitätssprache der deutschen Minderheiten. München 2014 (Argumente und Materialien zum Zeitgeschehen 92), P. 19–22. cf. Weber: Deutsche Minderheiten (Footnote 7), P. 37–38.

munity centres in German-minority settlement areas is to improve the range of German-language courses available, as they often need to compensate for the lack of mother-tongue teaching in public schools. These centres also fulfil an important community-building function in that they offer a forum for those living in diaspora to meet and maintain their cultural identity.

Promoting German-language media also helps to maintain language skills and customs, and to transmit knowledge of the history and traditions of the German minority populations. They provide, not only a forum for communication within the minority population group, but also a connection between the majority population and Germany. Support for new media gives an important boost to the involvement of the younger generation in a German minority population; this serves to develop networkers whose commitment is a central precondition for the preservation and further development of the specific minority culture. For German-minority groups to be able to take part in cultural debates and in political decision-making in their home country, and to give voice to the interests of their community in parliament and other representative forums, they need to not only be engaged as citizens, but also to have effective structures for self-administration. Support offered to minority populations seeks to strengthen such structures, since the associations, organisations and institutions of the German minorities play an important part, not only in the political sphere, but also in the civic life in each minority's home country. The German government places particular emphasis on supporting politically engaged German-minority associations, since it values their efforts to foster the process of European integration and the development of democratic and rule-of-law structures in their host-states. A further aim of the German government is to strengthen the church structures among the German minority communities: because of their public law status, and because of their longevity, not only do churches play a crucial role in promoting community life, but have often been the only institutions able to preserve the community's material cultural heritage. And finally, German governments estimate that their work supporting German minorities abroad serves three further purposes: it promotes transnational dialogue between civil societies, it contributes to healing historic animosity, and it deepens bilateral relations between Germany and its neighbours to the East.[89]

This summary of the political aims claimed by the German government clearly shows that it is seeking to minimise any possible conflict and to emphasise the value to Europe of maintaining cultural diversity. This also takes into account the fact that

89 cf. Koloman Brenner: Deutsch(e) in Mittel-Ost-Europa. In: Christoph Bergner, Hans Zehetmair (Eds.): Deutsch als Identitätssprache der deutschen Minderheiten. München 2014 (Argumente und Materialien zum Zeitgeschehen 92), P. 71–74. cf. Wakounig: Interethnische Beziehungen zwischen Minderheit und Mehrheit (Footnote 79), P. 239–258. cf. Koranyi: Migrating Memories (Footnote 62), P. 215–252.

there is a political consensus in Germany not to accept foreign policy tensions that could arise from the active promotion of kin-minorities abroad.[90] This principle is based on another broad political consensus in Germany, namely the continuation of the 'Ostpolitik' initiated by Willy Brandt. Before 1989, it was aimed at maintaining peace in Europe, reconciliation between Germany and its eastern neighbours and 'change through rapprochement', but after 1989 the latter was replaced by promotion of the eastward expansion of NATO and the EU. The first two objectives have remained an unreserved part of German Ostpolitik to the present day, even though Germany's political and economic weight has increased considerably since the end of the East–West conflict and reunification, and with it, its ability to exert influence in Eastern Europe. The German return to a policy of strength expected by several political analysts failed to materialise after 1990, especially as the Berlin Republic opted for continuity, and not just with Germany's ties to the West and its integration policy at European level. From Berlin's perspective, the eastward expansion of the EU helped to create an area of peaceful and democratic states on Germany's eastern border – Germany is intertwined with these states in many ways under the common umbrella of the EU and a new collective security order – and to promote economic transformation and development in Central Europe, thereby realising the main objectives of Ostpolitik since the 1970s. This German policy was stabilised by the successful integration of 16.5 million German refugees, expellees, ethnic German resettlers and late resettlers, whose representatives were included in Germany's external minority policy. Before 1989, the promotion of German minorities in Eastern Europe by the Federal Republic of Germany had to be limited to improving their humanitarian situation on the one hand, and expanding their opportunities to migrate to the Federal Republic on the other. This was particularly possible after the establishment of diplomatic relations with the countries of the Eastern Bloc. Completely new possibilities opened up after the fall of the Iron Curtain. This event offered German minorities certain opportunities to develop politically, economically and culturally in their home countries – as well as the option of migrating to Germany. The latter option was chosen by the vast majority, who were traumatised by developments after 1945 and had lost confidence in their host-states. After 1993, the German government endeavoured to limit the number of late resettlers entering the country to less than 100,000 per year by tightening the admission requirements; this was only achieved from 1998 onwards.

At the same time, this goal was achieved by improving the living conditions of the ethnic Germans outside Germany, as the federal government intended to open up

90 Further information about German minorities and the support offered to them by the German government is in: Bernd Fabritius (Ed.): Tätigkeitsbericht des Beauftragten der Bundesregierung für Aussiedlerfragen und nationale Minderheiten. Erstes Amtsjahr, April 2018 – April 2019. Berlin 2019. cf. Fabritius: Tätigkeitsbericht des Beauftragten 2019–2020 (Footnote 49), P. 18–39.

future prospects for them. However, Germany avoided improving the legal status of members of the German minorities who were unable or unwilling to leave for Germany, e.g. by granting them German citizenship, as some states in Eastern Europe did in the 1990s, for example Hungary, which came into conflict with neighbouring states. Germany thus made it clear that it did not want to abandon the principles on which its Ostpolitik was based. The German government was convinced that it could only offer German minorities the prospect of remaining if it combined concrete, bilateral aid measures, which have already been discussed in detail in this text, with an improvement in macro conditions. The EU's eastward enlargement and the Europe-wide improvement of rights for national minorities brought it a good deal closer to achieving these macro improvements.[91]

Players within the Federal German government

Three ministries within the German government are tasked with supporting German minority populations in Eastern Europe. The Federal Foreign Office funds cultural, scientific and media policy projects as well as measures to promote the language skills of German minorities (approx. EUR 2,8 million in 2024). Activities are implemented by intermediary organisations such as the Institute for Foreign Relations *(Institut für Auslandsbeziehungen)* in Stuttgart, the Goethe Institute in Munich, the Central Office for Education Abroad in the Federal Office for Foreign Affairs *(Zentralstelle für das Auslandsschulwesen im Bundesamt für Auswärtige Angelegenheiten)*, and the German Academic Exchange Service (Deutscher Akademischer Austauschdienst) in Bonn.[92]

The Federal Government Commissioner for Matters Related to Ethnic German Resettlers and National Minorities in the Federal Ministry of the Interior and Community is responsible for coordinating support efforts on behalf of the German minorities in Eastern Europe; some of these measures are implemented by intermediary organisations such as the German Society for International Cooperation (*Deutsche Gesellschaft für Internationale Zusammenarbeit*, GIZ). The resettlers commissioner, whose office was set up in 1988 and who is responsible for the four recognised national minorities within Germany since 2002, holds the office of German co-chair of the established bilateral governmental commissions for the affairs of German

91 For detailed information: Cordell, Wolff: Germany as a Kin-State (Footnote 18), P. 294–302, 306–308.

92 Ammon: Die Stellung der deutschen Sprache (Footnote 5), P. 264–266. cf. Andreas Meitzner: Die Rolle des Auswärtigen Amtes bei der Förderung von Minderheiten. In: Christoph Bergner, Hans Zehetmair (Eds.): Deutsch als Identitätssprache der deutschen Minderheiten. München 2014 (Argumente und Materialien zum Zeitgeschehen 92), P. 23–24. cf. Stiftung Verbundenheit mit den Deutschen im Ausland: Memorandum (Footnote 21), P. 3.

minorities. The commissioner supports cultural activities, projects fostering the self-administration structures of German minorities, and social and charitable activities. In 2024, the Federal Ministry of the Interior and Community supported the German minorities with around 25 million euros.[93]

In accordance with Paragraph 96 of the Federal Law on Expelled Persons (*Bundesvertriebenengesetz*, BVFG), the Federal Government Commissioner for Culture and the Media, who is a Minister of State in the German Federal Chancellery, promotes in the German minorities settlement areas projects to protect monuments (around 0.5 million EUR per year) and events to communicate German culture and history in Eastern Europe.[94] The German minorities in Eastern Europe are often taken into account in the Federal Government's concept for cultural and scientific funding under Paragraph 96 BVFG, which was updated in 2016.[95] The new Federal Government elected in 2025 plans to merge the responsibilities described above, which were previously divided between three ministries, into the Federal Ministry of the Interior.[96]

In order to manage the support for German minorities in coordination with the relevant neighbouring countries, so-called 'joint government commissions' are being established. Members of the commissions are drawn from representatives of the Federal ministries mentioned above and the institutions and associations of German-minority groups. They meet within the framework of the above-mentioned commissions for regular bilateral talks with the relevant ministries in the partner nations. So far, bilateral government commissions have been established between Germany and Kazakhstan, Kyrgyzstan, Poland, Romania, Russia, Hungary, Ukraine, and Uzbekistan.[97]

---

93 Fabritius: Tätigkeitsbericht des Beauftragten 2018–2019 (Footnote 90), P. 14–25. cf. Fabritius: Tätigkeitsbericht des Beauftragten 2019–2020 (Footnote 49), P. 18–39. cf. Stiftung Verbundenheit mit den Deutschen im Ausland: Memorandum (Footnote 21), P. 3. Further information on the current situation of German minorities and the support offered to them by the Federal German government is available via the homepage of the Federal Government Commissioner for Matters Related to Ethnic German Resettlers and National Minorities: https://www.aussiedlerbeauftragte.de/Webs/AUSB/DE/startseite/startseite-node.html (accessed 24.01.2024).

94 cf. the 'Bericht der Bundesregierung über die Maßnahmen zur Förderung der Kulturarbeit gemäß § 96 des Bundesvertriebenengesetzes in den Jahren 2021 und 2022': https://dip.bundestag.de/vorgang/bericht-der-bundesregierung-über-die-maßnahmen-zur-förderung-der-kulturarbeit/303353 (accessed 24.01.2024).

95 Deutscher Bundestag, 18. Wahlperiode, Drucksache 18/7730, 25.02.2016, 'Weiterentwicklung der Konzeption zur Erforschung, Bewahrung, Präsentation und Vermittlung der Kultur und Geschichte der Deutschen im östlichen Europa nach § 96 des Bundesvertriebenengesetzes': https://dip.bundestag.de/vorgang/weiterentwicklung-der-konzeption-zur-erforschung-bewahrung-präsentation-und-vermittlung-der/72691?f.deskriptor=Heimatvertriebener&start=25&rows=25&pos=31 (accessed 24.01.2024).

96 https://www.koalitionsvertrag2025.de/(accessed 01.07.2025).

97 Fabritius: Tätigkeitsbericht des Beauftragten 2019–2020 (Footnote 49), P. 18–39.

Conclusion

This review of the history of German minorities in Eastern Europe illustrates the importance of looking at history in any evaluation of the present. When assessing the extent of the groups claiming German ancestry or declaring that German is their mother tongue, both the relevant political situation and the historical background must be kept in mind, since any such claim – whether subjective or objective – can have associated advantages and disadvantages. This factor is particularly applicable in the case of so-called 'diaspora minorities', a category that encompasses all the German minorities in Eastern Europe. An examination of the history of these minorities highlights the many difficulties and challenges that they face in the present time. Between them, the consequences of the Second World War – initiated by Germany – and the Nazi annihilation policy carried out in Eastern Europe led to the end of a centuries-long history of Germans living in many parts of Eastern, East-Central, and South-Eastern Europe as they were expelled or driven to flee. Until the political turning point of 1989, the German minority populations who stayed behind suffered all kinds of repressive measures, from persecution and denial of their existence to consistent marginalisation. This discrimination, and the fact that they were banned from learning or speaking the German language, meant that many members of the German minorities stopped acknowledging their ethnic roots, and it became hugely challenging for them to maintain knowledge of their language.

It is important to bear in mind the relationship between the German minorities and the kin-state Germany, and the quality of the relations between Germany and the host-states of the German minorities, in particular the importance that each country assigns to their German minority population. This can be measured, for example, by whether members of the German minority get elected to senior political positions, such as Rudolf Schuster (President of Slovakia, 1999–2004), Ferenc Mádl (President of Hungary, 2000–2005) and Klaus Johannis (President of Romania 2014–2025).

It is a positive advantage shared by all German-speaking minorities in Europe that over 100 million people speak German as a mother tongue or a second mother tongue, and many millions more speak it as a foreign language. In economic terms, it is one of the most significant language communities in the world, such that German minority populations and their neighbours derive positive benefits from maintaining and/or acquiring the language, in terms of access to the labour market and education.

The bilingualism or multilingualism of all German-speaking minorities in Europe can be described as ambivalent. On the one hand, this enables the much-cited bridging function of these minorities between Germany and their respective home countries, but on the other hand it often represents a preliminary stage on the way to complete conversion to the majority language. Another factor limiting the maintenance of German in German-speaking minorities is that, in spite of their close economic contacts with Germany, the English language is gaining ground in everyday business dealings, so that German remains marginalised in the public sphere in the countries we have been looking at. The option to use bilingual place-name signs has done little to change this.

The German used by the minorities is therefore being reduced to a 'proximity language', i.e. a language that is limited to everyday communication amongst families, friends, minority group events, and church communities. German can therefore maintain its position as both a 'language of proximity' and a 'language of distance', i.e. a language that plays an important role in the economic or cultural life of the countries concerned, in those countries where a German-language education system exists, such as in Romania. Because of the diaspora situation, it is very challenging to maintain German-language institutions, educational establishments, and media.

The German minorities themselves, it is clear, see the continued existence of their own group to be the greatest challenge they face. Minority associations therefore now focus their attention on consolidating and extending German-language skills and on transmitting these language skills, and for each specific minority group to pass on knowledge of its history and traditions to its own younger generation. The German Federal Republic plays its part here through the support it gives to German minorities, without treating them as objects of further foreign policy objectives. However, all German governments after 1990 have emphasised that this support should be provided in harmony with the respective host-state of the German minorities and that the promotion should not cause any foreign policy tensions.

Politically, the aim of the German government in supporting German minorities in Eastern Europe is that members of those minority populations who have not chosen, or not been able, to migrate back to Germany are offered clear options enabling them to stay in their home country. The help offered is principally economic and social, and through projects that foster the German language and secure the German identity of the minority German population concerned. In keeping with the principle of promoting self-help, the German government encourages the establishment of future-proofed self-administration structures to enable the German minority in each country to contribute to shaping society in the country in which they live. The aim is to enable German minority populations to develop cultural bridges and networks and establish lasting civil society links between Germany and their home country. The success of these measures will, in the end, depend not only on Germany and the specific German minority population, but also, to a large extent, on whether they are supported by their host-state.

Dieter W. Halwachs

Roma – A Stateless European Minority

Roma, Sinti, Kale, Romanichal…

The Roma are often the focus of public attention, since they are probably the most numerous stateless minority in Europe, estimated to number as many as 12 million. The defining attributes of this group are nevertheless still not clear. There are three possible basic definitions:

1) A general social definition (they are marginalised groups, subject to discrimination)
2) A wide ethnic definition (they are marginalised groups of Indian origin, subject to discrimination)
3) A narrow ethnic definition (they are marginalised groups of Indian origin, subject to discrimination, and they call themselves 'Roma')

The general definition of 'Roma' replaces in all European languages widely used pejorative terms such as 'Gypsy'. 'Gypsy' is frequently used to describe socio-economically marginalised population groups who exhibit sociocultural difference, or have it attributed to them, and suffer discrimination as a result. This usage is present, for example, in the texts of the European Union:

> This study uses the term 'Roma' as the plural noun form, as well as to name the group as a whole, and 'Romani' as the adjective, in line with emerging and converging uses. 'Romani' is also used for the purposes of this report as the name of the Romani language. At a number of points in this study, the term 'Roma' or 'Romani' is used as shorthand for the broad umbrella of groups and individuals. In no way should this choice of terminology be taken as an endorsement of approaches aimed at homogenising Roma and other groups perceived as 'Gypsies' in Europe or at eliminating the rich diversity among Roma, Gypsies, Travellers and other groups perceived as 'Gypsies'.[1]

The institutions of the Council of Europe use 'Roma and Travellers' to designate all socio-economically marginalised and socio-culturally stigmatised groups that currently or historically displayed a nomadic or peripatetic way of life as itinerant work-

1 European Commission: The situation of Roma in an enlarged European Union. Luxembourg, 2004, P. 6. Available from: ec.europa.eu/social/BlobServlet?docId=99&langId=en, accessed 8 August 2017.

ers, and who have been subsumed into individual member states under one of the categories outlined here:

> The terms 'Roma and Travellers' are being used at the Council of Europe to encompass the wide diversity of the groups covered by the work of the Council of Europe in this field: on the one hand a) Roma, Sinti/Manush, Calé, Kaale, Romanichals, Boyash/Rudari; b) Balkan Egyptians (Egyptians and Ashkali); c) Eastern groups (Dom, Lom and Abdal); and, on the other hand, groups such as Travellers, Yenish, and the populations designated under the administrative term 'Gens du voyage', as well as persons who identify themselves as 'Gypsies'.[2]

If one overlooks the category "persons who identify themselves as Gypsies", and understands "Travellers, Yenish" and "Gens du voyage" as category d), then the definitions describe four groups that can be further distinguished according to geographical, historical and social criteria. The group identified in the above quotation under a) essentially corresponds to the wide ethnic definition as socio-economically marginalised groups and socio-culturally stigmatised population groups of Indian origin who have been present in Europe since the late Middle Ages and speak or have spoken Romani.[3] The noun *rom* means 'man/husband', or 'group member who is male' in the Romani language.[4] In the Kaale, Romanichal and Sinti dialects, the word simply means 'husband', so in the plural it cannot be used to indicate membership of the group. East European Romani speakers commonly describe themselves collectively as 'Roma', fitting the narrow ethnic definition given at the beginning of this paper. These groups are also described, however, by a great variety of names, and it is often unclear whether these are endonyms or exonyms. These range from occupational descriptions such as 'Čurara' ('sieve-maker', from Romanian *ciur*, meaning 'sieve'), 'Kovači' ('forge', from Slav *Kovač*), 'Lovara' ('horse trader', from Hungarian *lo*, 'horse') and names indicating origin such as Bergitka ('mountain', from German *Berg*) , referring to the Carpathian range in southern Poland, 'Mačvaja' from the Mačva region of Serbia, and names indicating status, such as 'Arlije' ('locals', from Turkish *Yerli*, 'indigenous'), 'Cerhari' ('tent-dwellers', from Romani *cerha*, 'tent'), 'Gurbet' ('foreigners', from Turkish *gurbet*, 'abroad').

2 CAHROM: Abridged Report of the 9th meeting. Strasbourg 2005, P. 13. http://www.coe.int/de/web/portal/cahrom, accessed 8 August 2017.

3 In German-speaking countries their language is usually called Romanes, but internationally it is mainly called Romani. The first derives from an adverb: Ďzanes *romanes?* "Can you [speak] roma?", the second is a nominalised adjective: *romani* čhib 'Roma-tongue/language'.

4 The most plausible etymology is the Prakrit word *ḍōmba*, paraphrased in the online version of the *Comparative dictionary of the Indo-Aryan languages* as "low-caste black-skinned fellow". (http://dsalsrv02.uchicago.edu/cgi-bin/philologic/getobject.pl?c.1:1:1686.soas, accessed 14 August 2017). In modern India, *Ḍōm* indicates a heterogenous ethnosocial group of (former) trading nomads belonging to the lowest caste, the Dalit, or so-called 'Untouchables'). Historically this included jugglers, basket weavers, cremators, musicians and so on.

Members of these groups also live now in Western Europe and in other countries where Europeans have immigrated.

The Sinti have mainly settled in German-speaking areas and their neighbouring regions in Western Europe. In France and Piedmont they call themselves 'Manouches' (Romani *manuš*, 'person'). There are also many small communities in countries that formerly had German-speaking population groups. The origins and meaning of the ethnonym, which has been in use since the late 18th century, are not fully known. The original self-description seems to have been Kaale (Romani *kalo*, 'black').[5] The same endonym is in use among the Iberian Calé and the Finnish Kaale, who are now found in Sweden also. It has also been used in Wales.[6] The name 'Kaale' is most likely to be an old endonym used generally by groups now living in Western Europe.

The most frequent self-description in Great Britain is 'Romanichals', which is echoed in the Scandinavian 'Resande', 'Travellers' as 'Romanisæl' and among an isolated group living in Greek Epirus as 'Romacel'.[7] This would appear also to be an old self-description that has been preserved among isolated groups. The second element, *chal/sæl/cel* can be traced back to Romani čalado, meaning 'family'. In British Romani, *chal* means 'person', so the group self-description can be translated as 'Roma persons'.[8]

The Romanichal, Kaale and Sinti do not use 'Roma' as a collective self-description, but it is widely used by the Bojash people living in Romania and the surrounding regions. In Hungary they are called 'Beás' and are officially in the register of recognised Roma nationalities, and some of the Bajaši in Croatian Međimurje describe themselves in the same way. As well as 'Băieşi' (Romanian *băiaş*, 'miner') the most frequent term used in Romania is 'Rudari' or 'Ludari' (Slav *ruda*, 'ore'); these last two are also most frequent in Bulgaria, and 'Rudari' is sometimes also used in Serbia. All these groups have in common that they originated in Romania and worked in the past as miners. Instead of Romani, the Bojash people living outside Romania speak ancient Romanian dialects strongly influenced by the local languages they are in contact with: Bosnian, Bulgarian, Croatian, Serbian and Hungarian. Due to migration during recent decades, there are numerous small groups also living in Western Europe.

---

5 The suggestion of *Sindh* (Sanskrit *sindhu*, 'river'), a province of Pakistan, as an origin is undermined by the use of the Slav suffix in the feminine singular *Sint-iza* (masculine *Sint-o*).

6 John Sampson: The Dialect of the Gypsies of Wales: Being the Older Form of British Romani Preserved in the Speech of the Clan of Abram Wood. Oxford 1926.

7 Romanichal mainly describe themselves as 'Gypsies'. On Romacel see Yaron Matras: Romacilikanes: The Romani dialect of Parakalamos. In: Romani Studies14(2003) 2, P. 59–109.

8 British Romani or 'Angloromani', like the 'Skandoromani' of the Resande and the Iberian Caló, is a para-Romani language: it is a variety of the local majority language – English, Norwegian, Swedish, Castilian, Catalan etc. – that includes lexical elements drawn from Romani.

The same is true of the Ashkali and Balkan Egyptians, who are described in the quotation above from the Council of Europe as an independent sub-group of 'Roma and Travellers', but are often subsumed under the wide ethnic definition of 'Roma'. Ashkali and Balkan Egyptians live in and around the Albanian-speaking region of Kosovo, where the minority group 'Roma-Ashkali-Egyptians' (RAE) was established thanks to the United Nations Interim Administration in Kosovo (UNMIK), and this has at least in part addressed the efforts to establish the distinction between the Ashkali and Balkan Egyptians and the Roma. Both groups speak Albanian rather than Romani and they are socio-economically more firmly established than the Roma, from whom they mostly distance themselves. The Ashkali are the descendants of blacksmiths who worked for the Ottomans; the Balkan Egyptians distinguish themselves as 'from Egypt' by means of alternative exonyms using etymological derivations such as Greek γύφτοι, Albanian *evgjitë, magjypë,* Turkish *kipti* and English *gypsy*.

Strategies of this kind are significant in any political discussion of the origins, homeland and/or kin-state of the Roma. The following discussion addresses the groups so far briefly introduced, which mainly correspond to the wider ethnic definition of Roma given in the introductory remarks.

Nation and territory

In the second half of the 20th century, a socio-political development began that led to the Roma identifying as an independent nation enjoying a shared history and culture and similar interests. The wider Roma community of individual communities, who previously had little or no sense of shared identity, has emerged as a distinct European population group or even nation. In the 1920s and 1930s, in the context of the nationalities policy of the Soviet Union, some elite Roma groups achieved emancipation and integration, but in all other cases even local efforts by communities to organise themselves have been few and far between. Many Roma have been restricted to a life as itinerant workers due to continuing socio-cultural discrimination – and even genocide under Nazism – so that for centuries they have lived a life of subsistence in small groups. As a result, the Roma enjoy neither the social structures nor the economic resources that would enable them to participate in political life. The development of a general understanding of themselves as an ethnic group with a shared origin, culture and language did not begin, as we have seen, until the second half of the 20th century. The process of becoming a *nation*, initiated in the1990s, has not yet been completed and is indeed highly controversial within the Roma community.

The difficulty of establishing the concept of the Roma as a nation lies on the one hand in creating a commonly understood equivalence between nation, state and territoriality, and on the other hand in the dual meaning of the concept of nationality, which can indicate membership either of an ethnic group or of a state – implying membership of a nation. On the basis of these ambiguities, it is possible to identify four types of nation:

– A nation with its own territory and statehood: a state nation. Example: Finland.
– A (state) nation within another state nation (often a neighbouring one): a minority with a kin-state. Example: the Hungarian community in Romania.
– A nation with its own territory but no statehood: stateless but territorial minority (nation). Example: the Kurds in Turkey, Syria, etc.
– A nation with neither territory nor statehood: stateless nonterritorial minority (nation).

The Roma fall into the last category: they are a stateless nonterritorial minority. Significantly, at the the Fifth World Romani Congress in July 2000 in Prague, delegates from a variety of European countries defined this population group as a nonterritorial nation. Symbols, flags and hymns were decided as early as the First World Romani Congress in 1971, and have been in general use since then. However, given that in the context of the European ideology of the nation-state the most commonly accepted definition of 'nation' is a narrow one, requiring a coherent unit comprising population, culture, language, territory and state, the framing of the Roma as a nation is clearly politically constructed. This leads to understandable difficulties: it would be very challenging for the Roma to conform a common culture, given that ethnocultural differences specific to different groups are as much influenced by local contact as the heterogenous Romani language is – a language that, moreover, is only actively used by a third of the up to twelve million Roma. Territoriality and sovereignty are not at issue, since the Roma are not under the aegis of a kin-state, nor is there any prospect that they might at some future point gain an autonomous territory that would enable them to acquire that benefit. Compensating for this status deficit – the relevance of which in this context remains unclear – in the process of their emancipation is one of the key concerns of representatives of a wide variety of Roma and other organisations and institutions. The question of their origin is also highly significant to their claim to nationhood.

Origin

It would be very rare now to encounter the kind of speculation about origins that appeared in the Weekly News *Temeswarer Neueste Mannigfaltigkeiten* in 1781:

> a discrete travelling people [arose] from the mixing of Ethiopians, Troglodytes and Egyptians, having some characteristics of each nation, and we can assume that today's Gypsies are their descendants.

For several centuries it has been known that the *Roma* are of Indian origin, since their language belongs to the Indo-European family of languages, but this is rarely discussed outside academic circles. For the Roma themselves, and for at least part of the wider public, the concept of an Indian origin arose first via the cultural definition in the Romani Movement. There were also significant contacts with India itself.[9] Indian Prime Minister Indira Ghandi made a lasting impression in her opening address to the Second International Roma Festival, held on 29 October 1983 in Chandigarh, the joint capital of the two Indian states of Haryana and Punjab. It has often been claimed that Ghandi addressed the Roma as "lost children of India". This is erroneous, but she did mention kinship ties:[10]

> Welcome to the Roma people to *Baro Than*.[11] Some of us have met before and some are new faces but all are here in the spirit of friendship. Why am I here? Because I feel a kinship with the Roma People. I have always admired their love of adventure, their closeness to nature and above all, their fortitude and resilience.

It would seem to be only a small step from 'kinship' with a state leader to 'kin-state', but in terms of *realpolitik*, India in modern times has little meaning for the Roma; it is simply a symbol of their origin.

The same is true of the origin myth of the Balkan Egyptians. There are references to the presence of population groups of Egyptian origin in South-Eastern Europe in Herodotus's description of Athens, in Philip's Macedonia and the Roman Empire, and right up to the Byzantine and Ottoman periods. Apart from the issue of differentiation from the Roma and the above-mentioned recognition of the RAE minority in Kosovo, in terms of *realpolitik* this origin myth also has little effect. In spite of the apparent efforts of representatives of the Balkan Egyptians, they were unable to interest Egypt's President Mubarak in acting as a protecting power for them.

The word 'Egypt' may well refer to the mountain named 'Gype' (thought to be in the Taygetus range) near the Peloponnese harbour of Methoni (called 'Modon' by the Venetians), which was used as a staging post by pilgrim ships sailing to Palestine. It is mentioned in 1495 in Alexander Pfalzgraf von Rhein:

> Modon is a very strong city / not very pretty / it is a bishopric / and there are in Modon many Jews and Greeks / but few Christians / and near Modon there is a mountain named Gype and there are about 200 small houses / or huts / where there are Egyptians who are heathens and some people who call the mountain and its environs / Little Egypt.[12]

9 India participated in funding the First World Romani Congress, held in 1971 near London.

10 From the journal Roma, 7/2, published in 1983 in Chandigarh.

11 The Romani *baro than* (literally: 'big place') is here a metonymic reference to India.

12 Quoted in: Rüdiger Vossen: Zigeuner. Roma, Sinti, Gitanos, Gypsies zwischen Verfolgung und Romantisierung. Frankfurt/M.1983, P. 22. For other mentions – including the so-called Romiti

Early reports say that the leaders of immigrant groups arriving in Central and Western Europe described themselves as dukes of Little Egypt, and this is very likely to refer to the Gype mountains.

The Ashkali claim a different geographical origin. The most commonly cited theory is that they came from the city of Ashkal, in the modern Iranian province of Gilan, in the 4th century BC at the time of Alexander the Great. Others believe they emigrated from Aşkale in the Turkish province of Erzurum during the Ottoman era. Some believe they came originally from Egypt, following Alexander the Great's second campaign through Ashkelon in modern Israel.[13]

The origin myths of the Ashkali and the Balkan Egyptians emphasise their indigeneity relative to the Slav population of the Balkan peninsula and the Roma, both of whom arrived later. It is not unusual for ethnic groups to have origin myths that place them in the region a long time ago, as such a history bolsters claims to sovereignty. Albanians claim to be the descendants of the Illyrians, the Romanians trace their roots to the Dacians and Thracians, the Slav Macedonians justify their recent claim for sovereignty by citing Philip's and Alexander's Macedonia in Ancient Greece. Some Bojash similarly see themselves as descendants of the Romanised Thracians of the province of Moesia in Ancient Rome and define their language as Moeso-Romanian. In addition to distinguishing them from other groups and proving their indigenous status, origin myths and roots that reach far into the past (whether fact or fiction) both confer prestige and construct identity. Any associated legitimacy granted by historic territoriality serves to bolster the self-confidence of individuals and the coherence of the group.

Status

Although territoriality is incompatible with the designation as a nonterritorial nation mentioned above, a historical presence on a nationally specific territory can give legitimacy to the status of individual groups as indigenous. This is especially relevant for the descendants of the Roma who migrated from the Balkans to Western Europe around the 15th century. This was the first of the three major waves of Roma migration within Europe:[14]

near Modon by Niccolò Frescobaldi as early as 1384 – see Angus Fraser: The Gypsies. Oxford 1992, P. 52f.

13 Further information on the Ashkali and the Balkan Egyptians, for example, in: Studii Romani: Identity Formation among Minorities in the Balkans: The cases of Roms, Egyptians and Ashkali in Kosovo. Sofia 2001.

14 This paper omits some groups whose migrations were imposed because of exclusion, expulsion and persecution. For Roma, migration is an involuntary and irreversible experience.

1) The first migration wave, mentioned above, started in the 15th century, and the descendants of these Balkan Roma migrants still reside in the areas to which they migrated.
2) From the middle of the 19th century, Vlach Roma emigrated from the principalities of Moldavia and Wallachia, and now live throughout Europe and beyond.
3) In the second half of the 20th century, Roma economic migrants and refugees migrated from South-East Europe to Western Europe.

The Roma population of Western European countries therefore includes members of three groups (Balkan Roma, Vlach Roma and South-Eastern European Roma), and these often also display internal heterogeneity.

Migrants who originate from the first wave, such as the Scandinavian Resande, identify themselves as a quasi-indigenous population group distinct from the Lovara and Kalderaš (Romanian *căldărar*, 'coppersmiths'), who arrived in Sweden and Norway from 1900; similarly, the so-called 'Ungrika Roma', who arrived in the Hungarian region from the 15th century onwards, claim distinction from the later arrivals, the Vlach Roma. The latter, in turn, perceive the long-established groups as at least partly 'assimilated' into the local population, and look down on them for it. They consider themselves to be 'true Roma' and thus superior to the indigenous groups. Both groups – first-wave migrants and Vlach Roma – moreover claim difference from economic migrants and refugees, due to their indigenous status. German Sinti especially emphasise both their indigenous status and their nationality, in order to establish difference from other groups. Some of their representatives, for example, refuse to acknowledge the collective description *'Sinti und Roma'* used in Germany.[15] The Iberian Calé and the British Romanichal consider themselves different from later Roma arrivals, but do not typically deploy strict differentiation markers. The Arlije 'locals' in the Western Balkans have a similar attitude to the later arrivals, the Gurbet 'foreigners' and the Cerhari 'tent-dwellers'.

At the national level, human rights campaigners argue that the Roma's indigenous status should entitle them to the same rights as the citizens of the state they reside in, and that politicians and the authorities are therefore obliged to foster their integration into the relevant nation-state.[16] The Roma do not always apply for national citizenship and documents, but these can also be withheld from them, and without them the Roma are unable to exercise their democratic rights or access the employ-

15 This strong awareness of status extends to establishing internal differentiation between the indigenous German Gadžkene Sinti and the so-called Lallere Sinti, whose ancestors came from what is now Czech territory.

16 This is highlighted in the definition as a *'Volksgruppe'* in the German-speaking area, especially in Austria, since the paraphrase 'group of a people' implies *inter alia* that a person belongs to an ethnic community.

ment market, education and social security benefits. Travel documents make it possible for a person to migrate away from poverty, discrimination and danger. Roma people often lack the necessary prerequisites for economic success and suffer persistent marginalisation and stigmatisation, which is often either caused or exacerbated by political tensions or even military conflicts. These factors combine to frustrate social integration, and indeed often to force them to migrate in order to survive.[17] The ability to travel and obtain visas, claim asylum and gain residence permits all depend on having a national citizenship.

This pragmatic definition of Roma as citizens of various individual states stands in contrast with the Roma Movement's definition of Roma as a nonterritorial nation. The supranational identity of the Roma has been promoted internationally in the context of the various World Romani Congresses, and especially by its sponsoring organisation the International Romani Union, and it is gaining traction in the context of the Council of Europe. In 1981 the Conference of Local and Regional Authorities addressed for the first time the cultural and social problems of populations of nomadic origin,[18] and this led in 1983 to the Recommendation on Stateless Nomads and Nomads of Undetermined Nationality by the Committee of Ministers. Two years later the Council of Europe published a study on the situation of "Gypsies and Travellers" in 21 member states.[19] The Group of Specialists on Roma/Gypsies and Travellers was set up in 1995 to propose solutions for improving the situation of these groups. Then, in 1998, the Framework Convention for the Protection of National Minorities was ratified. In the same year the European Commission against Racism and Intolerance (ECRI) adopted a General Policy Recommendation on Combating Racism and Intolerance Against Roma/Gypsies. In 2000, the Committee of Ministers agreed on a Recommendation on the Education of Roma/Gypsy Children in Europe, and one year later, a Recommendation on Improving the Economic and Employment Situation of Roma/Gypsies and Travellers in Europe. The 2004 partnership agreement with the European Roma and Travellers Forum (ERTF) established the Council of Europe as the most important political platform for a supranational European Roma Movement.[20] In 2011, the Council of

17 Nomadism among the Roma is a stereotype that arises from a survival strategy forced on them by external circumstances.

18 Information here and below from Jean-Pierre Liégeois: The Council of Europe and Roma: 40 years of action. Strasbourg 2012, P. 196f.

19 Jean-Pierre Liégeois: Gypsies and Travellers. Strasbourg 1985. The new title of the 1994 revised and expanded edition, *Roma, Gypsies, Travellers*, probably gave rise to the now current description 'Roma and Travellers'.

20 This partnership agreement was downgraded in 2014 into a cooperation between the Congress of Local and Regional Authorities of the Council of Europe and the ERTF. The Council of Europe meanwhile supports the European Roma Institute for Arts and Culture (ERIAC), now established in Berlin. In spite of all the problems within and around the ERTF, this development – the scaling

Europe established a permanent Special Representative of the General Secretary for Roma Issues, with a support team of over twenty people, and has raised the profile of a supranational European identity for the *Roma*. Roma political representatives have started to describe themselves as 'true Europeans' whose concerns can only be properly represented by supranational or international organisations.[21]

Affiliation

The Roma are fundamentally nonterritorial, in contrast to nearly all other European minorities, who are identified with a territory and sometimes a (usually neighbouring) nation-state. Being nonterritorial means that they also lack any form of kin-state that might take up and defend their concerns. The Roma are longstanding residents in all regions of Europe, but (due to existential threats) they are perpetually forced into diaspora. They can thus be characterised as both local and supra-regional, and they adopt this dual description in their attempts at self-definition. The resulting conflict between national and supranational European identity is due to:

1) their presence in all European states
2) their definition (both intrinsically and extrinsically) as an independent ethnic group
3) their indigenous status, as national citizens, and their associated citizenship rights.

This contradiction is resolved if one accepts that a homogenous identity is a construct of the nation-state ideology. The social reality acknowledged in modern societies is that individuals can have multiple identities. This then gives rise to the (at least) threefold identity of the Roma:

1) Group = ethnic identity
2) Citizens = national identity
3) Europeans = territorial identity.

These three identities are invoked by the Roma and their representatives to establish a coherent self-definition and political legitimacy, and indeed as a partial substitution for their lack of a kin-state.

Indigeneity provides an ethnocultural definition based on historical roots that differentiates between, for example, the Roma of Indian origin (potential kin state:

down of political collaboration in parallel with the strengthening of cultural activity – seems a clearly retrograde step and a weakening of the political agenda.

21 This includes not only the Council of Europe but also the EU, in particular the Framework for National Roma Integration Strategies agreed in 2011, and also the OSCE and the Contact Point for Roma and Sinti Issues of the Office for Democratic Institutions and Human Rights (OHDIR).

India) from Travellers or Balkan Egyptians (potential kin state: Egypt), or from Ashkali. Nationality provides an ethnonational definition based on indigenous status that can differentiate as foreigners, for example, Swedish first-wave migrant Resande from Roma and Kaale, and German Sinti from Roma. A national liberal definition, based on an actual place of residence, has an integrative effect and makes any country of residence a kin state. Alternatively, a supranational definition of Roma as a European nation makes the notion of a kin-state obsolete.

Against the background of Europe's nation-state reality, the national liberal and the supranational definitions seem utopian, but they are an essential condition for the integration of the Roma as citizens with equal socio-political and socio-economic rights. In order to preserve the socio-cultural aspects of their heritage, the integration process must also recognise their multi-faceted identity. Otherwise, social integration will be confused with cultural assimilation. This is true not only of the Roma, but for any community or individual in our modern urban information society.

Appendices

Melanie Frank

Report on the international conference "The Promotion of National Minorities by their 'Mother Countries' in Central and Eastern Europe in the 20th and 21st Century"

From 9 to 11 November 2016, the European Network Remembrance and Solidarity (ENRS, Warsaw), the Federal Institute for the Culture and History of the Germans in Eastern Europe (BKGE, Oldenburg) and the Institute for Foreign Cultural Relations (IfA, Stuttgart) organised the conference "The Promotion of National Minorities by their 'Mother Countries' in Central and Eastern Europe in the 20th and 21st Century", which took place at the Representation of the Free State of Saxony to the Federation in Berlin. The conference was made possible through cooperation with seven other institutions from Germany and abroad: the OSCE High Commissioner on National Minorities (The Hague), the Federal Union of European Nationalities (Flensburg), the European Centre for Minority Issues (Flensburg), the Institute of International Affairs at the University of Hamburg (Hamburg), the Institute of Social Policy at the University of Warsaw (Warsaw), the Department of History at the Pavol Jozef Šafárik University (Košice/Kashov), and the Institute of Minority Studies at the Centre for Social Sciences of the Hungarian Academy of Sciences (Budapest).

In order to adequately cover the topic of minorities and minority policy in Eastern Europe in accordance with its complexity and continuing topicality, the organisers invited representatives of European states and international organisations, civil society actors, representatives of academia as well as minority organisations from Central and Eastern Europe. The diverse formats of the conference enabled a multidisciplinary and multi-perspective exchange on instruments, actors and legal standards of minority policy. The scholarly value of the conference was improved by limiting the period of study to the time after 1989, the geographical area to Central, Eastern and South-Eastern Europe, and the theme to the promotion of national minorities by their 'mother countries'. In this way, the representatives of the subject's ethnology, linguistics, political science, sociology, geography, law and history were able to present their research results on (comparative) case studies, pan-European standards, historical references and political instruments in combination with a fruitful discussion.

On the morning of November 9, before the conference proper, a workshop was held for young academics on "Historical, recent and upcoming topics". The workshop was led by DAGMAR RICHTER (Heidelberg). Seven scholars from the United Kingdom, Germany, Hungary and Romania took part, specialising in European ethnology, history, political science, law and sociology. The presentations of the young researchers dealt with topics that would go on to be discussed in the subsequent conference panels, such as the consequences of new media for the standards and practices of European minority policy and the legitimacy of unilateral approaches in the minority policy of some kin-states.

The special position of national minorities was emphasised in the opening speeches of the Chairman of the Steering Committee of the European Network Remembrance and Solidarity JAN RYDEL (Warsaw), the Special Representative of the Federal Government for the German OSCE Chairmanship 2016, GERNOT ERLER (Berlin), the Representative of the OSCE High Commissioner on National Minorities, BOB DEEN (The Hague), the Federal Government Commissioner for Matters Related to Ethnic German Resettlers and National Minorities, HARTMUT KOSCHYK (Berlin), and the Head of Directorate 'History, Remembrance' at the Federal Government Commissioner for Culture and the Media, Berlin, ANSGAR HOLLAH (Berlin). On the one hand, national minorities can take on the role of bridge-builders both within a state and between their respective 'home state' and 'mother country'. On the other hand, they are exposed to the danger of being instrumentalised for nationalist policies by both the 'mother country' and their 'home state'. The special situation of national minorities results from their position within the 'triadic nexus', a concept introduced by the US sociologist Rogers Brubaker and frequently cited during the conference. The triadic nexus refers to the three-sided relationship between minorities, their 'home states' and their 'mother countries' in which each pursues their own, often competing interests.

GERALD VOLKMER (Oldenburg) reminded the audience in his introduction to the conference that the term 'national minorities' is a modern concept that should not hide the diversity of linguistic and cultural minorities. The organisers therefore made it their task to reflect the complexity of the topic through a multidisciplinary and multi-perspective approach. The opening lecture addressed the historical framework of current minority policy and thus laid an important common foundation for the contributions to come, which focused on a period of investigation after 1989. JENNIFER JACKSON-PREECE (London) showed that, after 1919, the rights of national minorities, which were to be protected by bilateral and multilateral agreements between the member states of the League of Nations, largely corresponded to the current state of institutionalisation of human rights. Against the background of poor inter-state relations, national minorities had been instrumentalised, serving governments as a supposed justification for aggressive foreign and repressive domestic policies. Jackson-Preece therefore concluded that, especially against the background of newly emerging and strengthening populist currents, it is important to monitor the compliance of Council of Europe and OSCE member states with legal standards to preserve social diversity.

Since the Second World War, a large number of bilateral treaties with clauses on minority protection have been concluded, and a multilateral level of minority protection has been created with the Council of Europe, the OSCE and – to a lesser extent – the EU. The first day of the conference ended with a panel discussion moderated by STEPHAN EISEL (Bonn), in which the guests on the panel and the audience discussed the significance of these multi- and bilateral approaches to minority policy and their relationship to each other. The discussion between GRZEGORZ JANUSZ (Lublin), STEFAN OETER (Hamburg) and PETRA ROTER (Ljubljana/Laibach) focused primarily on questions about the relationship between these two levels and with regard to the multilateral level, questions about the enforceability of international agreements. On the former, Janusz explained that bilateral agreements between two states have the potential to take into account specific conditions of the culture, language and religion of the minority concerned, which tend to recede into the background with pan-European standards. Oeter, on the other hand, emphasised that there was also close practical relevance at the multilateral level of the Council of Europe and that multilateral approaches could help to advance standards of minority protection at the European level. However, according to Roter, achieving this goal depends on the following factors: minorities would have to be able to participate in matters that concern them and society as a whole would have to create framework conditions to integrate minorities while ensuring their identity is preserved. This shows how decisive the political will is in implementing the protection of minorities.

The second day of the conference began with the panel "Concepts and Attitudes", chaired by FLORIN ABRAHAM (Bucharest). Multilateral agreements were the focus of the lecture by STEFAN OETER (Hamburg). He emphasised that despite the multitude of different instruments of minority policy in Europe, common goals, guidelines and standards were conceivable, and are already manifested in the relevant conventions of the OSCE and the Council of Europe. They are based on a common understanding of the goals of minority protection: the protection and promotion of cultural diversity as a characteristic feature of pluralistic societies and modern constitutional states. According to Oeter, there is no need for further standard-setting; rather, the decisive challenge lies in the implementation of these standards, which depends on the political will of the states. TOVE HANSEN MALLOY (Flensburg) explained in her lecture the extent to which unilateral legislation in favour of an 'own' national minority abroad could also become an instrument of peaceful minority policy, using the example of Romania, which had enshrined the principle of the primacy of international law in its *Minorities Act (2007)*. ZOLTÁN KÁNTOR (Budapest) illustrated a concrete form of the promotion of national minorities by their 'mother countries' by looking at Hungary's policy towards Hungarian minorities living abroad. Hungary's goal is to compensate for home states' efforts to assimilate minorities by supporting them to maintain their own language and culture, as well as to build a community between society in Hungary and the Hungarian minorities abroad. The demographic data, which form a central basis of minority policies, were analysed by KÁROLY KOCSIS (Budapest) in his subsequent lecture. He addressed the conditions under which Europe's ethnolinguistic heterogeneity arose. Kocsis emphasised that he expected a further decline in the number of members of national minorities as well as a decline in ethnic diversity as a whole for Eastern Europe, due, among other things, to the high level of migration from Eastern to Western Europe.

The second panel, chaired by MARTIN PEKÁR (Košice/Kaschau), focused on the instruments of minority protection. KYRIAKI TOPIDI (Lucerne) examined the issue of dual citizenship – not a classic tool of minority protection. With recourse to Benedict Anderson's concept of 'imagined communities', Topidi explained that minorities could also be considered an essential part of the society of several countries and that an institutionalisation of multiple affiliations through dual citizenship gives expression to this situation, through which the effects on interstate relations always had to be taken into account. Many instruments of minority protection aim at preserving and promoting minority languages. The contribution by HELMUT GLÜCK (Bamberg), whose paper was read by Matthias Weber (Oldenburg), dealt with the special relevance of language rights and the obligation of states not to leave the task of language preservation and transmission of the mother tongue to minorities alone. ATTILA PAPP (Budapest) looked at structural disadvantages for pupils with a minority language as their first language, which a monolingual school system in multilingual regions entails.

In the afternoon panel discussion, moderated by URBAN BECKMANN (Stuttgart), representatives of the German minorities and media from Eastern Europe spoke. BERNARD GAIDA (Opole/Oppeln), Chairman of the Federation of German Socio-Cultural Societies in Poland, spoke with the publisher of the Moscow German Newspaper, OLGA MARTENS (Moscow), and the Chairman of the Democratic Forum of Germans in Romania, PAUL-JÜRGEN PORR (Sibiu/Hermannstadt). The German foreign ministry was represented by the head of the department responsible for German minorities abroad, BERTRAM VON MOLTKE (Berlin). The discussion made it clear that the 'bridging function' of minorities within and also between states, which has been frequently mentioned since 1989, can only be fulfilled under certain conditions. In addition to the size of the minority and its self-perception and the perception of others, the minority's ability to communicate its own and general issues plays an increasingly important role. The panellists addressed the different starting situations when it comes to support by the home states, especially with regard to the financial resources of the media and the broadcasting times allocated to them.

The third section, chaired by ADAM WALASZEK (Krakow), was dedicated to the players of minority politics. PETER A. KRAUS (Augsburg) directed the focus to Western Europe. In the view of Kraus, minority conflicts in Western Europe differ from those in Eastern Europe because in Western Europe there are no 'mother countries' outside the state in which minorities live. Kraus pleaded for solutions that take greater account of the minorities' demands for broader political autonomy and more decision-making power over their own affairs. ANDRIS SPRUDS (Riga) also showed, in his lecture on the relations between Russia and the Baltic States, that the situation of minorities in Eastern Europe with a strongly involved 'mother country' differs from the constellation in Western Europe. Using the term 'soft power', coined by Joseph Nye, Spruds described the instruments that Russia has at its disposal to influence the political attitudes of the large Russian-speaking minorities, especially in Latvia. Contemporary crises in Europe played a role in the evening lecture "New Perspectives and Research" by KARL CORDELL (Plymouth). Cordell combined social constructivist perspectives with a look at the current majority and minority communities in Europe, especially the xenophobic sentiments in many European countries.

The first section on the last day of the conference, chaired by PAWEŁ HUT (Warsaw), also looked at the players in minority politics. CEZARY ŻOŁĘDOWSKI (Warsaw) compared the situations of Polish minorities in Belarus, Ukraine and Lithuania. Overall, for the Polish government, support for the Polish minorities in these three countries is a lower priority than maintaining good relations with these states. DIETER W. HALWACHS (Graz) used the situation of the Roma, a minority without a kin-state, as a contrasting foil and showed that the Council of Europe's definitions of 'Roma and Travellers' already lacked a discussion of the ethnic groups, languages and cultures subsumed under these terms. Halwachs analysed the extent to which the home states of the Roma fulfil their obligations to implement the Council of Europe's instruments for protection against discrimination. He showed that, at best, one can speak of a partial recognition of the rights of the Roma, but not of protection against discrimination.

The concluding panel discussion on "Potential Discrepancies Between the Goals and Actual Consequences in the Promotion of Minorities", was moderated by ROBERT SCHWARTZ (Bonn) and featured BERND FABRITIUS (Berlin), RAINER HOFMANN (Frankfurt am Main), JÁN VARŠO (Bratislava/Pressburg) and LORÁNT VINCZE (Flensburg). Hofmann named the promotion of an integrated society in the home country of the minorities as a central goal of modern minority policy. Against the background of this goal, any post-imperial interference in the affairs of another state should be critically evaluated. The decisive factor is whether there is a genuine will to protect and promote the minority. Any approach to minority policy must be fundamentally in the interest of the minorities. Varšo added that in addition to relations between the national minority, the majority society and the 'mother country' of the minority, observance of international law should always be in the foreground. Fabritius emphasised that first and foremost the protection of minorities must take effect in the home states on the basis of national law.

The promotion of national minorities by their 'mother countries' should only be a supplementary means, chosen in such a way that it does not have a negative effect on the relationship between minority and majority society or home state. With a view to the EU level, the participants made it clear that there was significant potential for multilateral minority protection here, but that France or Greece had so far prevented this. "The monocultural state must not become the future of Europe," Hofmann concluded.

The conference offered a varied selection of formats that provided important *insights* into the requirements and goals of sustainable minority protection. Speakers identified preservation of cultural and linguistic diversity as one of the most important elements of responsible protection of minorities, alongside the preservation of peaceful interstate relations already mentioned in the opening speeches. The question of how states could support 'their' national minority abroad without endangering relations with the minority's home state remains a research desideratum, especially when the government in the home country is increasingly using authoritarian means. The current research once again illustrates the special situation of national minorities in Central and Eastern Europe, which raises complex questions due to the clash of interests between the minorities, the 'mother countries' and the home states.

Melanie Frank

Report on the workshop for young academics

The European Network Remembrance and Solidarity (ENRS, Warsaw), together with the Federal Institute for the Culture and History of the Germans in Eastern Europe (BKGE, Oldenburg) and the Institute for Foreign Relations (IfA, Stuttgart), jointly hosted the international conference "The Promotion of National Minorities by their 'Mother Countries' in Central and Eastern Europe in the 20th and 21st Century", which took place at the Representation of the Free State of Saxony to the Federation in Berlin from November 9 to 11, 2016. Preceding the conference, on the morning of 9 November, a workshop for young academics was held. This workshop was titled "Historical, recent and upcoming topics".

The workshop leader, DAGMAR RICHTER (Heidelberg) addressed in her introduction the current political situation both in Europe and in the USA: xenophobia and nationalism are a firmly established element of current political debate. She discussed the importance addressing issues of rising nationalism and the implications of the current situation for minority affairs.

MARTA LORIMER (London) also addressed this question in a presentation of her work on the images of Europe used by parties of the extreme right. Using case studies from Italy, France and Slovakia, she is seeking to discover whether current developments prove the existence of a new nationalism distinguished by an ambivalent attitude to Europe.

The second presentation also foregrounded the way in which actors can subjectively assign meaning. Using an interpretative political analysis, MELANIE FRANK (Augsburg) demonstrated that actors involved in current language policy in Latvia interpret the language situation very differently. This ambiguity is among the reasons for the persistent discrepancy between legal norms and actual language usage in Latvia.

FATMA RESIT (Hamburg) turned our attention to the legal framework of European minority protection. She described a vital research gap: it is still unclear whether recent developments in the field of new media should feature in the European Charter for Regional and Minority languages.

KATHARINA SCHUCHARDT (Kiel) explained how difficult it is to find European guidelines that deal fairly with the current developments and heterogeneity of European minorities and their needs. Using an ethnographic approach, she revealed how processes of identity construction must be understood from the point of view of the minority group itself. Using the example of the German minority in Upper

Silesia, she showed that self-definition can uncover context-sensitive differences and understanding gaps.

In her dissertation, ESZTER HERNER-KOVÁCS (Budapest) shows that a minority can also be defined externally and instrumentalised as an object of the policy of a kin-state or motherland. She outlined the various facets of the Hungarian state's diaspora policy towards Hungarian minorities abroad, which include pursuing nationalistic strategies.

MĂRIUCA CONSTANTINS (Bucharest) focused her presentation on the Roma living in Romania. She spoke about the complex relationship between rights and diversity in Romania. Using the political theory of Will Kymlicka and Susan Moller Okin, she illustrated legal principles that enable distinctions to be made between cultural rights and individual freedom.

ADRIANA CUPCEA (Cluj-Napoca) expanded on Eszter Herner-Kovács' observations about unilateral approaches to minority policies. She used the example of Turkish kin-state policies in the Balkans, based on a case study on the Muslim community in Dobrogea (Eastern Romania).

The presentations by the young academics pointed towards topics that were addressed and discussed in the conference that followed, such as the impact of new media on the principles and practices of European minorities policy, and of the legitimacy of unilateral approaches by kin-states towards minority policies. Further foretastes of some of the key themes that were to be explored during the conference pertained to the construction, heterogeneity and complexity of minority identities as well as the risks for minorities, on the one hand of assimilation into majority populations, and on the other of being instrumentalised by kin-state governments.

Contributors

Prof. Dr. Karl Cordell
In a career spanning over 30 years, Karl Cordell co-authored and edited 15 books and wrote over 50 book chapters and peer reviewed academic papers. His most notable publications (co-authored with Stefan Wolff) were *Germany's Foreign Policy towards Poland and the Czech Republic* published by Routledge in 2005 and *Ethnic Conflict. Causes, Consequences and Responses* published by Polity Press in 2009. Together with Stefan Wolff he edited the Routledge published journal *Ethnopolitics* for over 20 years. He is currently Emeritus Professor of Politics at the University of Plymouth, UK.

Dr. Melanie Frank
Melanie Frank works in science management with a focus on internationalization. She studied European Studies and Political Science in Magdeburg, Montréal, and Heidelberg, and holds a Doctorate in Political Science from Augsburg University. Dr. Frank has published on linguistic diversity in democratic societies, exploring dynamics of inclusion and exclusion, and multilingual political mobilization. She examines language politics in Eastern and Central Europe through the lenses of democratic theory and comparative politics. In particular, she studied the role of language policies during regime transformations after the dissolution of the Soviet Union, with fieldwork in Latvia, Moldova, and Ukraine. She is the author of *Sprache im Spannungsfeld von Nation und Demokratie: Lettlands Sprachenpolitik seit Wiedererlangung der Unabhängigkeit* (Harrassowitz Verlag, 2023) and (with Peter A. Kraus) *The Politics of Inclusion, Citizenship and Multilingualism. In: François Grin, László Marácz, Nike K. Pokorn (Eds.): Advances in Interdisciplinary Language Policy. Amsterdam, Philadelphia 2022, P. 129–149.*

Prof. Dr. Dr.h.c. Helmut Glück
Helmut Glück (born 1949) studied in Tübingen and Bochum. State examination in German and Russian philology; 1975–1985 research assistant and university assistant at the University of Osnabrück; 1978 doctorate; 1984 habilitation at the University of Hanover; 1985–1991 lecturer at the Ain Shams University in Cairo and research associate at the Universities of Siegen and Duisburg; 1991–2015 Professor of German Linguistics and German as a Foreign Language at the University of Bamberg. Research stays and guest lectureships in Québec, Montréal, Cairo, Casablanca, Tbilisi, Urbino, Olomouc/Olmütz, Aarhus, Mexico D.F., Aix-en-Provence, Tallinn/Reval and Helsinki. His work focusses on the history of German as a foreign language, German grammar, writing as well as linguistic terminology and lexicography. He is the author of *Die Fremdsprache Deutsch im Zeitalter der*

Aufklärung, der Klassik und der Romantik. Grundzüge der deutschen Sprachgeschichte in Europa (Harrassowitz Verlag, 2013) and has edited a number of volumes on the history of German as a foreign language. Most recently, he edited the 6th edition of *Metzler Lexikon Sprache* (Metzler, 2024).

Prof. Dr. Dieter W. Halwachs

Dieter W. Halwachs (born 1956) is a sociolinguist. He was the head of the Plurilingualism Research Unit at *treffpunkt sprachen* / Centre for Language, Plurilingualism and Didactics at the University of Graz; a member of the Committee of Experts of the European Charter for Regional or Minority Languages of the Council of Europe and coordinator of various projects on minority languages, principally on Romani. His research interests include, *inter alia*, the politics of language, the linguistics of minorities, endangered languages and language contact. He is the co-author of *Kalderaš Romani* (LINCOM, 2015) and author of *Language Policy and Planning in Romani. In: Yaron Matras, Anton Tenser (Eds.): The Palgrave Handbook of Romani Language and Linguistics. Cham 2020, P. 429–457.*

Dr. Zoltán Kántor

Zoltán Kántor holds a PhD in Political Science. He studied in Timișoara/Temeswar (sociology), Budapest (political sciences), and Edinburgh (nationalism studies). His research interests are kin-state politics, theories of nationalism, national minorities, ethnic parties, Hungarians in Romania, citizenship and out of country vote. He is editor of several books on nationalism, national minorities, and kin-state politics. His articles were published in Hungary, Romania, Slovakia, Spain, Japan, USA, Russia, Germany, and Slovenia. He is the editor of the journals *Kisebbségi Szemle* (in Hungarian) and *Hungarian Journal of Minority Studies*. At present he is the director of the Research Institute for Hungarian Communities Abroad, a governmental think tank of the State Secretariat for the Hungarian Communities Abroad (Office of the Prime Minister), that focuses its research on the Hungarian minorities living in the neighboring states. He is also a lecturer (political sciences) at the Pázmány Péter Catholic University.

Prof. Dr. Martin Klatt

Martin Klatt (born 1964) is a Senior Researcher and Head of Research Cluster on Danish-German Minority Issues at the European Centre for Minority Issues (ECMI), Flensburg (since 2022); 2005–2022 Associate Professor at the Center of Border Region Studies, University of Southern Denmark, Sønderborg. Previous scientific positions as research fellow at the Schleswig-Holstein Institute for Peace Research (1996), the Research Department of the Danish Library for South Schleswig (1997–2000), assistant professor at the Danish Institute for Border Region Studies (2001–2005). Research activities concentrate on national minorities in border regions, regional cross-border cooperation, cross-border regions in history and today, and cross-border regional governance, for example as part of the international research project "European Non-Territorial Autonomy Network" (ENTAN), a COST Action examining the concept of non-territorial autonomy (NTA), from both a comparative and comprehensive perspective. Most recently, he co-edited the volume *Secondary Foreign Policy in Local International Relations. Peace-Building and Reconciliation in Border Regions* (Routledge, 2018). He is the author of *The Dilemma of Responsibility: The Role of Kin-States and Nation-States in Implementing Non-Territorial Autonomy Models to Realise Minorities' Linguistic, Cultural and Educational Rights. In: David J. Smith, Ivan Dodovski, Flavia Ghencea (Eds.): Realising Linguistic, Cultural and Educational Rights Through Non-Territorial Autonomy. Cham 2023, P. 43–56.*

Prof. Dr. Peter A. Kraus

Peter A. Kraus is a full professor of political science (comparative politics) and the director of the Institute for Canadian Studies at the University of Augsburg (Germany). In 2022 he has been the Joan Coromines Visiting Chair at the University of Chicago. He has also been the chair of ethnic relations at the University of Helsinki, an associate professor of political science at Humboldt University in Berlin, a John F. Kennedy Memorial Fellow at the Center for European Studies at Harvard University, a visiting lecturer at the New School for Social Research and a recurrent visiting professor at the Universitat Pompeu Fabra in Barcelona. He has published widely and in several languages on cultural diversity and identity politics, language policy and political linguistics, ethnicity, nationalism, and migration, the dilemmas of European integration, as well as problems of democratization and democratic theory. He is the author of *A Union of Diversity: Language, Identity, and Polity-Building in Europe* (Cambridge University Press, 2008). His most recent book publications include *The Catalan Process: Sovereignty, Democracy and Self-Determination in the 21st Century* (edited with J. Vergés, Barcelona: Institut d'Estudis de l'Autogovern, 2017) and *The Politics of Multilingualism: Europeanisation, globalisation and linguistic governance* (edited with F. Grin, Amsterdam: John Benjamins, 2018). Kraus has been the Chair of the Research Networking Programme "Responding to Complex Diversity in Europe and Canada" (RECODE, www.recode.info), funded by the European Science Foundation, and a member of the steering committee of the European Commission's Seventh Framework project "Mobility and Inclusion in Multilingual Europe" (MIME, www.mime-project.org).

Prof. Dr. Tove Hansen Malloy

Tove H. Malloy is professor of European Studies at the Europa-Universität Flensburg, Germany and External Lecturer at Roskilde University, Denmark. She was Director of the European Centre for Minority Issues in Flensburg (2009–2019) and has been a member of the Council of Europe's Advisory Committee on the

Framework Convention for the Protection of National Minorities for which she was elected Gender Equality Rapporteur (2011–2018). She is a political theorist by background specialising in the political and legal aspects of national and ethnic minority rights in international relations and international law, especially in the European context. She is the author of *National Minority Rights in Europe* (Oxford University Press, 2005) and has co-edited a number of volumes on minority rights protection and non-territorial autonomy as well as two textbooks. Most recently, she co-edited the *Research Handbook on Minority Politics in the European Union* (Edward Elgard, 2022). She holds a PhD in Government from Essex University, UK.

Prof. Dr. Stefan Oeter

Stefan Oeter (born 1958) studied Law and Political Science in Heidelberg and Montpellier from 1979–1983. After his legal clerkship (1984–1987) he was research associate at the Max Planck Institute for Comparative Public Law and International Law in Heidelberg from 1987–1999. Doctorate (Dr. iur.) in Heidelberg in 1990; Habilitation in Heidelberg in 1997; Professor of Public Law and International Law and Director of the Institute of International Affairs at the University of Hamburg since 1999; from 1999–2017 German member and (from 2006–2013) Chairman of the Independent Committee of Experts of the European Charter for Regional or Minority Languages of the Council of Europe; Chairman of the Historical Commission of the International Society for Military Law and the Laws of War; member of the Permanent Court of Arbitration, The Hague; member of the Academy of Sciences in Hamburg. Research interests: Comparative federalism research, protection of linguistic and cultural minorities, international humanitarian law, European and international economic law, theory of international law and international relations. Most recently, he co-edited the volume *Democracy and Sovereignty. Rethinking the Legitimacy of Public International Law* (BRILL, 2023). He is the author of *Minderheitenmedien zwischen medienökonomischen Effizienzanforderungen, Gerechtigkeitspostulaten und Spracherhalt. In: Philipp B. Donath, Alexander Heger, Moritz Malkmus, Orhan Bayrak (Eds.): Der Schutz des Individuums durch das Recht. Festschrift für Rainer Hofmann zum 70. Geburtstag. Berlin, Heidelberg 2023, P. 517–546.*

Dr. habil. Kyriaki Topidi

Kyriaki Topidi is a Senior Researcher and Head of Cluster on Culture and Diversity at the European Centre for Minority Issues (ECMI). Her research interests focus on diversity governance and minority protection rights and mechanisms. She has lectured extensively and researched in Public International Law, European Law, Human and Minority Rights as well as Comparative Law. Prior to joining the ECMI, she has occupied research and teaching positions in various academic institutions and is regularly engaged as a guest researcher and lecturer in numerous research institutes and faculties across the globe. She is also the author and editor of several volumes and articles. Since 2023, she co-edits the Routledge *Advances on Minority Studies* book series. Her latest co-edited volume *Minority Rights and Social Change: Norms, Actors and Strategies* focuses on the intersection of minorities with social movements (Routledge, 2024). At the ECMI, she is currently researching on minority identity and digital governance, preparing a monograph on Intersectional Discrimination in Platform Governance (BRILL, forthcoming).

Dr. Dr. Gerald Volkmer

Gerald Volkmer (born 1974) studied Law and History in Mainz and Frankfurt am Main. Doctorates in History (Dr. phil.), Johannes Gutenberg University, Mainz in 2004 and in Law Studies (Dr. jur.), Johann Wolfgang Goethe University, Frankfurt am Main in 2012. From 2005 to 2007 Assistant to the Director and 2007–2009 Director of the Institute for Transylvanian Studies at the University of Heidelberg. From 2009 to 2013 Researcher and Deputy Director of the Institute for German Culture and History of Southeastern Europe at the Ludwig-Maximilians-University Munich. Since 2013 Deputy Director of the Federal Institute for Culture and History of the Germans in Eastern Europe at the University of Oldenburg *(Leitender Wiss. Direktor).* Research interests: History of international and transnational relations in Central and Southeastern Europe, history of Romania, Hungary and the Habsburg Monarchy, legal and economic history of Central and Southeastern Europe, German national minorities in Central and Eastern Europe. He is the author of *Deutsche Minderheiten im Ausland. In: Aus Politik und Zeitgeschichte 67 (2017) No. 11–12, P. 38–46,* and *Die deutschsprachigen Minderheiten in der Europäischen Union. In: Oxford German Studies 48 (2019) No. 1, P. 17–53.*

Prof. Dr. Cezary Żołędowski

Cezary Żołędowski is a habilitated doctor of political science, professor at the University of Warsaw employed at the Faculty of Political Science and International Studies. Research interests: multiculturalism, theory of ethnic relations, ethnic relations in historical and contemporary perspective, the situation of national minorities in Poland and Polish minorities abroad, population issues, migrations and Poland's participation in international migrations. He is the author of *Poland in international migrations: the perspective of world systems theory. In: Miscellanea Geographica – Regional Studies on Development 24 (2020), No. 2, P. 94–103,* and *Problemy mniejszości polskiej w międzywojennej Litwie na łamach 'Spraw Narodowościowych' [Problems of the Polish minority in interwar Lithuania in the pages of 'Sprawy Narodowościowe']. In: Wojciech Lis (Ed.): Polacy na Kowieńszczyźnie – dawniej i obecnie [Poles in the Kaunas region – in the past and present]. Lublin 2023, P. 357–388.*

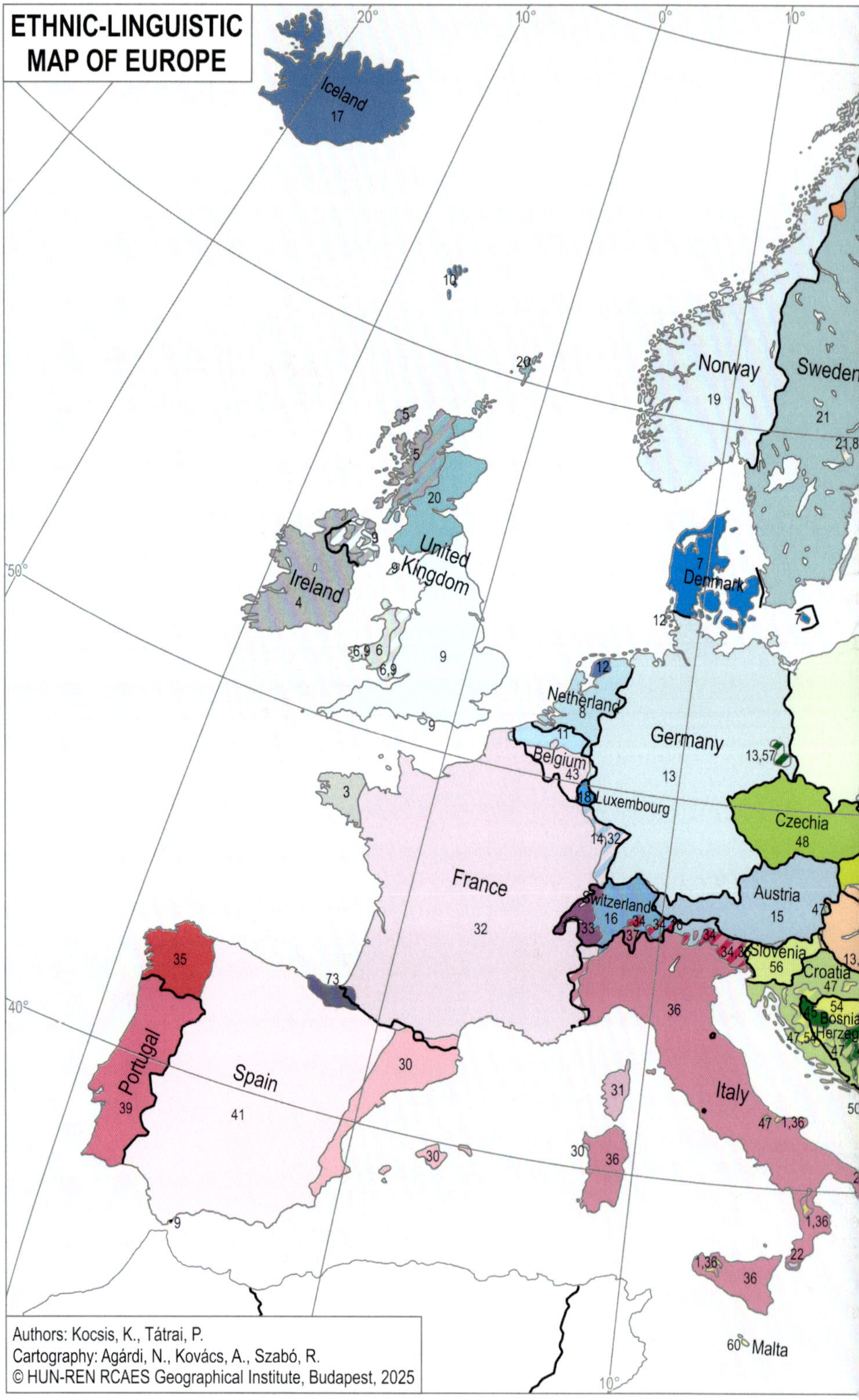
ETHNIC-LINGUISTIC MAP OF EUROPE
Iceland
17
Norway
19
Sweden
21
United Kingdom
20
9
Ireland
4
Denmark
7
Netherlands
8
Belgium
43
Luxembourg
18
Germany
13
Czechia
48
France
32
Switzerland
16
Austria
15
Slovenia
56
Croatia
47
Bosnia Herzeg
Portugal
39
Spain
41
Italy
36
Malta
60
Authors: Kocsis, K., Tátrai, P.
Cartography: Agárdi, N., Kovács, A., Szabó, R.

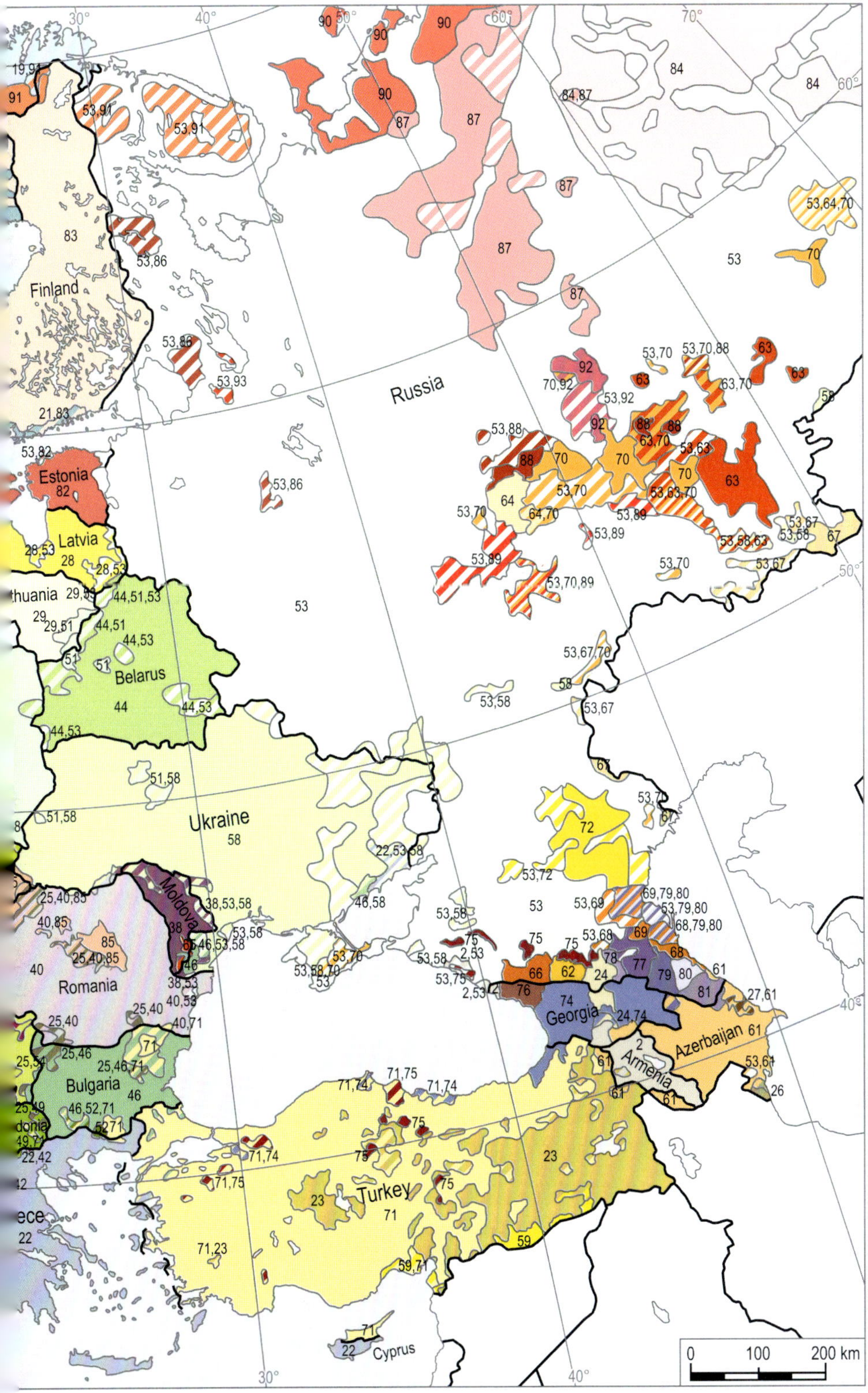

Finland
Estonia
Latvia
Lithuania
Belarus
Russia
Ukraine
Moldova
Romania
Bulgaria
Greece
Turkey
Cyprus
Georgia
Armenia
Azerbaijan
0 100 200 km

INDO-EUROPEAN FAMILY

Albanian group

1 Albanians

Armenian group

2 Armenians

Celtic group

3 Bretons
4 Irishmen
5 Scottish Gaels
6 Welsh

Germanic group

7 Danes
8 Dutch
9 English, Manx, Normandians, English-Scottish Ulsterians
10 Faroese
11 Flemings
12 Frisians
13 Germans
14 German-speaking Alsatians, Lotharingians
15 German-speaking Austrians
16 German Swiss
17 Icelanders
18 Luxembourgers
19 Norwegians
20 Scotsmen
21 Swedes

Hellenic group

22 Greeks

Indo-Iranian group

23 Kurds
24 Ossetians
25 Roma, Sinti
26 Talyshes
27 Tats

Lett-Lithuanian group

28 Latvians
29 Lithuanians

Romance group

30 Catalans
31 Corsicans
32 French, Occitans
33 French Swiss
34 Friulians, Ladinians, Romansh
35 Galicians
36 Italians
37 Italo Swiss
38 Moldavians
39 Portuguese
40 Romanians
41 Spaniards
42 Vlachs, Aromunians
43 Walloons

Slavic group

44 Belarusians
45 Bosniaks, Muslimans
46 Bulgarians
47 Croats
48 Czechs, Moravians
49 Macedonians
50 Montenegrins
51 Poles, Kashubians, Silesians
52 Pomaks
53 Russians, Lipovans
54 Serbs
55 Slovaks
56 Slovenes
57 Sorbs
58 Ukrainians, Rusyns

AFROASIATIC FAMILY

Semitic group

59 Arabs
60 Maltese

ALTAYIC FAMILY

Turkic group

61 Azerbaijanis, Karapak
62 Balkars
63 Bashkirs
64 Chuvashes
65 Gagauzes
66 Karachais
67 Kazakhs
68 Kumyks
69 Nogais
70 Tatars
71 Turks, Turkmens

Mongolian group

72 Kalmyks

BASQUES

73 Basques

CAUCASIAN FAMILY

Kartvelian group

74 Georgians, Laz

Abkhazo-Adyghian group

75 Abazins, Adygeis, Cirkassians, Kabardians
76 Abkhazians

Nakho-Dagestanian group

77 Chechens
78 Ingush
79 Avars
80 Dargins, Laks, Tabasarans
81 Lezghis, Aguls, Rutuls, Tzakhurs

URAL FAMILY

Finno-Ugrian group

82 Estonians
83 Finns
84 Khanty, Mansi
85 Hungarians
86 Karelians
87 Komis, Komi-Permyaks
88 Maris
89 Mordvinians
90 Nenets
91 Sami
92 Udmurts
93 Vepsians